Laure Junot

Philippine–Marie–Hélène de France (Madame Elizabeth), Sister of Louis XVI. (1764-1794).

Laure Junot
Duchess of Abrantès & Wife of General Junot
During the Napoleonic Age

ILLUSTRATED

Catherine M. Bearne

Laure Junot
Duchess of Abrantès & Wife of General Junot During the Napoleonic Age
by Catherine M. Bearne

ILLUSTRATED

First published under the title
A Daughter of the Revolution

Leonaur is an imprint of Oakpast Ltd
Copyright in this form © 2020 Oakpast Ltd

ISBN: 978-1-78282-942-3 (hardcover)
ISBN: 978-1-78282-943-0 (softcover)

http://www.leonaur.com

Publisher's Notes

The views expressed in this book are not necessarily those of the publisher.

Contents

Preface	9
Life in Paris Before the Revolution	10
The Terror	22
Violent Scenes in Paris	36
The Rising Star of Napoleon	53
Triumphs of Napoleon in Italy	62
Betrothal of Laura	68
A Mixed Party	85
Madame Person's Invitation	89
The Consular Court	97
Napoleon and Laura	107
Laura's First Child	121
Birth of Laura's Second Daughter	126
Narrow Escape of Laura and Caroline Murat	133
Junot and Laura at Arras	144
Illness of Laura	155
Laura Remains at Paris	163
The War	171
Fontainebleau	181
Meeting With Junot	196

Continuing Hardships and Dangers	206
Laura Returns to Paris	224
Return of Junot	234
Abdication of Napoleon	247
Laura Visits Joséphine at La Malmaison	259
Her Journey in Italy	272

THIS BOOK
IS DEDICATED
TO MY HUSBAND

THE TUILERIES.

THE STORMING OF THE BASTILLE.

THE BARRICADES

THE LOUVRE

Preface

It has always seemed to me that Laura Permon, afterwards the wife of General Junot and Duchesse d'Abrantès, was one of the most interesting women who belonged to the Court of Napoleon I.

And owing to the literary pursuits of her later years the story of her eventful life, filled from beginning to end with romance and adventure, can be told and realised more fully than is usual in such cases.

It was a stormy, brilliant career, chequered with good and evil fortune, poverty and splendour, perils and triumphs; but it was never dull. For *ennui* she had neither time nor inclination.

When her fortune disappeared with her husband's death and the downfall of the Empire, she turned her attention to literature, and besides various novels, several of which had at the time a considerable popularity, she wrote those voluminous and delightful memoirs to which she owes her lasting reputation as an author.

The first edition, in eighteen volumes, treating of the Revolution, the Directory, the Consulate, and the Empire; was published at Brussels in 1831-4; a second edition in twelve volumes was published at Paris in 1835.

In 1835-7 she wrote the *Memoirs of the Restoration*, also published in Brussels in seven volumes. From these are chiefly drawn the materials for this book; but I am also indebted to various other works of that time, such as *Mémoires sur la vie privée de Napoléon*, by Constant, *Mémoires de La Harpe*, *Les rois frères de Napoléon*, Napier's *Peninsular War*, and other books of the kind.

As this book is intended for the "general reader," who, as a rule, does not care to wade through long descriptions or many volumes, I have endeavoured to leave out anything he might consider dry or tedious, and to compress into a single volume the most interesting portions of the life of my heroine and the most important events in which she was concerned.

With regard to the way French names should be written in English books, although, as Mr. Wakeman observes, (*The Ascendancy of France,*

Preface), it must be to a certain extent a matter of custom, the names of countries, capitals, and a few other universally known places being always translated, I cannot agree with that most delightful historian that this practice should be extended to the names of ordinary places and of persons.

To me this entirely destroys the harmony of a book, for after all a man's name is part of himself If he is French or German or Italian, his name is *not* Henry or Frederick or Charles, but Henri or Friederich or Carlo, as the case may be. I have even seen the noble, picturesque name of "Louis" transformed into "Lewis"! In *Henry of Condé, Anthony of Bourbon*, or *Henry of the Rochejaquelein*, I fail to recognise *Henri de Condé, Antoine de Bourbon*, and *Henri de La Rochejaquelein*, nor could I ever quite realise *Lorenzo dei Medici* as *Lawrence of the Medicis* or *Masaniello* as *Thomas Lamb*.

The names of Laura, Laure, or Laurette all go well with the French *Junot* and Portuguese *Abrantès*. That of Napoleon is, of course, an exception. I have kept the Italian *Buonaparte* throughout, though it was Frenchified by Napoleon, who disliked the idea that he was not of French parentage.

THE ARC DE TRIOMPHE.

CHAPTER 1
Life in Paris Before the Revolution
1784-1789

Laura Permon was born at Montpellier, 1784. Her father, Monsieur Permon, who belonged to a family of finance, had started in life with neither birth, money, nor connections to push him on; but by his intellectual gifts and many attractions had made for himself, while still young, a sufficient fortune and a good position.

His wife, a beautiful Corsican of Greek descent, belonged to the noble family of Comnenus, for several generations settled in that island.

******

The settlement was made in 1676. The district of Paonia was given to the Greek colony, whose chief, Constantine Comnenus, and his heirs, were looked upon as royal, wore violet and scarlet, and received peculiar honours from their clergy. They carried on a feud with the Corsicans for a hundred years. Their claim to royal blood was recognised at the Court of Louis XVI.

******

At Ajaccio he met and fell in love with her. He at that time held a post in the administration of the government of Corsica, which had just been transferred by the Genoese to France. After their marriage they left Corsica and lived in France for several years, at the end of which M. Permon was sent to America with the French troops that took part in the war against England. His wife, taking her children with her, returned to her mother, resolving to pass the time of their separation in the home of her childhood, that romantic, beautiful land with its southern sunshine, great forests, and snowy mountains, to which she was passionately attached.

The head of her family was then her brother. Prince Demetrius Comnenus, and among the early friends with whom she renewed her intimacy was Laetitia Ramolino, now married to Charles Buonaparte, and the mother of several sons and daughters. During the absence of M. Permon, which lasted several years, these young people grew up in constant companionship with her own children.

When her husband returned, she accompanied him to Montpellier, where he had an appointment and where their youngest daughter, Laurette, was born. She was their fifth child, but they had lost two; there remained their eldest son, Albert, then sixteen years old, and a daughter some years younger, named Cécile.

The day after her confinement Madame Permon was seized with a terrible illness. For three months her sufferings were frightful, and the doctors could neither understand nor relieve them, when one morning a peasant who had come with fruit and vegetables for the house, finding everybody in despair and hearing what was the matter, desired to speak to M. Permon.

"I do not want any reward," he said, "but from what your servants tell me, I think I know what is the matter with your wife, and if you like I will cure her in a week."

On being questioned, he declared that his remedy was not in the least dangerous, but that it was a very painful one.

M. Permon sent for the doctors and consulted them. They advised him to allow the experiment to be tried, and Madame Permon having consented, the peasant departed for his own home and came back the next day with the herbs he had gathered. Mixing them with beer and flour into a sort of; paste, he heated it in the oven and applied it to the: part affected. As he had said, the pain it caused was frightful, but at the end of the week the invalid was cured, though still very weak. As for the child, she had entirely forgotten its existence.

One day, however, four months after its birth, she was sitting on her balcony with her husband, when the nurse passed underneath carrying the baby, which had been carefully kept at a distance, as M. Permon feared that his wife's sufferings had made her take a dislike to it, and that that was the reason she never mentioned it. But with a sudden exclamation Madame Permon, in great agitation, asked her husband whether she had had a child and if that were it. Her delight on its being brought to her knew no bounds, and from that moment Laurette was her idol from whom she could never bear to be separated.

In 1785 they established themselves at Paris, where M. Permon bought himself a place as *fermier-général*. Cécile was educated in a convent, but Laurette was brought up at home.

The Permons lived in a large *hôtel* on the *Quai Conti*, went a great deal into society, and entertained at home, giving dinners on a certain day of every week, according to the prevailing custom. The *salon* of Madame Permon was very popular with their numerous friends, of whom the greater part belonged to the *faubourg St. Germain*, but amongst whom were also to be found officials of the government, personages of "finance," scientific and literary men.

Madame Permon was a strange mixture of talent and ignorance. She was even heard to declare that she had never read any book but *Télémaque*, and yet was a thorough woman of the world, with manners and conversation as fascinating as her beauty, possessing to perfection what Napoleon afterwards called "*l'art de tenir salon!*"

The old *régime* was rapidly drawing to a close; already the dark clouds that were to usher in the new one were gathering on the horizon. It was a time of excitement and restless anxiety, people's minds were unsettled, there was a general feeling of uncertainty and changes to come; while amongst the masses sullen anger and discontent were steadily growing and assuming a more threatening attitude. Society in France was divided into opposite camps. Those who held to the old *régime* regarded with horror and dismay the new ideas and practices which seemed everywhere to be arising; and to this party belonged for the most part the French nobles and gentlemen, the clergy, and the peasantry in some of the provinces, especially in the west.

The party of the new *régime* was composed of many shades and varieties, the most violent and reckless of whom were advancing with rapid steps towards the Revolution. The moderate sections comprised many persons who were discontented with the present state of things either from some private grievance or from philosophic or benevolent reasons; whose ideal was a constitution like the English, which they vainly imagined possible to establish in France; who hailed with delight the dawn, as they supposed, of liberty and fraternity, but would have shrunk with horror from the bloodshed and cruelty for which they were unconsciously paving the way.

To one or other of these sections belonged a sprinkling of the more lax and freethinking of the clergy, a few nobles and gentlemen, either *mauvais sujets*, like Orleans and Mirabeau, or generous young enthusiasts such as Noailles and Lafayette; many literary men, most of the professional and mercantile classes, and the artisans, small shopkeepers, and other inhabitants of Paris and the larger towns, who afterwards formed the furious and bloodthirsty mobs of atrocious memory.

During the first part of their life at Paris, Monsieur and Madame Permon held opinions directly opposite to those which might have been expected from their early associations. Although belonging to a simple *bourgeois* family without any claim to ancient blood, he was by nature and education a refined and cultivated gentleman, with studious habits and quiet intellectual tastes. The manners, principles and aims of the revolutionary party were alike abhorrent to him.

She, on the contrary, noble by birth, but the wife of an official of finance, in spite of her social success occasionally met with some slight vexation or disadvantage which irritated and induced her, like many other women in the same position, to join in desiring the abolition of privileges and distinctions of caste.

With the growing spirit of atheism and blasphemy which characterised the revolutionary party, neither of the Permons had any sympathy. How deeply a large portion of French society was thus tainted may be gathered from the following account of a dinner-party given early in the year 1786 by a rich and learned member of the Academy to a large and brilliant circle of guests, including many of the most distinguished names in the social, political, and literary world. The banquet was magnificent, and after applause had greeted the impious. and licentious tales of Chamfort, the conversation became more and more animated, and amidst jests and laughter and the drinking of healths might be heard the praises of Voltaire and Diderot mingled with scoffs and gibes against religion.

One man declared that he was as certain there was no God as that Homer was a fool; another, with shouts of merriment, said that his barber, while powdering his hair, had remarked to him, "You see, sir, that although I am but a poor, miserable barber, I have no more religion than anybody else?"

It was agreed that the Revolution, which was to destroy superstition and fanaticism and establish the reign of pure reason, must be near at hand; the older part of the company lamented the improbability of their living to enjoy it; the younger rejoiced that they were likely to have that privilege. One of the guests, who had hitherto sat silent and pre-occupied, taking no part in what was going on, now replied in a grave and decided tone—

"Be satisfied, gentlemen, you will all see this great, sublime Revolution which you so much admire. You know that I am given to prophecy—and I repeat that you will see it."

"One need not be a conjuror to know that," was the retort.

"That may be," replied the former, whose name was Cazotte, "but perhaps one must be a little more than a conjuror for what remains for me to tell you. Do you know what will be the consequence of this Revolution to all of you who are here present?"

"Ah!" cried the *infidel* Condorcet with a contemptuous smile; "let us hear. A philosopher is not afraid of a prophet."

"Monsieur de Condorcet, you will die on the floor of a prison, of poison which you will have taken to avoid execution—from poison which the *happiness* of that time will oblige you to carry about your person."

There was a moment's silence, after which it was recollected that Cazotte was known to be a visionary, gifted with second--sight, professing to possess power to foretell the future. There was a general laugh, followed by exclamations against such gloomy prognostications.

"What has filled your head with prisons and poisons and executions?" cried one. "What has all that to do with the reign of reason and philosophy?"

"That is what I tell you. It is in the name of philosophy—of humanity—of liberty, in the reign of reason that these things will happen to you; and it will be the *reign* of reason indeed, for she will have her temples, and there will be no others in France."

"*Ma foi!*" cried Chamfort, with a sarcastic laugh; "you will not be one of their priests!"

"But *you* will, M. de Chamfort; and you will open your veins with twenty-two cuts of a razor, but you will not die till some months afterwards. You, M. Vicq d'Azir," he continued, turning to an eminent physician, "will not open your own veins, but you will cause yourself to be bled six times in one day during a paroxysm of gout, to make sure of your end, and you will die in the night. You, M. de Nicolai, M. Bailly, M. de Malesherbes, M. Roueler, will die on the scaffold—"

He was interrupted by a chorus of incredulity and disapproval. "Shall we then be conquered by Turks or Tartars?"

"Not at all. As I have told you, you will only be conquered by philosophy and reason. They who treat you so will all be philosophers with the self-same phrases upon their lips which you have been putting forth for the last hour. They will repeat all your maxims and quote Diderot and La Pucelle as you do."

"He must have gone mad!" whispered one.

"Don't you see that he is joking?" asked another. "And you know his jokes have always a good deal of the marvellous."

"Yes; but his marvelousness is not cheerful," said Chamfort, "it has too much of the gallows about it. And when will all this happen?"

"Six years will not have passed before all that I have told you shall be accomplished."

"Extraordinary miracles indeed! But you have not included me in your list," said La Harpe, who himself gives these details in his memoirs.

"But you will be there as an equally astonishing miracle. You will be a Christian."

"Ah, well! I am comforted," observed Chamfort. "If we are only to perish when La Harpe is a Christian, we are immortal."

In reply to the Duchesse de Grammont's remark that women were not likely to suffer in a revolution, he assured her that she would go to the scaffold, with many other ladies, in the cart of the executioner, with their hands tied behind them.

"Ah! I hope that in that case I shall have a carriage hung with black."

"No, *Madame*; higher ladies than you will go like you in the cart of the executioner with their hands tied behind their backs."

"Higher ladies! What! the princesses of the blood?"

"Still more exalted personages."

A sensation of terror fell upon the assembly, and the darkening countenance of the host proclaimed that the jest had gone too far. Wishing to appear indifferent to the growing apprehension, the duchess said carelessly—

"You see he will not even leave me a confessor."

"No, *Madame*, you will not have one; neither you nor anyone besides. The last victim to whom this favour will be granted will be—"

"Well! who then will be the happy mortal to whom that prerogative will be given?"

"It is the only one he will have retained," was the gloomy answer—"The King of France." (La Harpe: *Mémoires*, vol. i.)

Everyone rose hastily; the master of the house, approaching Cazotte, remonstrated with him in a tone of deep emotion.

Cazotte made no reply, but turned in silence to leave the room. As he did so, the Duchesse de Grammont observed that he had told them their fortunes but said nothing of his own; whereupon he reminded her of the siege of Jerusalem and of the man who for seven days went round the ramparts crying, "Woe to Jerusalem! woe to myself!" until a great stone struck and destroyed him.

So saying, M. Cazotte bowed and retired.

He perished as he had predicted, in the Revolution. He was arrested and liberated, but refused to share the joy of his family, telling them that in three days he should again be arrested and perish, which, like his other predictions, proved to be true.

This extraordinary story is verified not only by La Harpe, but by the Comtesse de Beauharnais, Vicq d'Azir, and others who were present, by the son of Cazotte, and by Madame de Genlis and many others who heard it told before the Revolution.

Laurette, or Loulou as she was called at home, was petted and spoiled by all her mother's friends who frequented the stately *salon* on the *Quai Conti*, and who used to bring her presents of *bon-bons* and costly playthings.

Amongst those whom she regarded with the greatest affection was the old Comte de Périgord, who had been Governor of Languedoc and with whom Madame Permon had begun a friendship at Montpellier which lasted for the rest of their lives. He was *cordon bleu* and a perfect specimen of the best type of a great French noble. His eldest son, the Prince de Chalais, resembled him. His younger son used to cause him much annoyance by a mania for everything English. He had been in England, ever since which he would have neither servants, horses, carriages, nor even saddles or whips that were not English, and although speaking the language very badly he would be heard, on leaving the theatre, to call out to his servants "Périgord House."

The Comtesse de Périgord had been a beauty of the reign of Louis XV. That monarch fell in love with her and wanted to make her his mistress, but as she did not wish anything of the kind, she retired from Court until he had transferred his attentions to somebody else. Her daughter, the Duchesse de Mailly, was one of the ladies of Marie Antoinette.

As soon as Madame Permon had established herself at Paris, she made inquiries after Napoleon, the second son of her friend Madame Buonaparte, then at the *École Militaire*. Her brother, Prince Demetrius Comnenus, told her he had met him directly he arrived, and taken him home to dine.

"I met him in the Palais-Royal, looking about him with his nose in the air—exactly the sort of figure to have his pocket picked. The lad seemed to me to be rather sullen and more conceited than is desirable. He declaims against the luxury of the cadets, and talks about a memorial he wants to write on the subject and send to the Minister of War. All that will only make his companions take a dislike to him and will probably lead to duels."

Napoleon was, in fact, at this time an irritable, touchy, discontented lad; unhappy on account of his poverty and inferior position in the college. His father had died at Montpellier in the house of the Permons, who had fetched him from the inn where he was staying and nursed him with the utmost kindness. Madame Buonaparte, left with eight children and very little money, was thankful to have her eldest daughter, Marianne, placed at Saint Cyr as "*élève de Saint Louis*" and her son Napoleon in the *École Militaire*. The brother and sister were *boursiers*, educated at the expense of the State, and as at both these institutions there were children of noble and rich families who had plenty of pocket-money and everything they wanted, the contrast was often painful, especially when there was a question of any subscription among the pupils.

LETITIA BUONAPARTE (NÉE RAMOLINO), MOTHER OF NAPOLEON.

The Permons, were very kind to them both. M. Permon, who knew all the authorities at the *École Militaire*, often got Napoleon leave to go out, and he was always welcome to spend as much time as he chose on the *Quai Conti* with his friend Albert Permon, who was about his own age and at the same college. Madame Permon, whose attachment to Corsica and to her early friends never varied, was anxious that her son should be intimate with Napoleon, but Albert, who had inherited the good qualities and charming manners of both his parents, at first assured them that it was impossible; that in spite of all his attempts Napoleon remained cold and reserved and seemed embittered by his dependent position.

His mother suggested that the fault might be in his way of going about it, but his father replied that he was not to blame, but that Napoleon, conscious that in Corsica the two families had been in the same position, fretted at the difference now between his own lot, a *boursier* at the college, poor and isolated, while Albert was well off, surrounded with indulgence, and constantly amongst his own relations. Madame Permon replied that if Napoleon's way of going on was caused by envy he must be a stupid, ill-conditioned boy; but her husband observed that it was human nature, and that he was no worse than others.

"Why has he been in a perpetual rage ever since he came to Paris? Why is he always raving about the 'indecent luxury' of his companions? Because at every moment their position contrasts with his. He thinks it ridiculous that these young fellows should have servants because he has none; he objects to entertainments because he cannot subscribe to them. I heard the other day from Dumarsay, the father of one of his companions, that a *déjeuner* was to be given to one of the masters, and that each of the pupils was to give a subscription much too large for those boys; Napoleon is quite right there. Well, I went to see him and found him more gloomy than usual. I guessed why, so I offered to give him the sum required. He became first red, then pale, and refused."

"You must have gone the wrong way about it," said Madame Permon. "Men are so awkward."

"When I saw the boy's high spirit," continued her husband, "I invented a lie, for which God will doubtless pardon me. I told him that when his father died in our arms at Montpellier, he gave me some money to be given to him on any occasion when he might need it. He looked at me fixedly, and replied that since the money came from his father, he would take it, but he could not have accepted a loan, as his mother had already too many expenses, which he ought not to increase for his own personal debts, especially if they were caused by the stupid folly of his companions."

His sister was not so scrupulous. One day Madame Permon, her brother, Prince Comnenus, and Napoleon went to Saint Cyr to see Marianne. She came to the *parloir* looking very sad, and having evidently been crying. When asked what was the matter, her tears broke out afresh as she explained that a certain Mademoiselle de Montluc was going to leave school, and the other girls intended to give a sort of farewell luncheon party in her honour. Marianne had not enough money to pay her subscription like the rest.

"I have only six *francs* left," she sobbed, "and my allowance won't be paid for six weeks. If I give the six *francs*, I shall have nothing left; besides, it is not enough."

Napoleon made a movement to put his hand in his pocket, but recollecting that he had no money, he stopped, blushed, and stamped his foot impatiently on the ground.

Madame Permon gave her the ten or twelve *francs* required, and when they were seated in the carriage on their way home. Napoleon broke into indignant remarks on the detestable management of the Government schools and colleges, such as Saint Cyr and the *École Militaire*; and his language became so violent and abusive that Comnenus, who was naturally hasty, exclaimed, "Hold your tongue! It is not your place, when you are being educated by the charity of the king, to speak as you are doing."

Napoleon turned crimson and then pale, and in a voice trembling with anger replied—

"I am not the pupil of the king, but of the State!"

"A fine distinction!" cried Comnenus. "What does it signify whether you are a pupil of the king or the State? Besides, the king is the State, and I will not allow you to speak so of your benefactor before me."

"I will say nothing to displease you, Monsieur de Comnenus," replied Napoleon, "only if I were master and made the regulations they would be altered for the general good."

Long afterwards the Emperor Napoleon, who never forgot the mortifications of his youth, entirely reorganised the administration of the military schools.

While he was at the college, he was disliked both by his superiors and companions, who declared him to be so unsociable that it was impossible to make friends with him, and that he did nothing but grumble and find fault. The consequence was to hasten the time of his exchange from the college to a regiment. There was a unanimous entreaty for his departure, a sub-lieutenant's commission in an artillery regiment was given to him, and he was sent to Grenoble.

Before he left Paris, he spent some days with the Permons. Cécile, then a child of twelve or thirteen, was being educated at the Convent of the Dames de la Croix, but often came home for holidays. She and Laura, who was much younger, were in the room when he entered, wearing his uniform for the first time with pride and delight. But unfortunately his boots were enormously large, and as his legs happened to be remarkably small and thin, they gave him a most ridiculous appearance, so that Cécile and Laura fell into uncontrollable fits of laughter, which made him very angry; but they only laughed all the more, and Cécile answered, "Now that you wear a sword you ought to be the '*chevalier des dames*,' and think yourself lucky that, they should joke with you."

"It is easy to see that you are nothing but a little schoolgirl," replied

Napoleon.

"And you are nothing but a puss-in-boots," retorted Cécile.

Napoleon became still more angry, but as Madame Permon joined in the general laugh, he said nothing. A day or two afterwards he brought Laura a toy he had caused to be made on purpose for her, representing puss-in-boots running before the carriage of the Marquis de Carabas, and for Cécile a beautifully bound copy of the story of *Puss-in-boots*, on seeing which Madame Permon observed—

"The story-book is *de trop*, Napoleon. The plaything for Loulou is all very well, but the story for Cécile proves that you have not forgiven her."

Time passed on, and the state of affairs grew more and more threatening. Everyone seemed to be living in an atmosphere of fear and foreboding, but no real measures of precaution or defence against the coming danger were adopted—it was like the calm of stagnation that often precedes a fearful tempest.

It was the 5th of May, 1789, when the States-General held their first sitting. The day before, the three estates, nobles, clergy, and *tiers-état*, or deputies of the people, were to repair to Versailles to attend Mass at the church of Saint Louis. It was to be an imposing sight, and Madame Permon was anxious to see it. M. Permon would not go. He disapproved strongly of the States being assembled just then, when the two parties were so inflamed against each other that danger was sure to arise.

Madame Permon, however, accompanied by her son and another officer, and taking Laura with them, drove to Versailles through the shouting, rejoicing crowds, whose hopes and expectations were centred in the new Parliament. Everyone seemed to be animated by the same joyful confidence; well-dressed women waving their handkerchiefs, the people cheering frantically as the deputies passed; everywhere a scene of enthusiasm.

Madame Permon, who had many friends in all the three orders, looked on with eager interest and sympathy. Laura was delighted with the splendid show, but Albert remarked the sullen, hostile faces of the deputies of the *tiers-état*, and thought of his father's words. On their return, he told him his impression, which M. Permon repeated on the following day to Necker, of whom he was a friend, exclaiming—

"Ah! what a mistake they have made in convoking that assembly in such a stormy time as this!"

"It is not my fault," replied Necker; "and yet I am responsible for it."

M. Permon's predictions were only too quickly fulfilled. The violence of the opposing parties in the new Parliament only accelerated the calamity it had been hoped it would avert, and on the 14th of July the Revolution broke out, in all its horror and fury, with the storming of the Bastille and the murder of its garrison. During the weeks and months that followed, life at Paris was like a perpetual nightmare.

One alarming event rapidly succeeded another. On the 1st of October a banquet was given at Versailles by the king's bodyguards to the *régiment de Flandre*, in the hall of the opera, at which the king, queen, and *dauphin* appeared. Their entrance was the signal for a frenzy of loyal demonstration. The band struck up the royalist air, "*Richard! O mon Roi,*" the young officers climbed into the boxes, maids of honour and ladies of the court tore up their handkerchiefs to make them white cockades, the *tricolor* was trampled underfoot.

When the news of this *fête* became known at Paris it aroused the rage of the populace. Furious, threatening crowds thronged the road to Versailles, and on the 6th the terrible procession re-entered Paris escorting the unfortunate royal family.

M. Permon, beside himself with grief and horror, was anxious to go to Versailles, but his wife, putting Laura into his arms, with tears and entreaties implored him not to leave them, till at length he yielded to her representations. They closed the shutters of the great *salon*, which looked on to the *Quai Conti*, before three o'clock in the afternoon, and remained indoors all the rest of the day, trembling at the cries and tumult outside.

CHAPTER 2
The Terror
1791

It would be scarcely possible now to realise the constant anxiety, alarm, and tension in which for so long a period people at that time went on living. There could be no peace or security night or day; it was dangerous to express unpopular opinions, and still more dangerous to make an enemy, however apparently insignificant. Sometime in the year 1791 a man named Thirion set up a little upholsterer's shop near M. Permon's house, and called to ask for his custom. The *valet-de-chambre* of Madame Permon replied that they had already an upholsterer, whom they certainly should not leave for a new one; whereupon the fellow became so violent and abusive that M. Permon, hearing the noise he was making, came to see what was the matter, and turned him out of the house, observing that he was not only mad but insolent. He soon forgot all about it, but Thirion vowed vengeance on him and his family.

In the following year M. Permon, alarmed at the aspect of affairs, made a journey to England accompanied by his son, taking with him a sum of money which he had realised in order to place it safely in London while the route was still open. Having transacted his business, and not liking to remain longer than a few weeks away, he returned to France, leaving Albert with orders to await his instructions, which he did in much anxiety, for a fortnight, at the end of which he got a letter from his father, telling him to take a letter he enclosed to his man of business in London and then return at once to France. When he arrived, on the morning of the 9th of August he found that his father had fought a duel with one of the officers of his regiment who had spoken slightingly of his political opinions in his father's presence.

As to M. Permon, who had fought plenty of duels and was said to be *de la première force*, an affair of the kind troubled him very little; he considered it impossible to allow remarks to the disadvantage of his son to be made before him, but he concealed the matter from his wife lest she should be frightened, and from the public because it was safer not to draw too much attention to one's proceedings just then.

The duel took place in the wood of Meudon; M. Permon was unhurt and his opponent wounded in the arm. Paris had just been divided into sections, and in the one in which his house was situated the upholsterer, Thirion, was an influential personage.

One morning soon after his return, as he was dressing, a domiciliary visit, ordered by the Commune, was announced, directed by Thirion, who presented himself at the door of his dressing-room attended by three others—his two brothers and his shop-boy.

The sight of this man so irritated M. Permon that he imprudently advanced with a threatening gesture and his razor in his hand, for he was shaving.

"I am here to carry out the law," cried Thirion.

"Well, and what does the law wish to express by such a respectable agent?"

"I am here to know your age, your qualifications, and the reasons for your journey to Coblentz?"

M. Permon, who, ever since he saw the fellow, had been longing to kick him out of the house, was speechless with anger. He laid down his razor and turned to the intruder, crossed his arms, and stood looking at him in silent contempt. At last he said, "You want to know my age?"

"Yes, those are my orders."

"Where are your orders?" asked M. Permon, holding out his hand. "Show them to me."

"It is enough for you to know that I am sent by the committee of my section; my presence here proves it."

"You think so? Well, I think the contrary. Your presence in my house is an insult, unless it is justified by an official order. Show it to me, and I shall forget the man and only recognise the public functionary."

"I tell you again," shouted Thirion, "that you have no occasion to see my order. Once more, will you answer my questions? What is your age? What are your qualifications? What did you go to Coblentz for?"

"And you, once more, will you show me the order by virtue of which you violate my domicile?"

"It is enough for you that I am here. What is your age?"

"If you ask me such a question on the part of a pretty woman, I am five-and-twenty. Otherwise," he continued, giving way to his indignation and seizing a large bamboo cane, "I will teach you that I am quite young enough to thrash insolent fellows," and as he spoke, he whirled the stick over the heads of Thirion and his acolytes.

Serious consequences might have followed had not Madame Permon come in at that moment and contrived to get her husband away into another room. Thirion departed with many threats, while Madame Permon and Cécile tried to calm M. Permon.

Presently Napoleon Buonaparte entered the *salon*, where he only found Laura, who was crying. He tried to comfort her, and asked what was the matter. When the child told him what had happened, he went and knocked at the door of her father's dressing-room, where the matter was explained to him.

"How abominable!" he exclaimed. "How infamous! Four men to come into the house without producing an order to legalise it! But you must complain. It's evident from what you tell me that the fellow has had a spite against you for some time, and thinks this is a good opportunity to revenge himself. There is no time to be lost; I will see about it, leave it to me."

Buonaparte left the house and went to the committee of the section, to whom he spoke strongly of what had taken place, but he saw at once that Thirion had been beforehand with him. However, he did not allow that to prevent his saying what he chose, but represented that the man's refusal to show his order might have had disastrous consequences, for if M. Permon had shot him he would have been within his right as defending his domicile.

Napoleon returned to the Permons, and said that there was so much agitation going on all around that he could not do much, but advised them to be on their guard. However, the terrible events that almost immediately took place drove every lesser matter out of people's minds.

The affair of Thirion happened early in August, and on the morning of the 9th Albert arrived from England. Cécile had left the convent and was now living at home, where the usual preparations, so far as was possible at such a time, had been made for Laura's *fête* which, as there was no Ste. Laure or Laurette, was observed on the 10th of August, the *fête St. Laurent*. Madame Permon wished it to be a day of which the child should have a happy remembrance, so her young friends were already invited to celebrate it, and from morning till night her little white bedroom was filled with flowers, toys, and *bonbons*. But now festivities and rejoicings were far enough from everyone's thoughts. From the early hours of the morning the increasing tumult filled the household with terror; the crash of artillery, shouts and cries, the groans of the wounded who were carried past under the windows.

Leaving the house shut up, M. Permon and Albert went out to see if they could be of use to any of their friends who might be in danger.

About midday Albert came in, bringing with him one of his brother-officers disguised in the great-coat of a *bourgeois*. The poor fellow had eaten nothing for forty-eight hours. They were looking for him, and if they found him, he would certainly be murdered. His family were under great obligations to the queen, and he had lately fought three duels in her defence, in two of which he had killed his opponent. He was in deadly peril. Madame Permon and Albert hid him in Laura's little room, giving the child careful instructions what to say if she were questioned. It was her first lesson in prudence and caution.

But the day passed on and M. Permon did not return. His wife and children waited in terror and anxiety hour after hour, Madame Permon crying and wringing her hands, Albert going every few minutes to the *porte cochère* to look out. Owing to the isolated position of the house he was tolerably safe there, and even ventured out on to the *quai*, but could learn nothing of his father. He was told of the slaughter of the Swiss guards, the storming of the Tuileries, the flight of the weak, vacillating Louis and the royal family to the Assembly. The fury of the conflict seemed to have abated, the firing was less frequent, but still scattered shots were to be heard every now and then, while groups of drunken, furious men and women roamed through the streets yelling and shouting out horrible blasphemies and threats.

Twilight was gathering when at last Albert saw a figure come cautiously round the corner, looking carefully about him on all sides. At once he recognised his father, who stopped on seeing someone watching at the door, but on Albert's calling to him as loudly as he dared M. Permon came forward quickly, told him to keep the door open, and turned back into the street round the corner to fetch a tall man whom he had left under shelter in the *Arcade de la Monnaie*. The man could hardly walk, but leaned on the arm of M. Permon, who brought him in with great care and helped him into his bedroom, desiring all to keep as quiet as possible and do what they could to help him. When he threw off the military cloak in which he was wrapped they recognised an old friend, M. de Bévy, one of the superior officers of the *gardes-du-corps*, pale, exhausted, and covered with blood.

"Poor Loulou!" he exclaimed, on seeing the trembling child, "it is a sad *fête* for you. Great God! what a *fête!*" His head sank on his breast, overcome more by the terrible events of the day than by his physical sufferings. There was no chance of anyone's escape that night, during the whole of which bands of ruffians, mad with wine and blood, were parading the streets outside with curses and cries.

Next morning came a messenger from the valet of Albert's friend, telling his master that he was in great danger, as search was being made for him everywhere. Then Albert recollected that an influential person whom he knew lodged near at hand. To him he went, and by his permission and assistance the young officer was first hidden in a safer place, and four or five days later enabled to escape to Germany.

As to M. de Bevy, he resolved to try to get to London, and M. Permon was occupied in writing him a letter of credit to take with him—for the house was no longer safe, and he must get away as soon as possible—when a footman came in saying that the butcher they employed, who was in the *Garde Nationale*, but a respectable, trustworthy man, had come to warn M. Permon that he had been denounced for giving refuge to the enemies of the people, adding that he was sure no one could wish to hurt him as he gave so much employment and did no harm to anyone, but he had better be on his guard. More than that the butcher dared not say, and M. Permon, who was never afraid of anything, would not pay any attention to his words. However, about an hour afterwards a friend arrived with a still more urgent warning and the promise of a passport for M. and Madame Permon to one of the southern towns, for it was all-important to get them out of Paris. This friend also promised to come and fetch them and get them safely out of the city, but said it was out of the question to take anyone else.

Madame Permon was distracted between the necessity of going with her husband and the horror of leaving her children at Paris at such a time. But there was not a moment to lose, and it was decided that Cécile and Laura should be placed in some obscure school and that Albert should lodge near them and look after them. M. de Bévy had found another refuge. Hurried preparations were accordingly made, and that same evening, after a heartrending farewell between the parents and children, who knew that it was very possible they might never meet again in this world, M. and Madame Permon left Paris, and the two girls were sent to a school in the *rue du faubourg St. Antoine*, kept by the Demoiselles Chevalier.

It was a new experience for them both. Laura had never been away from home before, and to Cécile, though she had been brought up at a convent, there was all the difference in the world between the household and establishment, of the *Dames de la Croix* and the second-rate school to which it was considered safest to send them, a religious house at such a time being, of course, out of the question.

Laura, who had never seen such a place, when she found herself without her nurse, surrounded by strangers and discomforts, cried bitterly. Cécile, who was old enough to understand the peril of their position, tried to forget her own sorrow to console her little sister. Albert and their nurse, Rénesson, paid them frequent visits. Shocked to find that they had sour apples, cheese, and other coarse food given them, she shed many tears, and insisted on bringing them such quantities of grapes, peaches, pears and cakes that Albert was obliged to diminish her supplies for fear of compromising the girls.

The only happy hours they had were during these visits, and after a short time they observed that their brother had become much more depressed and sad. They begged him to tell them what was the matter, and he replied that their father had been denounced in the section in a manner that rendered his position still more dangerous. The fact was that he had been told that M. and Madame Permon had been arrested at Limoges and were being brought back to Paris. However, this fortunately turned out to be untrue.

It was then the end of August, and affairs in Paris grew worse and worse. Albert drove every day to see his sisters in a carriage his father had lately had built. It was a *cabriolet*, very high and smart-looking, and was called a "*whiskey*"; and its appearance, with the livery which, in spite of the remonstrances of Cécile, he persisted in making the servant who accompanied him wear, excited the angry attention of the mob as he passed through the *faubourg St. Antoine*.

The Demoiselles Chevalier had in their employment a man named Jacquemart, who did all the rough work of the house. He was useful enough, as he seemed able to turn his hand to anything, but so hideously ugly and with an expression so sinister that Albert and his sisters regarded him almost with horror.

One day, soon after their arrival at the school, Jacquemart was carrying in some wood when Albert drove up at such a pace that, although he called to him to look out, the man, who was heavily laden, could not get out of the way in time. Seeing this, Albert, at considerable risk to himself and his horse, pulled up so suddenly that Jacquemart escaped without any injury but a slight bruise on the leg, and as he saw clearly what happened, he from that moment vowed gratitude to young Permon.

It was the 31st August, and although that day he had little or nothing to do at the place, Jacquemart was hanging about the courtyard and the entrance of the *pension Chevalier* from morning till evening, watching for Albert, who on that occasion happened to come later than usual. As he got down from his *cabriolet* Jacquemart came up to him and said—

"Don't go home this evening. Stay here and take care of your sisters."

Albert looked at him with surprise. He knew that an attack was expected that same evening, but he thought it would be directed towards the Temple—then the prison of the Royal family.

"What do you mean?" he asked.

"I advise you to sleep here," replied Jacquemart. "You will be near your sisters, and if they stand in need of protection—well, we shall be ready."

Albert, however, did not take his advice, but gave him an *assignat* of twenty-five *francs*, went in to see his sisters, and then returned home.

The next day, September 1st, was the eve of the massacres at the prisons. News that the Duke of Brunswick's army had crossed the frontier, and had even fought a successful battle at Longwy, excited the Parisians to still greater ferocity; arrests and murders were going on all over the town. Dreadfully alarmed for his sisters, Albert came to the school to see them at considerable risk to himself. Jacquemart was standing at the door of the courtyard, looking a most frightful ruffian; the Demoiselles Chevalier were terrified at his appearance but afraid to send him away. The girls were all dreadfully frightened.

"I did not tell you to come here today, but to stop here!" he cried when he saw Albert. "Why did not you attend to me?"

"And why did you tell me any such thing?" returned Albert. "Is Mademoiselles Chevalier's house especially threatened?"

"I don't know, but at such a time of horror as this there is everything to fear," answered Jacquemart.

Something not only in these words, but in the tone of voice and expression of the man's eyes, struck Albert. The voice was refined and cultivated; the expression was compassionate, even gentle.

"You are a good master and a good brother," continued this strange individual, "therefore you cannot fail in your duty to these poor little things. They have no one at Paris but you. Is not that so?"

It was late, and all over Paris cries and groans were heard. Mademoiselle Chevalier invited Albert to remain that night, but he refused, saying that he would come back in the morning. Cécile was terrified at Jacquemart in spite of what her brother told her, and the danger of going through the streets was very great; however, Albert persisted in going home, as he had to finish arranging some papers left by his father. They took a long time to arrange, so that when, the next day, he had burned all those marked by his father to be destroyed, looked over the rest and put them safely away, it was already three o'clock.

Then he got into his *cabriolet*, with his servant by his side, and drove towards the *faubourg St. Antoine*. The town was in a frightful state. They kept meeting groups of miscreants half naked and stained with blood, carrying on their swords and pikes pieces torn from the clothes of their victims, their inflamed faces, haggard eyes, and horrible expression making them hideous to behold.

The farther he went the more numerous they were, and Albert, in desperate fear for his sisters, from whom he had so rashly allowed himself to be separated, pushed on as fast as he could, resolved to get to them at all hazards. At last the *cabriolet* was stopped by a crowd of these bloodstained villains, who were howling, singing, and dancing. They looked like devils. Calling out that here was an aristocrat, they surrounded the *cabriolet* with frightful yells. At that moment a head with long, fair hair, raised on a pike, approached Albert till it touched his face, and with a terrible cry he recognised the head of the Princess de Lamballe. He fell senseless on to the bottom of the *cabriolet*, while his servant urged on the horse, knocking over the ruffians who stood nearest, and driving as hard as he could, feeling all the time that a man had got up behind them, and hoping he would fall off. However, when they stopped at the door of the Demoiselles Chevalier the man jumped down, took the insensible form of Albert in his arms as if he had been a child, and carried him into the house, muttering, "Monsters! they have killed him too, poor lad!"

It was Jacquemart. Who he was and what he was doing there was a mystery that was never solved. It was evident that he had no bad intentions, and the Permons always supposed that he was concealing himself in this disguise. He disappeared, and they saw him no more.

Albert meanwhile had been carried, pale and senseless, into the house, to the terror of his sisters and the rest of the household. The shock brought on a serious illness, during which he was nursed in the house of a doctor, and his mother was communicated with at once.

Madame Permon, who was at Toulouse with her husband, soon returned to Paris to look after her son. When he was well enough to be moved, she set off for Toulouse, taking all her three children, escorted by M. de Luppé, a friend of her family.

Their journey having been accomplished in safety, Madame Permon looked about for an apartment, and finally established herself and her household in one of those enormous old-fashioned *hôtels* built round a great courtyard, with ample room to accommodate four families, one of whom occupied one side or end. Each was, in fact, like a separate house, with its own entrance, hall, and staircase. The Permons were fortunate enough to get one of these, and to settle themselves in it for the present.

M. Permon's health had been seriously affected by all he had gone through, and there was, of course, no society just then. Almost everybody had either lost some near relation or was in deadly fear for one or more in prison or in exile; and the more retired and quiet people's lives were the safer it was for them. Although they had escaped from Paris, the danger was by no means at an end. The fury of the Revolution was raging at Toulouse also. The proconsul, a venomous little scoundrel and a violent Jacobin, soon began to annoy them and cause them much uneasiness, but by good luck they had a friend, a Corsican named Salicetti, who was powerful and influential enough to protect them if he chose, and was now at Paris engaged in the trial of the king.

It was true that there had been a coolness between them in consequence of some discussion which took place at the Permons' house in Paris; still he was an old friend and a countryman, and to him Madame Permon, after some consideration, decided to write. It was well that she did so, for they were in a dangerous position. M. Permon was in extremely bad health, and Albert was so delicate that if he were forced to join the army he would probably die of consumption. By the next post arrived a letter from Salicetti, in which he assured them of his satisfaction in being able to help them. He wrote and recommended them to the especial protection of the authorities of Toulouse, made Albert his own secretary, and sent him his nomination and three months' leave of absence. It was then about Christmas time.

The trial of the king caused the greatest anxiety and grief to M. Permon, and his execution filled him with profound depression. He wanted to go back to Paris to see if he could not do something at least for Madame Elizabeth, to whom he was deeply grateful for some kindness and help he had received from her in past years. Madame Permon represented that it would only be throwing away his life to no purpose.

"You will destroy yourself and do her no good," she said, with tears, when he was on the point of setting off for Paris. "You cannot possibly save her; and what is to become of your children?"

M. Permon allowed his wife's entreaties to prevail and remained at Toulouse, shut up in the house writing a book on education and teaching Laura, who was the only person always allowed to be with him. The child would sit silently studying while his fits of melancholy dejection lasted. There was a great difference between the ages of the three surviving children of M. and Madame Permon; Albert being, when they took up their abode at Toulouse, twenty-four years old, Cécile sixteen, and Laura nine.

They remained at Toulouse until the fury of the Revolution had abated—eventful years full of excitement and emotions. The powerful protection of Salicetti ensured their safety; they found and made a small circle of friends, and the old southern town, with its ancient houses, grey cathedral, and lovely walks by the river and in the neighbourhood, very soon seemed friendly and familiar to them. M. Permon never left it during that time, but Albert was away at Paris with Salicetti, and on one occasion Madame Permon, after an attack of inflammation of the lungs which left her chest delicate, went to Cauterets in the Pyrenees, taking Cécile and Laura with her, to their great delight.

M. Permon could not go with them, not being then allowed to leave Toulouse. His health did not improve, and the perpetual seclusion in which he lived began to excite attention and comment, and to constitute a fresh danger for himself and his family.

The *Procureur de la Commune* was a certain Conder, a shoemaker, who though a violent republican was an honest man and had befriended them on several occasions, having received from Madame Permon a promise that they would not emigrate.

One day he came to see her and warned her that disquieting reports about her husband were going about the town.

"It is said," remarked Conder, "that he is saturated with aristocracy. I declared that it was not true, but that he was a good republican. Of course, I know," he added, with a smile, "that that is not exactly so, but one can't always tell the exact truth. But if you will take my advice, force the *citoyen* Permon to go to the theatre now and then. If he would do me the honour to accept a place in my box—" and he hesitated in some embarrassment.

Touched by the kind intentions of the man, Madame Permon caught him by the hand and expressed her gratitude, promising that they would accept his invitation. But it was not so easy to manage her husband, who, when he heard her proposition, remained silent, and on her asking impatiently what he was going to do, replied with a shrug of the shoulders—

"What a question? What would you have me do? The *citoyen* Conder invites the *citoyen* Permon to his box at the theatre; therefore, he must go there, since it is better than being dragged to prison, for I have the choice, I suppose? It is another Thirion! Oh! Marie, Marie, could you not have spared me this?" And he walked up and down the room in despair.

"Charles," said Madame Permon, "you are making a mistake. Is it likely that I should have entertained a proposal that could be insulting to you? Of course not. Conder—"

"My dear Marie," interrupted her husband impatiently, "let the man make you some shoes, but let me hear no more about his box at the theatre. I am tired of it."

He said no more, and Conder was told that he was too ill. It was fortunate that although the worthy *procureur* saw clearly enough how the matter stood, he did not resent it, or at any rate took no steps to revenge himself, as he might easily have done. Soon afterwards Madame Permon received a letter from Salicetti warning her that there were rumours of royalist plots and conspiracies, that her husband was an object of suspicion owing to his persisting in shutting himself up in the way he did, and that it was absolutely necessary that he should at any rate receive people at his house. "Your *salon* was charming at Paris, why should it not be the same at Toulouse?"

At last M. Permon, to whom she showed this letter, perceived the danger to which his obstinacy was exposing them all, and consented to open his house. Madame Permon knew a great many people in Toulouse by this time, and, as Salicetti had predicted, her *salon* was soon as popular as before.

She had met in Toulouse, by chance, a cousin of hers, a Signorina Stephanopoli, who had left Corsica and married a French naval officer, M. de Saint-Ange. He had retired and bought a *château* near Toulouse, where he lived with his wife and children.

The cousins were delighted to find each other again, and frequently met and talked about old times and their beloved Corsica.

"Well," said Madame de Saint-Ange one day, "it seems there is one of Laetitia Ramolino's sons who is getting on well. I should not wonder if some day he were to be a *général de division*. I should never have guessed it. I should always have thought that the one to raise the family would be Joseph. And the archdeacon—"

"Oh! do let the archdeacon alone!" exclaimed Madame Permon. "It was bad enough to hear everybody always talking about him in Corsica."

"Well, the canon, then, if the word archdeacon annoys you," replied Madame de Saint-Ange, laughing. "He is their uncle, and authority enough in the family for me to quote him about the children; and he thinks, as I do, that Joseph is the one formed to distinguish himself. See how handsome he is and what charming manners he has, whereas Napoleon, although he is your *protégé*, is as ugly as a penguin, as obstinate as a mule, and very rude besides."

The Permons, after the warning of Salicetti, went into society and entertained a good deal. One evening they were going to have a dinner-party, and amongst others they expected was M. de Regnier, commandant of the place, an old soldier whom M. Permon particularly liked. Half an hour before dinner he sent a note saying that a friend of his had just arrived, having been sent to him on a matter of business, and as he could not leave him, he must beg to be excused.

Madame Permon asked him to come and bring his friend with him, observing to her children that an adjutant-general, a friend of M. de Regnier, was sure to be some tiresome old man who would spoil the party. They had intended to have music, which he would not care for; he would have to play *reversi*. "An old infantry officer can always play *reversi*, and always cheats too," she added.

Albert was just then at home on leave, and was devoted to music. He played duets with Cécile, who was a pupil of Hermann, a brilliant *pianiste* and a very attractive girl. Without regular beauty, she was slight and graceful, with fair complexion, dark blue eyes, and the *cheveux blonds cendrés* so much admired in France.

When M. de Regnier arrived, instead of a tiresome old man, his friend proved to be a very good-looking young one, extremely fond of music. Cécile was dressed in pink *crêpe*; she played, sang, and looked like an angel—at least in the opinion of M. de Geouffre, who immediately fell in love with her.

Next day he called on Madame Permon, and after that he came perpetually, sometimes with M. de Regnier, sometimes without him.

Madame Permon saw with disapprobation the reason of these constant visits. Both she and her husband had the strongest objection to a son-in-law in the Republican Army, and yet she was afraid to put a stop to his coming.

M. de Regnier knew this well enough. However, after some difficulties he yielded to the entreaties of his friend and went to see the Permons about the matter. As he had expected, they both refused at once. "But what have you against him?" asked M. de Regnier. "He is well born: I tell you he is one of the Geouffres de Chabrignac of Limousin. Several of them have emigrated. He has a tolerable fortune and a nice place near Brives-la-Gaillarde. He is well thought of in the army, and very high up in it for his age; he is certain of promotion. He is clever and handsome too, which is no drawback to a marriage. Come, Madame Permon, let me persuade you."

But it was no use, they still refused, and no representations either from M. de Geouffre or anyone else for some time had any effect.

Cécile, however, had fallen in love with him, and fretted in secret at her parents' decision. She was a gentle, timid girl, very much afraid of her mother; and Madame Permon, though she had a great affection for all her children, committed the fatal error of not treating them alike.

The great difference in their ages probably exaggerated this tendency, besides which Cécile had been brought up away from her, but Laura was never out of her sight. At any rate, while she treated the latter with great indulgence, she was strict—almost severe—with the former, so that Laura, a clever, merry, high-spirited child, was devoted to and perfectly at ease with her mother, while Cécile was shy, reserved, and in considerable awe of her. So, Cécile did not venture to oppose her parents' decision, or even to let them know that she was unhappy, only as time went on everyone remarked on her melancholy and altered looks. Her father's health was so bad at that time that she saw scarcely anything of him. Albert was away and Madame Permon did not notice that anything was amiss.

M. de Geouffre, however, persevered all the more, and about six months after his first offer he got a friend of his to go to Madame de Saint-Ange, who readily promised to help him.

She went to see the Permons, and observed how ill and languid Cécile looked.

"Panoria," she said one morning to Madame Permon, "when are you going to marry Cécile?"

"What a question!" replied her cousin. "You know very well that I have refused."

"Have you looked at your daughter? Don't you see how she is changed? Do you know that you are answerable for what she suffers?"

"Kalli," said Madame Permon, much disturbed, "I leave you to manage your own family, and I wish you would not concern yourself with mine."

"Indeed! Well, if you take it in that way, I am accustomed to be frank, and I tell you that you are not a good mother."

"Kalli!"

"No, you are not a good mother. Send for your daughter; ask Loulou what sort of nights her sister passes, and then say what you like."

Madame Permon, who had no idea of the state of things and no wish to make Cécile unhappy, called Laura, and from the questions she asked discovered that Cécile spent the nights in crying and lamenting, but had forbidden her little sister to say anything about it. Filled with remorse, Madame Permon then sent for Cécile, and assured her with tears that since it appeared she had set her heart upon this marriage it should take place; and at the end of another month the wedding was celebrated, and Cécile, now Madame de Geouffre, took up her abode in the Hôtel Spinola, the headquarters of the district her husband commanded.

The death of the queen, and still more that of Madame Elizabeth, caused a shock to M. Permon from which he never recovered. Gradually his health failed so completely that he seldom came down even to dinner, but remained almost always in his bedroom or study.

And though the fall and execution of Robespierre caused a paroxysm of joy and relief throughout the country, and the worst of the Terror was over, all danger was by no means at an end. The executions at Paris, though less numerous, had not ceased, and at first people dared not express the delight they felt at the death of the tyrant. Until France was delivered from the tyranny of the convention there could be no real security for anyone.

CHAPTER 3
Violent Scenes in Paris
1793-1795

In this atmosphere of suspicion, anxiety, and danger people all over France went on living for a considerable time longer.

M. Permon was kept informed of what was going on at Paris by his lawyer, M. Brunetiere, a man of great experience and capacity who belonged to the Chatelet, knew everybody and had dealings with all the powers and authorities. All letters, however, had to be exchanged with the greatest precaution. Though the Terror was over, it might at any moment break out again.

Letters were sent concealed in pies, in cakes, in poultry, in the linings of coats and dresses, in hats and bonnets. With the box or parcel was generally sent a letter, saying, "In compliance with your order I send you" such and such a thing. Now, as he had ordered nothing, the receiver of such a notice knew that a letter of importance was to be found somewhere in the article sent. Madame Permon, however, did not like the dresses, bonnets, &c., that came to her from Paris being pulled to pieces to look for letters in them. On one occasion she wore a headdress for a fortnight before she told her husband that it came from Paris and allowed the letter it contained to be taken out.

It is true that just then nothing of great importance was going on.

At length the time arrived when they were to leave Toulouse. Calmer days seemed to be approaching. M. Permon received pressing letters from different friends urging him to return to Paris, telling him that he was certain of a distinguished post. For all that, he sadly replied it was too late, but he would, if it were possible, go back there to die.

It was arranged that he should go to Bordeaux, where he had some affairs to settle, while his wife should proceed with Laura to Paris to see whether it would be safe for them to live there again. Upon her report their future plans were to depend.

Albert was now at Paris; he had just left Salicetti, and was thinking of going on some business to Holland. He took an apartment for his mother in the Hôtel garni de la Tranquillity, Rue des Filles-Saint-Thomas. They were pleasant rooms on the second floor looking into the garden, and there she installed herself with Laura, a maid and *valet-de-chambre*, and began to receive the visits of such of her friends as had survived the horrors of the Revolution.

Amongst them was the old Comte de Périgord, who had just got out of prison, where his life had been saved by his valet, Beaulieu. Without him, he would have been even more lonely and desolate than he had now become. His wife and daughter were dead, his sons had emigrated, he had lost almost all his fortune, his health was impaired.

When his master was arrested, Beaulieu devoted himself to his service. He contrived to bring him everything he wanted, and watched over him unceasingly.

The Comte de Périgord, like many others, was always writing to the members of the Committee of Public Safety protesting his innocence and asking for justice. These petitions he gave to Beaulieu to post or deliver.

But Beaulieu had been told by a friend of his own, a relation of the man in whose house Robespierre lived, that this importunity had been the destruction of many of the prisoners, who might very likely have been forgotten, and so escaped, had not their first petition recalled them to the recollection of the tyrants, and the following ones irritated them, so that they often signed their death-warrants to get rid of them.

Beaulieu did not tell his master this, but he put all the petitions into the fire as fast as he received them, and the old count could not imagine why he never obtained any answer. Beaulieu did everything he could to ensure his being forgotten. He bribed the prison officials, and whenever the Comte de Périgord began to be well known in one prison he managed to get him transferred to another. When the Terror was at an end and the prisons were opened he remained with his master, still taking care of him; and another of his servants, directly he knew that the count was free, came back and lived with him in the house of his friend, the Comte de Monchenu, who was still well off, had given him shelter and shown him unceasing kindness and friendship.

Napoleon, directly he heard of the arrival of Madame Permon, hastened to see her, and was received by her with great pleasure. He was then, as Madame de Saint-Ange had said, decidedly plain; thin, sallow, sickly-looking, and slovenly in his dress, his boots were badly made and he wore no gloves because he said it was a useless expense. He had been arrested on an accusation of being a spy and for other matters by order of Salicetti, about whose conduct in the affair Napoleon felt all the more bitterly as they were compatriots and friends. Napoleon had been in considerable danger, and when Madame Permon alluded to the matter he remarked with a momentary smile, "He wished to ruin me, but my star would not let him. However, I ought not to boast of my star, for after all what is to be my fate?"

Napoleon resumed his former intimacy, and was constantly at Madame Permon's house. For advice and assistance, she depended chiefly upon M. Brunetiere, who already repented of having counselled her to return to Paris, where everything was still so unsettled and threatening.

The Royalists were beginning to raise their heads again; their young men went about with hair powdered and plaited, sometimes with a comb in it, dressed in grey coats with black collars and green cravats, armed with thick sticks, for they were continually getting into fights, which they very often provoked.

There was great distress owing to the scarcity and dearness of provisions. Cécile managed to send flour to her mother in secret from the south, but it was unsafe to do so, as it was forbidden, and a heavy penalty attached to it. The people were becoming more and more irritated and menacing, the convention was constantly being invaded by the sections, and gangs of drunken women began to go about again crying out for bread and shouting, "Down with the Republic!"

"*Ma foi!*" exclaimed Napoleon one day, when he came to dine with Madame Permon; "I don't know who they are so furious with, but they are like demons. I have just met a section of the *faubourg St. Antoine*, which was the second volume to the troop that I wish they had commissioned me to receive at the Tuileries on the 10th of August."

They dined hastily, and then went out towards the Tuileries, to get news of what was going on, Napoleon giving his arm to Madame Permon, Albert taking Laura.

Before they had gone far, they heard horrible cries and shouts, women and children yelling against the convention, recalling the days of the Terror; therefore, Napoleon said to Madame Permon, "You had better go back; this place is not fit for women. I will take you home, and then go and find out what is the matter and bring you word."

They returned accordingly, and Napoleon went out with Albert, but neither of them could get back that night. They went to the convention, where fortunately a man of sense and moderation was presiding; the people were yelling like maniacs for the Constitution of '93.

Salicetti was one of those often to be seen at Madame Permon's evenings, but he was gloomy and absent, and whenever any political discussion went on, especially if he and Napoleon took part in it, there was always a tone of bitterness and personality incompatible with the old ideas of well-bred, pleasant society.

Madame Permon, who saw all this with impatient disgust, tried in vain to establish in her present *salon* the charm and ease of the Hôtel Conti. She forbade any politics to be discussed by the miscellaneous groups who drank tea and ate ices in her rooms, and Napoleon, who was entirely of her opinion, tried to help her and to lead the conversation to other topics. But it was impossible, for, with the best intentions, what else was there to talk about?

Literature seemed to be dead—there were no new books except a few translations of English novels; the theatres produced nothing worth speaking of, although now there were plays going on every night, concerts at the *conservatoire*, and even balls. Everyone's mind was preoccupied and filled with the same subjects, to which, do what they might, the conversation always returned. Napoleon came every day to the Permons, and did not seem much more contented than in the old days of the military school. It was true that he was already a general, though not yet six-and-twenty; but the proceedings of Salicetti had for the time ruined his career: he had very little money, and his family could not send him any, as they had become involved in the political troubles of the day, had been forced to leave Corsica, and were now living at Marseilles.

There Joseph had just married Mademoiselle Clary, the daughter of a rich merchant, and sent what help he could from time to time to Napoleon.

Often in the evenings, as the young general walked on the boulevards with his friend Junot, and watched the *jeunesse dorée* riding and driving past in all the luxury it was no longer dangerous to display, he would inveigh against injustice and inequalities of fortune and abuse the young dandies with their ridiculous dress and absurd, lisping speech, for it was then the height of fashion to leave out the letter *r*, and to speak of a *mi'acle, a pa'fum,* and so on.

Junot, whose family was better off, shared everything sent him, as well as all he won at *trente-et-un,* &c., with Napoleon, whom he adored.

Napoleon, in addition to other troubles, had at this time an unfortunate love-affair going on, and Junot was deeply in love with Napoleon's second sister, Pauline, who was remarkably beautiful, but whom he could not afford to marry. To his entreaties that Napoleon would write for him to Madame Buonaparte about Pauline, he only replied—

"I cannot write to my mother to ask her any such thing. You say you will have twelve hundred *livres de rentes.* Very well; but you have not got them now. Your father is in good health, and you will have to wait a long time. In fact, you have nothing but your lieutenant's epaulette. As to Paulette, she has not even as much as that. Therefore consider—you have nothing, she has nothing, what is the total? Nothing. You cannot marry at present. Wait, perhaps we shall have better days, my friend. Yes, we shall have them, if I have to go to another part of the world to find them."

For some time, public affairs seemed to have calmed down, but every now and then some new riot or commotion broke out, recalling to people's minds the fearful days of the Terror, which were past but might return. One day Laura was sent out by her mother to buy some ribbons, gauze, and artificial flowers, under the care of her maid, Mariette. They went in a cab, and as they were coming back along the boulevard, they met a troop of drunken, furious women, yelling and shouting against the convention, and crying out for the Constitution of '93.

Mariette began to cry, but Laura, who had plenty of spirit, said nothing, even when fifty or sixty of them surrounded the carriage, and one, who was the wife of the driver, ordered him peremptorily to get down and open the door.

"But I have a fare in the carriage. And there you are shouting like a fury as usual!"

"I tell you that I am tired, and these *patriotes* too, and we are going to this cursed convention to make them give us bread, *jour de Dieu!* (expression taken literally from the *Memoirs* of the Duchesse d'Abrantès) or the President shall know the weight of my arm as well as you do. Come! no more 'ifs' and 'buts'! Open your *whiskey* at once, I tell you!"

Laura wanted to give the driver twenty *francs* and walk home, but he would not listen or understand. He tried to force his way through the crowd, whereupon his wife herself opened the door and let down the steps. Laura jumped out, beckoning to Mariette to follow, but she was afraid to move.

"Come! room for the good people," cried the woman; but on seeing Laura she took her in her arms. "Why, what's the matter, my chicken?" she said consolingly; and turning to her husband she exclaimed, "And you, animal! couldn't you have told me it was a child like this you had in your carriage? Rabbit's brain! Do you think I am going to put *that* out to walk, stupid? And she is frightened, poor little cat! Is it your mamma inside there, *mon chou?*"

"No, *citoyenne*, it is my maid."

"Well, what is she crying and making all that noise for? One would think she had lost both father and mother."

"Look here, Marianne," cried another woman, opening the opposite door, "she is begging for mercy. The fool thinks we are going to kill her! Perhaps she is a princess in disguise!" And they all began to laugh at Mariette, who cried all the louder.

"Come! will you be quiet, you idiot!" cried another. "Hold your tongue and come out!" and she seized hold of her arm. Mariette screamed and fell on her knees in the carriage.

"Well! what is it?" cried the proprietress of the cab. "Leave the girl alone. Do you think I'm going to make *that* go on foot? Why, she can hardly hold herself up. And then this child!" as she felt Laura tremble. She was a tall, handsome woman, with fine eyes, teeth, and complexion, and the strength of a giantess. Her language, like that of her companions, was interlarded with oaths and blasphemies, but her dark eyes rested compassionately upon Laura.

"Come, get back into the *coucou, mon chou,*" she said, "and go to your mamma; but tell her not to let you run about with nobody but God to take care of you, for you might just as well be quite alone as with a canary like that, or that rabbit of a coachman either! Where did you take them from?" she added, turning to her husband.

"Rue des Filles-Thomas, close to the Théâtre Feydeau."

"Well, then take them back there. I am going with the others, and you can come after me. The more the better."

And lifting Laura in her arms, she embraced her, thrust her into the carriage, put up the steps, shut the door, and with two or three oaths called out to her husband in a voice like thunder, "Drive on!"

Madame Permon was waiting at the entrance of the house in great anxiety, having heard that there were disturbances in the streets.

Laura jumped out of the carriage, threw herself into her arms and burst into tears, having had, as Napoleon laughingly observed, too much pride to cry before the fishwives.

Her mother said that she had shown the spirit of a Spartan, for which she was very much pleased with her.

The state of affairs continued to be disturbed and dangerous. There were insurrections every day, and the strife between the two parties in the convention grew more and more bitter. Among the members were now some men of moderate views and respectable character, but most of them were weak and vacillating. Those of the party known as the *Montagne* comprised the ferocious and violent ruffians such as Collot-d'Herbois, Billaud-Varennes and Barrère, who flattered the mob, and whose aim was to bring back the Terror. To this party Salicetti also belonged.

People of all shades of opinion were in the habit of coming to the *salon* of Madame Permon in the evening, and among them Salicetti, to whom Madame Permon felt herself too much indebted for the protection he had given them to do anything to discourage his presence in her house. But as events grew more and more startling, she felt an unconquerable repugnance to receive as a friend a man who was doing his utmost to bring back the Terror, and she was considering whether she should not speak to him on the subject, when the matter was decided by the following circumstances.

After violent scenes, in which the *Montagne* supported all the demands of the mob, the convention awoke to the critical state of affairs, and gave orders to General Pichegru, who in a few hours arrested the leading members of the Terrorist faction. But the city was seething with rage and excitement, there was a general call to arms, the air was filled with shouts, cries, and the ringing of the tocsin, an armed mob poured out of the *faubourg St. Antoine*, urged on by the conspirators who were driven to desperation, and had promised them the sack of Paris. There was a universal dread of a worse calamity even than that of 10th August, '91. Roused by this frightful danger, the respectable citizens—all, in fact, who had anything to lose—formed themselves into armed and organised bands, and prepared to defend their lives and property.

Madame Permon and Laura remained, of course, shut up at home all day, having done their best to hide their most valuable things. Towards evening Albert, whom they had not seen all day, came in to get some food, exhausted with hunger, having eaten nothing since early morning, for at that time the *cafés* and restaurants, now so universal, were few and scattered. Just as he was finishing his repast Napoleon arrived in the same state. He sat down to the table, telling them, whilst he ate, of the frightful commotion going on in the streets. He asked if they had seen Salicetti the last day or two, and remarked that he had ruined his career.

Albert Permon tried to make an excuse for him, but Napoleon interrupted.

"Hold your tongue, Permon, hold your tongue! That man has been my evil genius. Dumerbion liked me, and would have given me active service. No, I may pardon, but I cannot forget it; that is another thing."

About midnight he and Albert went out together; the streets were still full of excited crowds, a few shots were heard, but the *Montagne* had fallen, the convention was victorious, and for the time the danger was over.

The next day Madame Permon had some people to dinner. It was a sort of farewell party, as she and Laura were to start for Bordeaux four days afterwards to spend some months with M. Permon, and then return with him to Paris. About six o'clock Madame Permon was in her drawing-room, only one person having arrived, when Mariette came and whispered in her ear that there was someone in her bedroom who wanted to speak to her alone.

When she went in she saw a figure standing half-concealed by the curtain of the window. He stepped forward, making a sign to her to keep silence, and she recognised Salicetti. He was deadly pale, his black eyes burning, his lips white.

"I am proscribed," he said in a low, rapid voice, "and that means condemned to death. Gautier met me on the boulevard and warned me. Madame Permon, I have not deceived myself in trusting to your generosity. You will save me, will you not? I need scarcely remind you that I saved your husband and son."

Laura had come in and shut the door. The three stood looking at one another. Through the closed door were heard the voices of the guests assembling in the drawing-room. Madame Permon took her unwelcome guest by the hand and led him into the room beyond, which was Laura's, where they could not be heard.

"I will not waste time in talking," she said. "All that I have is at your disposal. But beyond my own life I value my son and daughter. I am ready to risk my life for you. But if I hide you here only for a few hours—this house will not conceal you longer—I shall not be able to save you, and I shall not only bring my own head to the scaffold, but my son's. I owe you gratitude; say yourself if it ought to go so far as that."

"I would not run you into danger for the world," he replied. "This is my plan and my only hope. This house, being an *hôtel garni*, will never be suspected; the landlady naturally wants to make money. I will give her plenty. Let me be hidden here for a few days, then you are going to Gascony, take me with you and you will save my life. If you refuse me shelter even for a few hours, when I leave this house I shall be arrested, condemned, and perish on the scaffold from which I saved your husband and son."

"Salicetti," said Madame Permon, "there is neither pity nor generosity in what you say. You know my position and take advantage of it. Once more, what can I do in an *hôtel garni*?—a house filled with people from all the provinces, inhabited by your enemies, for you know very well that Buonaparte is one of them. Besides, the landlady is far from sharing your opinions, and is it likely that any promise of yours would induce her to help you at the risk of her life? Everything round us bristles with difficulties."

At that moment someone opened the bedroom door. Madame Permon rushed forward to stand at the inner door, but it was only Albert who came to see why dinner was not served.

"Everybody has come," he said, "except Buonaparte, who has sent an excuse."

Madame Permon clasped her hands tightly, and for a moment raised her eyes to heaven. Albert looked at her in astonishment, but she signed to him to be silent and desired him aloud to order the dinner to be taken in at once. Then, taking a letter from the mantelpiece she entered the drawing-room with it in her hand, saying to the assembled guests that her daughter Cécile had just sent her a messenger from the South with a turkey and truffles, which, if they did not mind waiting, they could have for dinner. This she said because the man who was present when Marietta called her was a chattering, gossiping person, who would be a danger.

Everybody preferred not to wait for the turkey, which she proposed they should eat the next day instead; so, asking leave to finish her letter, she returned into the bedroom, softly bolted the door, and told Salicetti that fortunately Buonaparte was not there.

"Now what is to be done?"

"If you don't refuse to save me, the thing is certain. Do you consent?"

Madame Permon was silent for a minute, and Laura saw by her changing colour the violent agitation she felt. Salicetti, interpreting her silence as a refusal, took up his hat, muttered some words, and turned to go, but Madame Permon caught him by the arm.

"Stay!" she said; "this roof must shelter you. My son must pay his debt, and I must pay my husband's."

"Well, then, it is all settled: there is nothing more to say. Go to dinner, and Marietta will look after me."

Madame Permon stopped for a moment in her own room to regain her composure. Her eyes rested in despair upon Laura, who was clinging to her, for she well knew the danger she was incurring. However, she controlled herself, and no one who saw her bright face and heard her merry laugh could have guessed the deadly fear that made her heart sink. The dinner was gay and animated. M. Brunetière was of the party, and the conversation turned upon Salicetti, of whom he spoke with contempt and reprobation.

At last the evening came to an end, and when everybody was gone Madame Permon told Albert what had happened. He was horrified at the danger for his mother and sister, but there was no time for fear or hesitation; something must be done. They sent for Madame Grétry, their landlady, who was an excellent woman. At the first mention of a proscribed person she exclaimed—

"I have what you require, but for that it will be necessary that Madame Permon should change her apartment. It is a secret place which has saved more than four people already in the Terror, and it will save others yet, as long as I live in this house."

They changed their apartment accordingly without delay, giving out that they wanted a larger one, as M. Permon was coming to Paris, and they arranged that they should pretend to get a second letter from him, saying that after all he was not coming, and summoning them to Bordeaux. Meanwhile Salicetti was put in the secret chamber, which was lined with tapestry and carpets to deaden any sound.

Next morning Napoleon appeared with a large bouquet of violets for Madame Permon, an attention so unwonted on his part that they all laughed, in which he joined, sayings "It seems to me that I don't make a good *cavaliere sirvente*."

He then began to speak of Salicetti, observing that he wondered how he and his friends liked being arrested themselves, and that they were reaping the fruits of their own actions.

"What! is Salicetti arrested?" cried Madame Permon, with an air of surprise, signing to Laura to shut the door.

"Why, didn't you know that the warrant was out against him yesterday? I thought you knew it so well that he was hidden in your house."

"In my house! "exclaimed Madame Permon. "In my house! Napoleon, my dear boy, you must be mad! In my house! Why, I haven't got a house. My dear general, I must really beg you not to make such a joke about me to anyone else. What have I done to you that you should amuse yourself by endangering my life, for that is what it comes to?"

Napoleon got up and stood in silence, looking at her with folded arms for some moments. Then he said—

"Madame Permon, Salicetti is hidden here. Don't interrupt me; I don't know it positively, but I say that he is hidden here, because at five o'clock yesterday he was seen on the boulevard speaking to Gauthier, who warned him not to go to the convention, and he went in this direction. He has not been to the *Palais Égalité*, and he has no friends here intimate enough to risk their own safety and that of their family by receiving him, except you."

"And by what right should he have come to me?" replied Madame Permon. "He knows our opinions are not the same. I was just leaving Paris, and if it had not been for my husband's letter, I should have set off tomorrow morning for Gascony."

"By what right should he come to you? You may well say so, my dear Madame Permon. To go to an unprotected woman whom a few hours' shelter given to a proscribed man who well deserves his proscription would compromise, is a mean, cowardly action of which nobody else would be guilty. You are under an obligation to him; it is like a bill he holds, and which he comes like a bailiff and orders you to pay. Was not that it, Mademoiselle Loulou?" he said, turning abruptly to Laura, who was looking at some flowers, and pretended not to hear.

"Laurette," said her mother, "General Buonaparte is speaking to you, my child."

Laura turned to him with a slight confusion, but Napoleon, taking the child's hand, said to her mother, "I beg your pardon, I was wrong, and your daughter has given me a lesson."

For more than two hours he remained there, Madame Permon denying that Salicetti was in the house; Napoleon, who did not believe it, saying, "Madame Permon, you are a remarkably good woman and he is a scoundrel. He knew you could not shut your doors against him, so he endangered you and this child."

Madame Permon tried to throw him on a false scent by declaring that Salicetti had been there and gone away. At last Napoleon departed, Salicetti having heard through the partition that concealed him the whole of the conversation.

For several days he stayed there, to the great inconvenience of the Permons. Laura was dreadfully afraid of him: she said in after-years that he was to her like a vampire. His principles and ideas were odious to them all, and he was constantly saying something that horrified and disgusted them. The execution of those who were condemned and had been arrested took place. Albert, who knew one of them and went to the scaffold out of kindness to be of some consolation to him, returned much overcome, his overcoat stained with blood, so close had he stood to him. The account he gave of what had passed was too much for Laura, who clung to her mother trembling and sobbing.

Then Salicetti had an attack of fever and delirium. Without any religion and stained with crime, his ravings, curses, and blasphemies were horrible to listen to. At last he was well enough to travel, and it was arranged that they were to set off on their journey to Bordeaux one night, taking Salicetti disguised as a valet, whose name, Gabriel Tachard, he assumed. He was to try to embark at one of the southern ports, those of the north being too strictly watched.

Napoleon had never been deceived by Madame Permon's assurances about Salicetti, and when he asked her at what time she was going to start, and she replied at midnight, as it was better in hot weather to travel at night and rest by day, he remarked sarcastically that it was an excellent idea, and asked if it were her own.

"Whose else should it be? Loulou's?"

"Why not? Mademoiselle Loulou has excellent ideas sometimes; especially when she likes me a little."

"But I like you very much always!" cried Laura.

There had been much trouble and difficulty in hiring a valet, very dark and about thirty years old whose description in the passport would suit Salicetti and then getting the man another place. However, it was done, and all other arrangements completed. Madame Grétry had been lavishly rewarded, but was thankful to see them going, as she had not a moment's peace or safety while Salicetti was there. The day before their departure Napoleon proposed to go with them, saying—

"I will go and see my mother while you are at Bordeaux and Toulouse, and then return with you all to Paris. I have nothing to do, thanks to that scoundrel who has ruined me."

They spent the next day in packing, much disturbed by the continued visits of friends who came to say goodbye. At half-past six they sat down to dinner with several people, among whom were M. Brunetiere and Napoleon. At ten Madame Permon dismissed everybody, saying that she had several things to finish and promising to be back in September or October. When Napoleon took leave of her he held her hand and said in a low voice—

"When you come back here remember this day and say to yourself that today I have given you more than I thought I possessed. Perhaps we may never meet again; my destiny will surely call me far away from Paris before long, but wherever I go you will have a true friend."

They set off, with Salicetti on the box of their travelling-carriage, and were soon safely out of Paris. The first time they changed horses the postilion, who was going back to Paris, brought a letter to Madame Permon.

"It cannot be for me," she said; "it must be a mistake."

"No, no, it is no mistake—at least if you are the *citoyenne* Permon."

On hearing this she remembered that Napoleon had told her he would send her a letter. She took it, therefore, offering him five *francs*, which he refused, saying that he had been paid by the young man.

"Really," said Madame Permon, "one would think I was a young girl being carried away from her lover by her parents. Did anyone ever hear of such a thing?"

She could not see to read the letter, and it was not until the day had dawned that she was able to do so. It was as follows—

> I have never liked to be taken for a dupe, as I should be in your eyes, if I did not tell you that I have known for more than three weeks that Salicetti was concealed in your house. Remember my words; on the *I prairial*, Madame Permon, I was morally certain of it. Now I know it positively. Salicetti, you see I could have repaid you the injury you did me, and by doing so I should have revenged myself, while you did me harm without any provocation. Which is the finest part to have played, yours or mine? Yes, I could have taken my revenge, and I have not done so. Perhaps you will say that your benefactress has been your salvation. It is true that she was a powerful consideration, but

alone, disarmed, and proscribed, your head would have been sacred to me. Go in peace, and find a refuge where you can learn better and more patriotic feelings. My lips are closed for ever upon your name. Repent and appreciate my motives. I deserve it, for they are noble and generous. Madame Permon, my best wishes follow you and your child. You are feeble and defenceless. May Providence and the prayers of a friend be with you. Above all, be prudent and never stop in large towns. *Adieu; recevez mes amitiês.*

Madame Permon passed the letter to Laura, telling her in Greek to read it.

When they stopped to breakfast, she showed it to Salicetti, who exclaimed, "I am lost! Ah! they are mad who believe in the prudence of women!"

"You are more imprudent than any of us, *mon cher*," remarked Madame Permon; "at the same time you pay my daughter and me a great compliment, for you must have great confidence in our generosity when in return for all we have risked you speak in that injurious manner."

Seeing his error, he hastened to apologise, saying that he was alluding to Mariette, but Madame Permon only shook her head, saying—

"You had much better appreciate the noble conduct of Buonaparte, which is admirable."

"Admirable!" was the disdainful answer. "What has he done? Would you have had him betray me?"

"I do not know what I would have of him," returned she, with a contemptuous smile, "but I know that what I wish about you is that you were grateful."

The secret had been betrayed by Mariette to the servant of Napoleon, who was in love with her, in spite of her affection for her mistress and Laura, who by her culpable folly had been placed in the most serious danger. Madame Permon would certainly have lost her life if they had been discovered, and nobody in the house would have escaped altogether. They travelled safely to Bordeaux, and on stopping at their usual hotel found that M. Permon was in the country.

A friend of his, M. Emilhaud, told them that they had tried in vain to find a vessel going to Italy; there would be none for a fortnight, neither was there any starting, except for England, St. Domingo, or America. Salicetti would not go to any of those places and would run great risks by staying in Bordeaux.

But the valet of M. Permon arrived with a message from him that he had succeeded in arranging with a man to let them have a sort of yacht to go up the Garonne to Toulouse and on by the canal to Carcassonne. The carriage could be put on board the yacht and they could land and drive on to Narbonne or Cette, where there were certain to be boats sailing for Venice and Genoa. This would be much safer than the road from Bordeaux to Montpellier. The valet, Landois, told Salicetti that he was being looked for and must embark at once. They went on board at night and Landois with them. The carriage was put on deck and covered up, so that no one could tell what it was from the shore, and they started.

It was a lovely night. Laura and her mother sat on deck talking in low tones as the boat glided through the water, and gazing at the quiet country through which they were passing, illuminated by the bright southern moonlight. Tall trees throwing their dark shadows on the dewy grass, silent fields and woods, here and there an old gabled house or *château* ruined by recent violence, a sleeping village, a church bearing marks of desecration, its windows and doors shattered, grass and weeds growing in the ancient porch, while its priest was either murdered or far away in prison or exile and his flock left to live and die like heathens and savages.

These reflections led them to speak of Laura's first Communion, for which she had passed the usual age, but which the danger—in fact, the impossibility—of attending to religious duties had hitherto prevented.

She was most anxious that it should be no longer delayed, and her mother promised directly they returned to Paris to arrange about it.

Just then Salicetti came on deck, and hearing what they were saying, began to make blasphemous remarks. The customs and manners in which Laura had been educated not permitting a young girl to give an older person the sort of answer he would certainly receive in our own day under such provocation, she got up without speaking, turned away and went down to the little cabin she shared with her mother, where she sat by the open window looking out.

Presently she heard Salicetti, who had taken her place by her mother under the awning on deck, carrying on a conversation which she could not help hearing, but which filled her with horror.

As at first they spoke in undertones, she did not distinguish what they were saying, but as they went on and conversed in a more audible manner, it became evident that she was the subject of discussion and that it was a project of marriage for her that Salicetti was pressing upon her mother, in reply to whose objections that she could not endure him and was too young, he said that she had the spirit of a heroine, with talents and intelligence far beyond her age, that he admired her all the more for hating the man whose presence was a danger to her mother, and that he would give Madame Permon an estate in Normandy and pay all the expenses of her daughter's education in Paris if she would consent to bring her to Italy in two years, supposing he were not by that time free to return to France, concluding with the representation that it would be foolish to refuse such an offer, as M. Permon was ruined and could give Laura no *dot*, whereas she could secure to her all these advantages and a good-looking husband of two-and-twenty.

"It cannot be himself, then," thought Laura with a sigh of relief, and just then Madame Permon brought the conversation to an end by saying that she did not wish to be separated from her child and declined to sell her, besides which the matter was for M. Permon to settle and she was perfectly willing to abide by his decision. She then rose, wished Salicetti goodnight, and came down to the cabin, where Laura told her that she had overheard the conversation and asked who was the young man in question.

"I did not quite understand," replied her mother; "one of his nephews or cousins, he says, but I believe he means himself"

"You must be joking!" exclaimed Laura; "why, he is old enough to be my father!"

"I am not joking at all," answered Madame Permon, "but whether it is he or another, I am not going to allow my Loulou to be taken from me in any such way. Come and kiss me, my child."

Laura clung to her with the passionate affection she had always felt for her mother, and the affair was at an end.

The party arrived safely at Carcassonne and drove to Narbonne, but no boat for Italy could be found there. They accordingly went on to Cette, or rather to Meze, which was a kind of suburb of that place, and took up their abode in a lonely inn surrounded by a salt-water marsh. The landlord at once went down to the port and found that a boat would sail at nine that night for Genoa.

Salicetti even then wanted to wait two days longer for the Trieste boat, observing that the solitude of the inn made it safe enough; but Madame Permon's patience was exhausted, and she replied that it did not suit her to stay any longer in that inn, that the wind might not be favourable in two days, and that he must go that evening.

The inn was not luxurious, but they sat down to an excellent dinner of fish with the captain of the ship that was to take Salicetti. He showed no surprise on seeing the servant dine with them or at anything that passed. Such incidents were easily accounted for at that time.

Directly after dinner the captain announced that the wind was rising and he should sail in an hour. Laudois and some of the people of the inn carried the luggage on board. Salicetti thanked Madame Permon, sent a message of thanks to Napoleon, asked permission to embrace Laura, and followed the captain into the boat that pushed off towards the ship.

Full of delight and relief to have got rid of him and to feel themselves once more in safety, Madame Permon and Laura slept at the inn, and the next morning went on to Montpellier, enjoying the delicious climate and the beauty of the country through which they travelled.

At Montpellier they found a letter from M. Permon saying that he was still detained at Bordeaux but if Laura wanted to go to the fair of Beaucaire they could do so.

The two little towns of Beaucaire and Tarascon stand opposite each other, their houses washed by the Rhone, which flows between them.

The fair of Beaucaire, like those of Leipsic and Frankfort, had long enjoyed a European reputation. To it came traders from London, Paris, India, Russia, in fact from all parts of the world. One of the attractions was a strange kind of mediaeval procession called the *Tarasque*, which, however, did not take place that year, much to Laura's disappointment. The disturbed state of the country made the merchants and everybody else uneasy and spoilt the fair.

They only stopped in the quaint old town long enough to see it, and then went on to Bordeaux, where at length they found M. Permon, delighted to meet them again but looking extremely ill. He listened with great interest to their account of what had happened, and when his wife told him of Napoleon's generosity and Salicetti's slighting observation, he said, "I have nearly always remarked that those who find the noble or generous conduct of others a mere matter of course are incapable of it themselves. And a person who has nothing to revenge cannot put himself in the place of one who holds in his hands the fate of the man who has ruined him."

CHAPTER 4
The Rising Star of Napoleon
1795-1798

Shortly after these events the Permons returned to Paris, staying on their way at the *château* of Madame Saint-Ange, who led a simple country life there with her husband and children. Long afterwards, when Madame Saint-Ange was staying at Laura's house in Paris, and saw her hurrying home to dress for some court festivity with scarcely time to speak to her children, she said to her, "Well, are you happier now than when you played with your cousins and gathered mulberries at Saint Michel?"

They arrived at Paris early in September, and stopped at the Hôtel de l'Autruche (formerly called Hôtel d'Autrichè),

The journey had been very tiring, and when Albert came to see them, he was shocked at the appearance of his father.

They sent immediately for their own doctor, who asked for a consultation, but a bad attack of fever still further reduced his strength.

Napoleon came directly he heard they were in Paris and visited them every day, sending them the news of what was going on in the morning when he could not get there early, for Paris was again in a disturbed and dangerous state.

He was sitting with them one evening when M. Permon was so much worse that Madame Permon wanted the doctor. Albert was not there, and none of the servants dared go into the streets. Napoleon said nothing, but ran downstairs. It was pouring with rain, and there were no cabs to be got, but he returned, wet through, with the doctor.

Paris was now like a besieged city. All night the challenge and reply of the sentinels could be heard under the windows. There was a strict search for arms, and every man fit for service was summoned to the section.

M. Permon was very ill one afternoon in October, when three fellows forced their way into the *salon* in spite of the representations of the landlord, demanding with brutal insolence why he had not presented himself, and on being told that he was ill in bed tried to enter his room.

Napoleon arrived and found Madame Permon defending the door, her indignant defiance having for the moment stopped and disconcerted the ruffians. He managed to clear the house, promising to go himself to the section and complain of them to the President, but

adding—

"Everything is on the brink of an explosion in Paris today; you must be most careful in all you do or say. Albert ought not to go out. You must see to all that, Mademoiselle Laurette, for your poor mother is in a dreadful state."

Madame Permon had, in fact, a bad attack of spasms, to which she was liable after any great agitation.

M. Permon became worse and worse all night, and in the morning the well-known terrible sound of the drums and the hurrying tramp in the streets filled them with fear.

M. Permon, aware of his own danger, sent for his lawyer, but he could not be found, the streets were very unsafe, and as twilight drew on, though the theatres were open, the tumult increased.

Napoleon had been in two or three times; he came while they were at dessert, drank some coffee, ate some grapes, and hurried out again, saying that if there was any interesting news he would come back. However, he did not return, and everything looked more threatening; the street was bristling with bayonets, and they were making barricades under the windows.

NAPOLEON AT ARCOLA

All that night and all the next day the preparations and commotion went on, and about four o'clock in the afternoon the first shot was the signal for a cannonade which seemed to come from all over Paris. The night that followed was a fearful one to Laura.

Amidst the deafening noise of the cannon she watched by the death-bed of her father, while her mother seemed in nearly as desperate a condition. The next morning the firing ceased, order and calm were re-established, but M. Permon only lived a day or two longer, the agitation of that time had been too much for him. His family were broken-hearted, and during this time of sadness Napoleon was continually with them and showed them all the affection of a son and a brother.

Ever since they came to Paris Albert had been arranging about a house for them, and had taken one in the Chaussée-d'Antin, which, without being very large, had room enough for Cécile and her husband also, whenever they should come to Paris.

Into this house they moved, glad to get away from the Hôtel de l'Autruche, with its sad associations. But now arose another trouble, the weight of which, in spite of her extreme youth, Laura was obliged to bear. The affairs of M. Permon were in such a state that when he died there seemed to be nothing left from which any income could be derived.

When Albert told his sister the result of the examination of their father's papers, she at first declared that it was impossible.

"Left nothing!" she exclaimed. "And the money he took to England?"

"There is not a deed, not a paper, not a trace of it. My father always paid everything as long as he was at Bordeaux, and since he came to Paris has told Brunetiere nothing. Mother, as you know, never spoke to him about money or business. As to me, if he told me nothing when we were in England, he was not likely to do so since."

"My God!" exclaimed Laura, "this will kill mother. She will never be able to bear hardships."

M. Permon had, in fact, had the foolish and mischievous habit—which, however, is far less common in France than in England—of entirely concealing all his money matters from those to whom it was of vital importance to know them. His wife, when he married her, was nothing but a beautiful child, brought up in the greatest simplicity in Corsica, who knew nothing even of household management, and spoke only Italian and Greek.

It was some time before she could speak French properly, and her husband had got into the way of managing everything, even the household arrangements, while he surrounded her with every luxury and pleasure, expecting her to do nothing but amuse herself, entertain, and make the house pleasant.

Albert and Laura resolved that for the present they would tell her nothing about the disastrous state of their affairs. They had plenty of ready money to go on with for some time, and Albert decided to apply to Napoleon, who would get him a post which would enable him to support his mother and sister.

For Napoleon had now not only the will but the power to help them. An extraordinary change had of late been taking place in his habits, circumstances, and position. Far removed were the days in which it had been a kindness to ask him to dinner, and when, as he could not afford to take a cab, he would come into the room with wet boots, which creaked as he walked about and smelt when he sat by the fire to dry them, excruciating the ears or the nose of Madame Permon, whom he was then so anxious not to displease.

Now, almost suddenly, he was an important personage, was well dressed, always came in a well-appointed carriage, and had a suitable house in the rue des Capucines. He came to see them every day just the same, only that now and then he brought one of his *aides-de-camp*, or his Uncle Fesch.

Paris was suffering from scarcity of food; there was great distress in consequence, which Buonaparte did his best to relieve. He caused distributions of bread and firewood to be made, and often gave Laura tickets for poor families to obtain them.

Many difficulties beset them in the arrangement of their new home. Madame Permon, knowing nothing about the state of their affairs, supposed that they were sufficiently well off. As to the money her husband had placed in England when he saw that things were going wrong, he had, contrary to his custom, told her about it; but his unfortunate folly in never having explained or taught her anything about business matters had made her incapable of comprehending them, consequently she neither understood nor remembered what he said. Accustomed to the most lavish expenditure, she now insisted on furnishing her house with all the luxury usual at the time she first came to live in France at the end of the reign of Louis XV., when the splendour of the French monarchy was at its height.

She had a box at the *Théâtre Feydeau*, for as her deep mourning prevented her opening her *salon* or going into society, the solitude of her life preyed upon her spirits and health. She went there every evening for two or three hours, and was generally joined by Napoleon. One day he told her that he had a project to unite their families by marriage.

"I wish," he said, "to marry Paulette to Permon. He has some fortune (the state of his affairs was not yet known); my sister has nothing, but I am in a position to do a great, deal for my family, and I can give her husband a good post. It is a marriage that would make me happy, and you know how pretty my sister is. My mother is your friend. Come, say yes, and the affair shall be arranged."

Madame Permon said neither yes nor no, but replied that Albert was his own master, that she would, not influence him either way, but that it depended upon him.

This marriage would have been suitable enough in many ways, but Napoleon next proposed to marry Laura to Louis or Jérôme, his two youngest brothers.

"Jérôme is younger than Laurette," replied Madame Permon, laughing. "Really, Napoleon, you are like a high priest today, marrying everybody, even the children."

He laughed too, but with an embarrassed air, and proceeded to propose that she should herself marry him.

Such was her astonishment at this suggestion that she first looked at him with stupefaction and then went into fits of laughter. Perceiving, however, that he was offended at this, she hastened to explain that she was the person who would be made ridiculous by such an arrangement.

"My dear Napoleon," she said, when she stopped laughing, "let us be serious. You think you know my age. Well, you do not; but I tell you that I might not only be your mother, but Joseph's. Let us leave off such jokes. I don't like them."

Napoleon assured her he was not joking, that he cared nothing about her age as she did not look thirty; that he wanted to marry a woman who was good, pleasant, charming, and belonged to the *faubourg St. Germain*. He begged her to reflect, which she promised to do, but gave him no hope of a favourable result to her reflections, assuring him that she had no pretensions to gain the heart of a man of six-and-twenty, and that she hoped this would not disturb their friendship.

But by this and another circumstance which took place, the long, affectionate, and intimate friendship which had always existed between them was destroyed. They were never upon the same terms again. It happened in this way.

A cousin of Madame Permon, a certain Dino Stephanopoli, had lately arrived from Corsica, and asked her to help him to get a commission in the army. She applied to Napoleon, who promised, to obtain it without delay from the Minister of War. Two days afterwards Madame Permon inquired if he had attended to the matter, and he told her that he had done so, that he had the promise of the brevet from the War Office, and would bring it himself the next day.

That next day was, however, the one of his unexpected proposals of marriage, and when, after Madame Permon's unfavourable reception of them, he was sitting next her at dinner, she recurred to the subject, asking him where was the *brevet*, which she considered already hers.

Napoleon, who did not seem altogether to like this peremptory manner of demanding rather than asking a favour, pushed away his plate with an impatient frown, and Madame Permon, who would not realise the changed position of the extraordinary genius whom she was accustomed to treat like a wilful lad in need of advice, proceeded to make some half-laughing but reproving remark upon his irritation. He excused himself, promising the *brevet* for the next day without fail.

That, evening when he was gone Madame Permon confided to her son the proposals of marriage she had received from Napoleon, and asked him whether he wished to accept his offer of Pauline as his wife, but he declined.

On Monday morning Napoleon rode up to the house, surrounded by a brilliant staff of officers, with whom he entered the room, and approaching Madame Permon in the highest spirits kissed her hand, paying her at the same time various compliments.

Unluckily, she had just received a long letter from Stephanopoli full of ridiculous complaints of the delay in getting his commission. Irritated by this, she snatched away her hand and asked for the *brevet*

He replied that it was not ready, but that she should have it on the following day, whereupon Madame Permon who was hasty, impetuous, and accustomed to have her own way, flew into a passion, refusing to listen to his explanations, and giving vent to her anger in reproaches and taunts more vehement than dignified, while the conversation which was going on around them stopped, and amidst an embarrassed silence all eyes were turned towards them.

M. Chauvet, a friend of both, interposed, and tried to make peace, but Madame Permon would not hear him and went on with her unfortunate and unsuitable remarks in the hearing of Napoleon's *aides-de-camp*, in spite of the remonstrances he addressed to her in an undertone and in Italian. Seeing that she was impracticable, he observed that he should hope to find her calmer and more just another day, and was about to kiss her hand in farewell, but she again snatched it violently away and folded her arms with a scornful smile.

With an impatient gesture Napoleon bowed and turned away. M. Chauvet, seeing that the affair was serious and that he was going slowly downstairs, was anxious to recall him, but Madame Permon's foolish obstinacy and loss of temper would not allow him to do so.

Albert had, unfortunately, been absent at the time, and was in despair when on his return in the evening his mother told him what she had done, but the mischief was irreparable. For several days they did not see Napoleon; then he called when he knew they would be at the theatre, after which his visits ceased. Shortly afterwards they heard that he had been made commander-in-chief of the army in Italy, and before his departure they only saw him once under the most melancholy circumstances.

It was on the 1st February, 1796. Madame Permon and Laura had gone up to the second floor of their house, which was occupied by Albert, as he had a bad cold and could not come down. Therefore, they dined and spent the evening in his rooms and were talking and laughing merrily. Madame Permon had an excellent marriage in view for Albert, and was saying that if Laura were also married early there was no reason why she should not have five-and-twenty grandchildren.

Cécile had been confined about a month since, and Madame Permon, remarking that she would make a charming young mother and that she would like very much to see her and her little son, leaned back on her sofa and fell into a reverie. It was about nine o'clock, and at that time, especially in that quarter of Paris, there was not much traffic in the streets. There was a long silence, which was suddenly broken by a loud knocking at the door, which startled them all.

"The noise has made me feel quite ill," said Madame Permon. "Who can be so ill-bred as to knock in that way?"

Steps were heard on the stairs, and a moment after a letter was handed to Albert.

"Ah! news of Cécile," said he; "it's from Brive, and in Geouffre's handwriting."

"Whom has he lost?" asked Laura, for the seal was black.

Albert tore open the letter and turned deadly pale.

"What does he say?" cried Madame Permon, starting up in alarm.

"Cécile has been ill, but is better," faltered Albert; but his mother caught the letter out of his hand and with a terrible cry threw herself upon her knees. Cécile was dead.

Her illness had been sudden, and her husband and all her family were plunged in the deepest grief. M. de Geouffre came to Paris soon afterwards to see them, and promised later on to bring the little Adolphe, to whom Laura was always devotedly attached.

Napoleon, on hearing next day of this new calamity, came at once to see them and behaved with much kindness, but Madame Permon was too overcome to talk to him, and he left Paris almost immediately. He was then married to Joséphine de Beauharnais.

They were obliged to explain to Madame Permon the disastrous state of their affairs, but the far greater sorrows she had suffered rendered her almost indifferent to this, though she made retrenchments in her expenditure. Just at that time the death of her old friend, the Comte de Périgord, brought another blank into her life. She became ill again, and the doctors ordered her to Cauterets.

Albert had refused a post in India, as it would have separated him for fifteen years from his mother and sister, but he now received the offer of one in Italy, for which they believed Napoleon was responsible. This he accepted, and accordingly preparations were made for their departure to their different destinations.

If it had not been an absolute necessity Albert would not have left his mother to the sole care of Laura, then not thirteen years old. But it could not be helped, and Laura was far older than her years; so, with many directions and promises to write constantly they took a mournful leave of each other and started, he for Italy and they for the Pyrenees.

They made a long stay at Cauterets, and the health of Madame Permon seemed to be quite restored by the mountain air, the change of scene, and the excitement of the journey.

They then returned to Paris and took up their old life, so far as the altered state of society and things in general permitted.

Among their friends at Paris were the Saint-Mesmes, a Marseillaise family, with whom they were on intimate terms. The custom of having two or three children only had not yet begun in France, and M. and Madame de Saint-Mesmes had six or seven. Two of the girls were nearly of Laura's age, and for their religious instruction there lived in the house a Benedictine nun, Sister Rosalie, whom M. and

Madame de Saint-Mesmes had protected during the Terror, and who was deeply attached to them in consequence.

The churches were now beginning to be re-opened, though still only here and there; and it was proposed that the confirmation and first communion of the children, so long deprived of those holy sacraments, should be celebrated.

Sister Rosalie was collecting a class of young girls for preparation, and invited Laura to join.

The nearest church to be had was still at a considerable distance from the Chaussée d'Antin, being the Church of *Bonne-Nouvelle* in the *quartier Poissonière*, in the sacristy of which the class was held every morning at half-past eight by the curd of the parish, M. de Cani, an excellent man, who was adored by his parishioners and had risked his life rather than leave them during the late perilous times.

Early in the morning Sister Rosalie went round to the different houses to fetch the young girls and take them to the church, where, gathered round the venerable priest, who had just escaped the perils of proscription and was ready, like the early confessors of the Christian faith, to risk his life again at any moment, they listened to his instructions with the enthusiastic devotion called forth by the dangers and persecutions which surrounded those who dared to profess a religion in the reign of "liberty, equality, and fraternity." The preparation went on for six weeks, and the day appointed for the first communion was Easter Monday, 1798, the confirmation to take place on Easter Tuesday.

Years had passed since any such spectacle had been seen in France, and immense crowds assembled to witness it. The church of *Bonne-Nouvelle* on both days was so crowded that the children could hardly pass up to the altar, and the bishop who confirmed was obliged to stand to administer that sacrament upon the steps outside the church. Multitudes of people, delirious with joy, were thronging the streets outside, pressing into the church, many of them shedding tears as they recognised a child, a sister, a niece or a grandchild among the veiled, white-robed girls kneeling at the altar, once more covered with lights and flowers.

Here and there among the crowd were heard muttered prayers and ejaculations from unwonted lips and murmured wishes from strange, rough-looking spectators that the prayers of the innocent children might help them too, whilst women held up their little ones to the bishop, exclaiming, "Bless him, bless him, *Monseigneur!* Alas! we shall perhaps never see you again!"

CHAPTER 5
Triumphs of Napoleon in Italy
1798-1800

The news from Italy was one long triumph. Battle after battle was won by the young Corsican leader, now the idol of France.

He had been very good to Albert, receiving him as an old friend, and seemed much surprised that Albert, who was very intimate with Joseph Buonaparte, thought it best, in consequence of the quarrel between his mother and Napoleon, to bring a letter of recommendation from the former to the latter.

"What is this letter for?" said Napoleon when he saw it. "Why should you feel such distrust of yourself?"

Albert replied that he was afraid the unfortunate altercation with his mother might have disposed the general unfavourably towards himself, to which Napoleon replied, laughing, that he thought no more about it, and was afraid Madame Permon bore him more ill-will than he did to her, which was perhaps natural, as she was in the wrong.

Albert had a post at Massa-Carrara, where he entangled himself in a love affair with the wife of his landlord and ran away with her, to the indignation not only of her husband but of General Lannes, who was quartered near Massa, and was in love with her too. They pursued and brought back the young people, but the affair caused Madame Permon much uneasiness, and her health was beginning to be seriously affected again.

Napoleon was received in triumph on his return from Italy, and entered Paris amidst the acclamations of the people.

The Parisians, so long deprived of gaiety and amusement, threw off the gloom and restraint under which they were becoming every day more impatient, and celebrated their victories by the most brilliant festivities. One *fête* succeeded another; money was lavishly spent; everybody joined eagerly and much more indiscriminately in whatever pleasures came in their way than would have been dreamed of twenty years earlier.

Although she was only fourteen years old, Laura went everywhere with her mother. One night, at a great party given by Talleyrand, who was then Foreign Minister, at the *Hôtel Galifet, rue du Bac,* they met Napoleon walking with the Turkish Ambassador. Madame Permon, who was with M. de Caulaincourt, bowed and was passing on, but General Buonaparte came up, and, looking at her with much admiration, for she was one of the handsomest women present, he shook hands and remained for some minutes talking to her and Laura, thereby drawing the attention of everybody upon them.

Soon after this, Madame Permon became so dangerously ill that for some time her life was despaired of. It was a terrible position for a girl scarcely more than a child. Albert was still in Italy, and their mother depended entirely upon Laura, who, with the help of their faithful Alsatian maid, nursed her night and day for six weeks. At length, however, contrary to the expectations of the three doctors who attended her, she began to recover, and by the end of the autumn she was well again.

That winter was a very gay one. The expedition to Egypt was decided upon, but thousands of families were rejoicing at the return of fathers, husbands, brothers, and sons; the air was full of triumphs and victories; everyone was in the highest spirits.

French society was at this time in a singular state. Everywhere the strange mixture of classes and opinions, brought about by the events of the last few years, had entirely altered the composition and tone of the *salons* of Paris. In that of Madame Permon, like many others, now congregated a miscellaneous crowd whose principles, education, manners, and habits were so different as to render impossible the sort of harmonious intimacy and confidence which had formerly been usual, but on the other hand produced a great deal more variety, interest, and excitement than were to be found in the old state of things.

Thither came officials of the new government, officers of the army—many of them risen from the ranks, visionary artists and literary men, to whom even all the horrors only just past had not taught wisdom, and who still hankered after a Republic; idiotic young men who called themselves by classical names, wore Greek and Roman costumes in the streets of Paris and believed themselves to be capable of regulating the affairs of the State; and lastly those old friends and acquaintances of Madame Permon who belonged to the *faubourg St. Germain* and formed the largest part of the society that gathered round her.

Since the rapid rise of Napoleon, Madame Buonaparte and her other sons and daughters had come to Paris. Joseph, whom, much to Napoleon's displeasure, the rest of his brothers and sisters persisted in regarding as the head of the family, was handsome, pleasant and courteous in manner, a great favourite amongst his friends and family, but with no particular talents or ambition. His wife was a gentle, sweet-tempered woman, whose sister, Desirée Clary, had just been married to Bernadotte, afterwards King of Sweden.

Lucien Buonaparte came next to Napoleon in birth and talent. He was upright and honourable, but a fanatical Republican, who called himself Brutus, indulged in all sorts of preposterous follies, and married the daughter of the innkeeper in the little village of Saint-Maximin, which he persisted in calling Marathon, and in which he had some kind of employment. His proceedings excited the vexation of his family, especially of Napoleon, who was very angry but could do nothing with him. Louis was at this time about eighteen years old. He was plain, delicate, shy and reserved; had simple tastes, hated society and public life, but was by many people said to be the best of his family. Jérôme, of whom there is not much good to be told, was then a boy at school.

If Napoleon's brothers were wanting in ambition, the same could not be said of his sisters, all of whom were inordinately vain, extravagant, and greedy for power and money.

The eldest, Marianne, or, as she was sometimes called, Elisa, was now Madame Bacciochi. She seems to have been the least attractive of the three, and was not generally liked. Pauline, now the wife of General Leclerc, was extremely beautiful and remarkably silly; she was Napoleon's favourite. Annunciata, afterwards called Caroline, was then at the famous school of Madame Campan at Saint-Germain.

Madame Leclerc came constantly to the house of Madame Permon, who was very fond of her, and who also visited all the other members of the family except Napoleon, with whom the quarrel she had made about Stephanopoli had never been made up.

The family and the wife of Napoleon hated each other. Joséphine, widow of the Vicomte de Beauharnais, was a Creole, and several years older than her second husband. She was pretty, charming in manner, and kind-hearted, but thoughtless, frivolous, and extravagant. Napoleon had the greatest aversion to her mixing herself in any way in political matters, and desired that she would not speak of them at all, saying, "Whatever you say is supposed to come from me; therefore say nothing upon those subjects, so that my enemies, by whom you are surrounded, may not be able to draw silly conclusions from your remarks."

It was not in Napoleon's disposition to feel deep or lasting affection for anybody but himself, and his ideas about women belonged rather to the Oriental character than to Western civilisation; but at this time, and in his own way, he loved Joséphine. As he told Madame Permon, he wished to marry a woman of the old *régime*, and just then

JOSÉPHINE, EMPRESS OF FRANCE, WIFE OF NAPOLEON I, NÉE TASCHER DE LA PAGERIE, WIDOW OF ALEXANDRE, VICOMTE DE BEAUHARNAIS (1763–1814).

he found this marriage suited his plans; notwithstanding which, nothing irritated him more than for it to be said, as it continually was, that he derived any advantage or assistance from his wife, her connections, or friends; he was also jealous and tyrannical. Joséphine, however, was much attached to him, and so were Eugène and Hortense, her son and daughter by her first husband, who had perished in the Revolution.

One of the most intimate friends of the Permons was the old Marquis de Caulaincourt, who lived within a hundred yards of them, and was constantly in their house. His children and Laura were like brothers and sisters, and she always called him "*Petit Papa.*" He wore the dress and preserved the manners of the stately Court of the Bourbons, and seemed to belong to a bygone age, though he was an old friend of Joséphine, and allowed his sons to serve under Napoleon, which many young men of good family were now anxious to do.

There were many others, however, who held aloof, and the greater number of the returned *émigrés* hated Napoleon and looked with disdain upon his family, who were already beginning to give themselves airs of royalty, which made them ridiculous in the eyes of all who had known the real court and royal family of France.

Amongst these was Madame de Contades, daughter of the brave

Marquis de Bouillé, who commanded in the affair of Varennes, when the king and queen so nearly escaped, and might have succeeded in doing so if Louis had possessed any spirit or decision of character.

Madame de Contades, without being a beauty, was a woman of striking appearance and much admired. She was one of the lately returned *émigrés*, detested the very name of Napoleon, made light of his victories, and laughed at his family, refusing even to allow that Madame Leclerc was beautiful.

Just after the departure of Napoleon and the army for Egypt, Madame Permon gave a ball, which was attended almost exclusively by the *faubourg St. Germain*, the only exceptions being a few men who danced remarkably well and went everywhere, and the Buonaparte family.

Madame Leclerc spent a whole week in arranging a *toilette* for the occasion, which she declared would immortalise her, and about which she made as much fuss and mystery as if it were an affair of State. She asked Madame Permon to allow her to dress at her house for fear anything might injure its freshness on the way; and when she thought the right moment for her appearance had come—that is to say, when the rooms were tolerably full and yet not so crowded as to prevent her from being observed—she entered the ballroom and made her way to the place reserved for her by Madame Permon.

A murmur of admiration greeted her, and she was soon surrounded by a group of men, some of whom had left Madame de Contades to come to her. She had certainly succeeded in making the sensation she wished: everyone was talking about her and admiring her beauty. Presently she moved her seat, and took possession of a large sofa in the *boudoir* of Madame Permon, which, being much more empty, she thought would allow her *toilette* to be seen better than the crowded ballroom, especially as it was brilliantly lighted. All sorts of remarks of another description mingled with the admiration expressed for her beauty and dress, many of the woman exclaiming at the insolent extravagance of the *parvenue*, who only three years ago had scarcely food to eat.

Madame Permon was in anxious distress lest she should hear any of these observations, when Madame de Contades, who had the greatest contempt and dislike for Pauline Leclerc, and was further irritated because two or three of the men who were talking to her had left her to join Pauline, came up and stood near, looking at her and admiring in an audible voice her dress, her face, her *coiffure*, her whole appearance, in fact, till suddenly she exclaimed to the man who stood by her, "*Ah!*

mon Dieu! what a pity! But how can such a deformity have escaped notice? *Mon Dieu!* how unlucky!"

Everybody turned to see; all eyes were fixed upon Pauline, who became crimson, while Madame de Contades, with her looks directed to her head, repeated in a compassionate tone, "What a pity!" and someone asked, "But what is it? What do you see?"

"What do I see? Could anyone help seeing those two enormous ears planted on that head? If I had ears like those, I should have them cut off, and I really must advise her to do the same."

There was an end of Pauline's success for that evening. She began to cry, and went to bed, where Madame Permon came to see her the next morning and listened for some time with patience while she abused Madame de Contades, for she was fond of Pauline and thought she had been hardly dealt with but when, after saying that she could not see what people found to admire in Madame de Contades, and that there were many far more attractive women at the ball, Madame Leclerc proceeded to single out a certain Madame de Chauvelin who was plain, short-sighted, and had a bad figure, Madame Permon exclaimed impatiently—

"But, Paulette, my dear child, you are mad, quite mad!"

"I assure you, Madame Permon, that Madame de Chauvelin is very well dressed, is clever and not sarcastic."

"Whether she is well dressed or not has nothing to do with the question. As to wit, I know she has plenty; and if you think that she does not laugh at anything ridiculous that comes in her way, just as much as Mérote (Madame de Contades) you are uncommonly mistaken, my poor Paulette. And if her short sight prevents her seeing, her husband has very good eyes, and can see everything for her, I can tell you."

That Madame Permon, charming as she was, could not have been altogether discriminating in her attachments is shown by her affection for Jérôme Buonaparte, a spoilt, troublesome boy with neither brains nor gratitude, and for Pauline Leclerc, a frivolous, empty-headed woman, who cared for nothing but dress and flirting, and could not bear any one to be admired but herself She even envied her young sister Caroline, and grumbled when their mother took her for a holiday.

One evening at Madame Permon's Madame Buonaparte came in with Caroline, whom she had brought from Madame Campan's school. Caroline had a lovely complexion and fair, curly hair, which excited the admiration of a man who was talking to Pauline. Therefore, when Caroline, in rather a rough, awkward way, ran up to her to kiss her, Madame Leclerc pushed her sister away, exclaiming—

"*Mon Dieu!* Mamma, you really ought to teach Annunciata not to be so brusque. She is just like a peasant of Fiumorbo!" (A savage district in Corsica.)

Caroline turned away with tears in her eyes, and Madame Buonaparte said nothing, though much displeased at this scene.

Some of the best balls given at this early period after the Revolution were those of Madame de Caseaux, whose husband had been President of the Parliament of Bordeaux. She received nobody who did not belong to the *faubourg St. Germain*. Her daughter Laura and Melanie de Périgord were the most intimate friends of Laura Permon. There were subscription balls at the house of M. Despréaux, the fashionable dancing-master, which were attended by all his pupils and by many others besides.

CHAPTER 6
Betrothal of Laura
1800

Out of the strife, disorders and confusion that for some years had prevailed in France a new calamity had arisen. A band of robbers called *chauffeurs*, whose crimes made them the terror of the whole country, now infested not only the provinces, but Paris itself. Numbers of those atrocious characters produced, or at any rate brought forward by recent events, flocked to join them, and they now formed a large and powerful body of daring miscreants, from whose depredations and cruelties nobody seemed to be safe.

In country places the villages and farms paid them blackmail, or if any refused to do so, they were very likely to be surprised some night, the house set on fire, and the inhabitants murdered in their beds. They were never caught, for no one dared to give evidence against them, nor even to refuse to shelter them from justice.

In different parts of Paris and the suburbs horrible murders kept taking place, now and then even of a whole family, and still the perpetrators were never discovered. Even the sentinels or watchmen posted about the city did not seem to do much good.

There was one a short distance from Madame Permon's door, in spite of whose presence one night, at about half-past twelve, while several people who had been spending the evening with her were still there, cries for help were suddenly heard in the street and some of the servants waiting downstairs for their masters, rushing out, found a man robbed and nearly murdered, whom they were only just in time to save, very suspiciously near the watchman in question.

Just after this, Madame Permon, having accidentally struck her head against the marble of her chimney-piece, had a dreadful abscess, which for many days caused her frightful suffering, and left her so weak and ill as to require great care and perfect quiet.

Albert was at this time living with his mother, and was occupied in the affairs of some friends of his who were starting a bank in Paris. They lived at Toulon, Bordeaux, Narbonne, and Nimes, and had placed the direction of their business in Paris in his hands. One evening he came in with a *commissionaire* usually employed in the house, carrying a heavy iron-bound box or safe, and early the next morning he went out, taking the same man and returning accompanied by him, this time laden with a box still heavier than before.

"Let him have a glass of wine, Laura," said he. "Here, drink, my good fellow; you are very much overheated, take care."

"*Dame!*" exclaimed the porter. "I am accustomed to heavy loads. I'm not a fine *muscadin* like you; you couldn't carry a quarter of what I carried just now."

Albert laughed, and going closer to the man, whom he knew and trusted, he said significantly, but most imprudently, "I carried more than double."

The man started and exclaimed, "Impossible! Ah! yes, yes, I understand."

He turned to go downstairs, but came back after a few steps and said—

"Am I to go and order your *cabriolet, citoyen* Permon?"

He asked this question because Albert was in the habit of going into the country every *décadi*, and staying away for at least one night. He replied in the affirmative, and the *commissionaire* went as usual to order one from the livery stables, as Albert always on those occasions left their own horses for his mother. Then he went to his mother's room to wish her goodbye. But he found her weak and low-spirited, and when she heard he was going away she looked ready to cry, and said she had scarcely seen him for two days. Without telling her, he sent away the *cabriolet* and went back to her room, where he sat with her most of the day playing the harp to her and amusing her. Later on, several friends came in, and she was so cheered up, that when she went to bed, as she drank the bowl of milk, she always took the last thing, she remarked that she felt much better, and should sleep well.

Albert went up to his rooms on the second floor, the servants went to bed on the third floor, where they all slept. The ground floor consisted only of the porter's lodge, a subterranean kitchen, store-rooms and offices. The first floor had two doors opening on to the landing of the staircase. One led into an ante-room, through which people passed into the dining-room, then the drawing-room, the *boudoir*, Madame Permon's bedroom, Laura's study, her bedroom and another room in which she also kept some of her books, her globes, &c. All these rooms opened out of each other, and the last named had also a door leading on to the landing, opposite the first named.

Laura sat by her mother till she fell asleep, and then retired to her own room and took a book, meaning to sit up for a time in order to be sure that the invalid wanted nothing more. But Madame Permon slept on tranquilly; no sound broke the silence but the measured tread of the sentinel by the Capucine church, his monotonous "*Qui vive?*" or now and then a carriage driving rapidly by. Little by little even this sound ceased. Laura looked at the clock; it was a quarter to one. She got up with a yawn, intending to go to bed, but suddenly became conscious of feeling very hungry. Having sat up at night so much lately, she had required supper, and had given orders that some fruit or comfitures should always be put in her room the last thing.

It was evident, however, that they had this time been forgotten, but as she looked round the room, her eyes fell upon the key of the opposite door leading into the dining-room, which was always left there to enable her to pass that way in the morning to practise on the piano without disturbing Madame Permon by going through her room.

Laura remembered that there was always something to be found in a cupboard in the dining-room, so, taking her candle, she opened her door, crossed the landing, and unlocking the door opposite, went in, and as she expected, found some bread and preserved strawberries. Having put these on the table and sat down to eat them, she remembered that her mother might awake, call her, and be frightened if she did not answer. So, taking all the things back into her own room, she returned to fetch the sugar, which she had forgotten; and then locking and bolting the doors, she sat down again with great satisfaction to her strawberries.

Presently she heard a noise at the bottom of the house, and it immediately struck her that the servants must be sitting up playing cards in the kitchen, contrary to her express order that all of them, cook, coachman, footman, and lady's maid, should be in bed and the lights put out by midnight.

She listened, and in a few moments heard stealthy steps upon the staircase.

"Just as I thought!" muttered Laura to herself. "Well, I shall catch them in the act." And creeping up to the door leading on to the staircase, she noiselessly drew back one bolt, waiting to draw the other until the whole procession should be close to it.

Just then a sudden sound told her that someone had stumbled over Madame Permon's bath, which was always put out on the landing at night.

Irritated at the noise, which might awaken her mother, Laura drew back the other bolt, and was just turning the handle to open the door when all at once it flashed into her mind that the servants knew where the bath was, and consequently were not likely to fall over it, and that even if they did they would have laughed, whereas no sound of the kind was heard.

But if not the servants, then who, or what?—and softly, with trembling hands, she slid back the bolts, and waited, almost paralysed with terror, listening while the steps passed her door and began to go up the staircase to the second floor. Being of wood, it creaked beneath the heavy footsteps, which she was now quite certain were not those of the servants, unless, indeed, Antonio, Albert's Venetian valet, who knew that the money was in his master's rooms, was acting as their guide.

But the noise ceased, and for nearly ten minutes Laura heard nothing. She began to wonder whether her fears had got the better of her reason, and the steps were after all only those of the servants. Persuading herself that this might really be the case, she sat down, and was just finishing her strawberries when she heard the steps coming down again. This time there was no mistake. What was to be done? The history of one murder after another committed by the *chauffeurs* came into her mind. Only the week before, near Orléans, they had killed two persons who had given the alarm, and at Croissy, where they had murdered several people, they had placed a sentinel in the courtyard with orders to shoot the first person who tried to get out.

If she were to give the alarm, Albert, hearing her voice, would open his door, come out, and be murdered at once.

Laura stood close to the door listening. The *chauffeurs* came quietly down, avoiding the bath, and stopped on the landing between her door and that of the dining-room. Two of them sat down upon a step, and by putting her ear close to the door, which was so thin that it could have been broken open, she heard a good deal of what they said, and soon made out that Antonio was not among them, but that they supposed Albert to be absent, and knew that there were from 70,000 to 75,000 *francs* in the house, which only the porter could have told them. They went on swearing at the Le Dru locks on Albert's door, which had prevented their opening it, and said that it was getting towards dawn (it was July); that it was not worthwhile to go into Madame Permon's room, and that that door belonged to *la petite*.

After a moment's silence she caught the words, "Well, tomorrow!" and heard some pieces of iron cautiously put down on the step. Then she discovered that they were going to force the door of the dining-room opposite to get the plate, and in a moment, seeing that this would open her mother's room to them, she rushed through the inner door of her own and stood by her bed, calling gently to her.

"*Mon Dieu!* what is the matter?" exclaimed Madame Permon, waking up and seeing her daughter half-undressed, with a candle in her hand and a terror-stricken face.

"The house is full of robbers!" answered Laura. Madame Permon sat up, seized hold of the three bells by her bed and rang them till one broke.

"In God's name keep quiet!" cried Laura, catching hold of her; "you will kill Albert!"

"How? What? Where?" cried Madame Permon, while the sound of the *chauffeurs* running downstairs was immediately heard, and it was evident that whilst two of them were sitting by Laura's door the rest were occupied in trying to force the locks of Albert's room. Madame Permon continued to ring and call until the whole house was disturbed. Albert opened his door, in which a burglar's tool was sticking; the servants rushed downstairs; and Laura threw open the window of her study just as the two last of the band jumped over the wall which separated the courtyard from a large woodyard, in which they had hidden themselves among the narrow paths made by the piled-up faggots. By means of these faggots they had got over the wall into the Permons' courtyard, and once there it was all easy enough.

The door of the woodyard was open when Albert, with some of the police, went in to wake up the caretaker and his family, all of whom seemed to be fast asleep, and suspiciously ignorant of what had happened. A whole heap of burglar's tools were found by Laura's door, and one of the police brought in a faggot stained with blood, one of the villains having fallen and hurt himself in his flight. None of them were taken.

Madame Permon suffered less from the effects of this adventure than might have been expected, but it was a long time before Laura could get over the terror she had gone through, especially when she reflected that she had narrowly escaped meeting the *chauffeurs* on the landing between the dining-room and her bedroom, or throwing open her door and appearing in the midst of them; and that while she was getting her strawberries and sugar in the dining-room they were actually in the house.

An attack of fever was the immediate consequence of all this, and when she and Madame Permon were well enough they went to Dieppe for a change, but for a considerable time she had a horror of crossing the landing from her room to the dining-room, or of sleeping in the dark.

But although she had borne this terrible shock so much better than her children had anticipated, the health of Madame Permon, always extremely fragile, and severely tried by the many sorrows and vicissitudes of her past life, had now become seriously impaired. She frequently suffered great pain, and spent most of the day lying on a sofa or in an armchair, going out very little.

Albert and Laura devoted themselves entirely to her, and her unfailing spirits, love of music, and the interest she took in everything that went on, made her easy to amuse.

Every evening her *salon* was as full and as pleasant as ever; some of her intimate friends came almost invariably, and the time was passed either in conversation, music or dancing.

Laura was now nearly sixteen, and Madame Permon feeling that her own life was uncertain, and that her daughter had no fortune, was anxious to establish her suitably as soon as possible.

Two marriages were proposed to her, one of which came to nothing for want of sufficient fortune. The other suggested husband, though his position and income were satisfactory, was so much older than Laura, that Madame de Caseaux and other friends remonstrated, declaring he was old enough to be her grandfather!

Like most well brought up French girls of the time, Laura was quite prepared to marry as her mother directed, but to this particular man she took such a violent dislike that although it never occurred to her that she could refuse to marry him if her mother insisted upon it, she declared that it would make her miserable for life, and threw herself at the feet of Madame Permon, who yielded to her entreaties and broke off the negotiations with reluctance.

Just then General Junot returned to Paris. He was a good-looking man of eight-and-twenty and a great favourite of Napoleon, who was now First Consul, and who had made him Commandant of Paris, desiring him to look out for a wife without delay, and adding that he must be sure to choose a rich one.

Junot replied that she must also be one who pleased him, and proceeded to make inquiries on the subject, whilst he occupied himself in arranging a *hôtel* and establishment on a sumptuous scale.

One day he happened to be at the house of a lady who was a friend of the Permons. To her he confided his wishes.

"Have you been to see Madame Permon since you came back?" she asked.

"No; and I reproach myself every day on that account. Why do you ask?"

"Because I think her daughter would exactly suit you."

"Her daughter! But she was only a child when I went to Egypt."

"She is not a child now, but a young girl. She is sixteen. I am very anxious to arrange a marriage for her myself at this moment, only her mother is so obstinate about one she has set her heart upon in which there is not common sense, for the man is old enough to be her father. Now mine is a very nice young fellow and one of the first names in France."

"Then in that case what can I do?" said Junot. "You tell me of a woman who has twenty suitors. I don't like so much competition. Besides, Mademoiselle Loulou, as I believe she is called, will be sure to be a pretentious, spoilt little person, insupportable. No, no! *Je vous baise les mains!*" And he rose and took his leave.

But the next visit he paid was to a Madame Hamelin, also a friend of the Permons, who immediately began the subject.

"Ah!" she said, "there is a young person I should like you to marry—but she is engaged, it is no use thinking of it."

"Then if she is going to be married cannot you tell me her name?"

"Oh! *mon Dieu,* yes! You knew her when she was a child. It is Mademoiselle Permon."

Junot laughed, and went on to ask several questions about the young girl, which ended in, his promising to go with Madame Hamelin to Madame Permon's one evening. But meanwhile he consulted another friend of Madame Permon, who told him that she was bent upon carrying out the marriage which was not then broken off; and feeling certain, from what he knew of her, that she would persist in having her own way, he made an excuse and did not go to her house until the following September.

On the 21st of that month about a dozen people were in Madame Permon's *salon*, talking, laughing, and acting charades, when suddenly the door opened and General Junot was announced.

There was a dead silence, for Junot, who had expected to meet two or three people he knew there, had mistaken the day and found nobody who did not belong strictly and entirely to the *faubourg St. Germain* set.

For a general of the Republic to appear unexpectedly in a circle of *émigrés*, most of whom had only returned within six months, was undoubtedly awkward, and for the moment he looked embarrassed, but Madame Permon, perceiving the situation, received him with such grace and courtesy and so many friendly reproaches for his delay in coming that he was at once at his ease, and before he left ventured to invite her to go the next day to the *Hôtel de Salm* to see the procession pass from the *Musée des Augustins* to the Invalides with the body of Turenne, which had been saved when the tombs of Saint Denis were desecrated by the brutal mob in the Revolution, hidden for a time in the *Jardin des Plantes*, and was now to be buried again with military honours.

Junot, as Commandant of Paris, was the director of that ceremony, and was not unwilling that his distinguished position should be recognised by Madame Permon and her daughter, to whom he paid marked attention. They found a private room reserved for them at the *Hôtel Salm,* to which he had sent chairs, cushions, a reclining chair for Madame Permon, and his German valet to await her orders.

For the next ten days he never missed an evening at Madame Permon's, where he sat by her side talking to her or to any of his acquaintance he met there, but never speaking to Laura or approaching the group of young girls among whom she was. On the 1st of October Madame Permon gave a dance, at which the De Caseaux were among the first to arrive, and Mademoiselle de Caseaux, taking Laura apart, complained that she had treated her with a want of confidence in not telling her of her approaching marriage.

Laura at once feared that the marriage she so dreaded was again in question, and her face of consternation made her friend exclaim—

"Isn't it true, then? Are you not engaged to General Junot?"

"General Junot!" cried Laura, much relieved. "Are you out of your senses? Why, I hardly know him. And is it likely that he would want to marry a girl with no fortune when he is the favourite of the First Consul and one of the first *partis* in Paris? When did you hear that wonderful news?"

"M. d'Aubusson de la Feuillade told us today at dinner," replied the young girl, whose mother just then approached and repeated her daughter's remark.

"It must be a trick to torment me!" exclaimed Laura. "And you, *Madame*, who are always so kind, how can you believe any such thing? Is not Laura my best friend and if there were any secret of that sort would not she be the first to know it?"

Having convinced and embraced her friends, Laura begged them to say nothing to Madame Permon, who would be sure to be angry and vent her indignation upon someone, most likely upon M. d'Aubusson, who had just come into the room.

General Junot presently arrived, apparently in high spirits, and made his way to Madame Permon, by whose side he remained, talking and laughing with her and paying her great attention.

"*Dieu me pardonne!*" exclaimed Laura de Caseaux; "one would think M. d'Aubusson had made a mistake and General Junot was go-

JUNOT, GOVERNOR OF PARIS AND DUC D'ABRANTÈS.

ing to marry your mother."

"Well, it would not be surprising," replied Laura Permon, "for my mother is charming; and see how pretty she looks this evening."

Madame Permon, in fact, looked lovely; her illness had not yet injured her beauty, to which nothing could be more becoming than the style of dress she had latterly adopted: long, flowing *peignoirs* of the finest Indian muslin, trimmed with Malines or point lace, with a headdress of the same lace.

M. de Trénis, who was celebrated for his dancing, came up and asked Laura to dance a *gavotte* with him, and when she refused appealed to Madame Permon, who desired her to do so. Can one imagine in these days a man with whom a girl had refused to dance asking her mother to make her, and that mother complying with his request?

The evening was as amusing and successful as Madame Permon's parties always were. When everyone was gone, and Laura found herself alone in her room, she began to think that perhaps she had better tell her mother what was being said; so the next morning she related to her all the remarks of Madame de Caseaux and her daughter, and as she expected Madame Permon put herself into a state of excitement and irritation, declaring that such a report would do Laura harm, and must have been set about by somebody who had a spite against them.

"And then if General Junot marries Madame Leclerc, which I hear is very likely, people will say that his marriage with my daughter has been broken off!"

"Really, mother," said Albert, "you are not reasonable. Just for a few words carelessly spoken—"

"It is all very well," replied she; "but do you suppose that just at the time when your sister has obstinately refused one good marriage and circumstances have prevented another, it is likely to be very pleasant for me to hear her name connected with that of a man she can never marry at all? No, no; it is most disagreeable."

"Perhaps you are right," said Albert. "I did not think of that. What is to be done?"

"*Oh, mon Dieu!* it's very simple. I shall tell Junot how it is, and ask him to leave off coming here."

Albert smiled, hesitated, and turning to Laura told her that her drawing-master had come and was waiting for her. Laura ran away to her lesson, forgetting all about the question under discussion, and Albert, when she was gone, told his mother that it would be a pity to act as she proposed.

"Eh! Why not, if it suits me?" was the answer.

"You must do as you choose, mother; but I can't change my opinion."

"At any rate give me a reason."

"Well, if you really want to know, I think Junot is in love with my sister."

"You don't say so!"

Albert said nothing, but walked slowly up and down the room.

"What makes you think so?" continued his mother.

"Has he said anything to you?"

"Not a word, but what I have noticed is quite enough for me. However, I may be mistaken. But I will go this morning and see Madame Hamelin; if there is anything in it, she will know and she will tell me the truth. I shall ask her in the interest of Laurette, and she is very fond of her."

"Ah!" cried Madame Permon, "such happiness is not reserved for me before I die. I would rather have Junot for my son-in-law than any man I know. Poor Laurette! No, no, my son, you are mistaken."

At that moment a carriage drove up to the door. Madame Permon, who was still in bed, was about to ring and say she could not see any one, when Albert looked out of the window and exclaimed, "It is Junot!"

"Junot!" cried Madame Permon. "What can he want at this time? Yes, yes! let him come up," as her maid came to ask if she would see the general. "And you stay here, Albert."

Junot very soon made his appearance, and sitting down by Madame Permon explained that he had come to ask her consent and Albert's to Laura becoming his wife. After their consent had been given and they had all embraced each other and regained their composure, he asked, as a special and unusual favour, to be allowed to speak to Laura himself, and hear her decision from her own lips.

Madame Permon exclaimed that such a thing was unheard of, but on his saying that he only wanted to ask her in the presence of her mother and brother, Madame Permon gave her permission, and Albert was sent to fetch Laura. When Junot repeated his offer, entreating her to say whether she would marry him of her own free will, she was so astonished, confused, and frightened that she became crimson, sat speechless for a few moments, and then jumped up and ran upstairs, where Albert followed and found her hidden in an attic, crying.

Junot meanwhile was filled with consternation, reproached himself vehemently for distressing her, and stamped his foot on the ground with an exclamation more suited to a barrack-room than the society in which he now was. Madame Permon remarked that she had told him his plan was absurd and that she would advise him not to use such expressions before Laura, who would not like them at all; and Albert, returning from upstairs, announced that his sister was perfectly willing to accept him.

Madame Permon's next question was how he had gained the consent of the First Consul, to which he replied that he had not asked for it.

"What!" exclaimed Madame Permon. "He does not know it? And you come and ask for my daughter in marriage. Allow me to say, my dear general, that your conduct is very thoughtless."

"May I ask in what I am to blame, *Madame?*"

"How can you ask? Don't you know the coolness and misunderstanding which have succeeded the friendship that existed between the First Consul and me? Do you suppose he will agree to my daughter becoming your wife, more especially as she has no fortune? And what shall you do now if he refuses his consent?"

"I shall do without it. I am not a child, and in the most important event in my life I shall consult my own happiness, not petty quarrels which don't concern me."

"You say you are not a child," cried Madame Permon; "and yet you reason as if you were six years old. Can you break with your friend and protector because you want to make what he will call a bad marriage?—that is to say, a marriage without fortune, for this is the reason he will give you; he is not likely to tell you it is because he does not like me. And what will you do when he gives you the choice between my daughter and himself?"

"He will never do so," replied Junot, "and if he could so far forget my services and my attachment, I should still be a faithful son of France, who would never repulse me. And I am a general."

"But do you think we could accept such a sacrifice? Although my daughter is only sixteen, you cannot have so misjudged her as to imagine she would so abuse her influence over you."

"My dear general," interposed Albert, "it seems to me that you have been rather hasty in this matter, but I think it can easily be arranged. I do not agree with my mother that the First Consul is likely to interfere in a question of this kind."

Junot looked at his watch, seized his hat, and said, "I will go to the

Tuileries. The First Consul is not yet at the Council. I will speak to him and be back in an hour."

He ran downstairs, sprang into his carriage, drove to the Tuileries, and meeting Duroc, inquired for the First Consul. Shortly afterwards he was shown into his study.

"*Mon Général!*" he began, "you said you wished to see me married. Well, the thing is done—I am going to marry."

"Ah! ah! And have you, by chance, just carried off your wife? You look very much excited."

"No, *mon Général* ——"

"And who are you going to marry?"

"Somebody you knew as a child and liked very much, of whom everyone speaks well, and with whom I am madly in love. It is Mademoiselle Permon."

Napoleon started up and caught Junot by the arm. "Who did you say?" he cried.

"The daughter of Madame Permon, the child you have held so often on your knees, *mon Général*"

"It is not possible! Loulou cannot be old enough be married. Why, how old *is* she?"

"Sixteen next month."

"But it is a very bad marriage for you; she has no money. And besides—how can you wish to; son-in-law to Madame de Permon? Don't you know that, woman though she is, you will have to do what she pleases? *C'est une rude tête.*"

"Permit me to observe, *mon Général*, that I do not marry my mother-in-law. And then I think—" and he hesitated.

"Well, *après*, what do you think?"

"I think, *mon Général*, that the disputes between you and Madame Permon have perhaps given you prejudice against her. I know she is surrounded by many old friends, and I see the love her children have for her."

Gradually Napoleon yielded to the representations of Junot, and ended by saying that he would give him a hundred thousand *francs* for the *dot* of his *fiancée* and forty thousand for the *corbeille*, and the affair was settled.

The mother, brothers, and sisters of the First Consul were delighted at the marriage, but for some reason it did not please Joséphine, and the friends of Madame Permon urged her to push on the preparations for the wedding and let it take place, as Junot desired, before Laura's sixteenth birthday, lest by any intrigues it might be broken off. Madame Permon scouted the idea of any such danger and declared that considerations of this kind were beneath her own and her daughter's dignity, but the precarious state of her own health made her anxious to get the wedding over, and she promised Junot that it should be on the twentieth of that same month.

When Laura was told this, she objected vehemently, and declared with tears that she did not want to be married till after Christmas. Albert tried to comfort her and induce her to be married on the day fixed, and M. de Caulaincourt, who had just come to dinner, added his persuasions to the rest, assuring her that she must be a good child and be married when her mother wished, and that now she was engaged the sooner the wedding took place the better, as nothing was less *convenable* than a young *fiancée* who went all the winter from one *fête* to another and was neither *dame* nor *demoiselle*.

By which arguments Laura was so far convinced that she consented to the thirtieth of the month being decided upon.

Many of Madame Permon's friends of the *faubourg St. Germain* strongly disapproved of Laura's engagement, saying that although her father had been *bourgeois*, her mother was not, and that she would have done much better to marry her daughter in her own set.

Madame Permon paid no attention to what they said, but hurried on the preparations for the wedding. She and Junot vied with each other in the splendour of the *trousseau* and *corbeille*.

Junot's family had come to Paris for the marriage. They were people entirely different from Laura and her mother in education, habits, and social position; but his mother was a woman so kind, gentle, and unselfish, that Laura very soon became extremely fond of her. She got on very well also with his brother and sisters, and managed to keep on good, terms with his father, an ill-tempered, disagreeable old country lawyer, who must have been a considerable trial. In fact, she was extremely good to them all, to the great relief of Junot, who had looked forward with much uneasiness to their meeting.

At the signing of the contract Laura heard with astonishment her mother's lawyer, when he read the document aloud, announce that she had a *dot* of 60,000 *francs*, derived from money left by her father, 12,000 *francs* for her *trousseau*, and 50,000 *francs* from M. Lequien de Bois-Cressy, an old friend of her father's, who hoped to become the second husband of Madame Permon should she be restored to health, and settled this sum on Laura as his future stepdaughter.

Knowing perfectly well that her father had left nothing for her to inherit, but that her education and all the expenses of her mother and herself had been paid by Albert, she asked as soon as she could speak to him alone, what was the meaning of it.

"Say nothing about it," replied he. "You know that my mother and you are all I have to care for in the world, and your happiness is my first consideration. The thing is simple enough, dear child. You are making a great marriage, greater than we could have hoped for. Junot insists on *communauté de biens* between you. It would not do for you to bring nothing into such an arrangement, it would be out of the question; therefore I am giving you some money I have to dispose of. If ever we find that sum my father placed in England, you can repay me; if not, it is yours—I make you a present of it; but as it would not be proper that you should receive your *dot* as a present, I made Tricard say that it came from our father."

Next day, according to the usual custom, Junot and Albert took the contract to be signed at the Tuileries. Napoleon spoke very kindly of Laura and her mother, and ordered it to be read to him. When it was finished, he took Albert by the arm, drew him on one side, and said—

"Permon, I remember quite well that your father left nothing at all. At the time of his death I used to be at your mother's every day, and you know, doubtless, that I then wanted to marry you to my sister, Madame Leclerc, and betroth Mademoiselle Loulou to that *mauvais sujet,* Jérôme."

He did not mention the other marriage he wished to make on that occasion. "Well," he continued, "Madame Permon told me that her husband left no fortune whatever, so what is the meaning of all this?"

Albert explained, begging that the First Consul would not mention the matter.

"You are a good fellow, Permon, you are a good fellow," said he; "and you let yourself be forgotten, but I shall look after you. Why have I never seen you at the Tuileries since I have been there? However, your brother-in-law will now remind us of each other."

Not long afterwards Albert received the appointment of Commissary-General of Police, of which posts there were only three in France.

Two days before Laura's wedding a circumstance took place which very nearly broke it off.

As Commandant of Paris, Junot had the right to be married at any *mairie* he pleased, and as he had a friend, M. Duquesney, who was mayor of the 7th *arrondissement*, he asked Madame Permon whether she thought Laura would mind the ceremony being performed there.

Madame Permon said she did not think so, but would send for Laura, who replied that her mother must settle all that, the only objection she saw being that it was rather far to go, adding—

"If that *mairie* were as near as our church, I should not be afraid of tiring my mother." So saying, she left the room without noticing Junot's look of astonishment. When she was gone, he turned to her mother and asked if she expected the marriage to take place in a church.

"In a church?" cried Madame Permon, starting from her chair. "And where else do you suppose she intends to be married? Before your friend with the scarf? My dear child, you must have lost your senses. Did you imagine for an instant that not only my daughter, but her brother or I, would allow a Republican marriage? Such a thing is absolutely against our principles, and I can tell you that Laura will not thank you if you suggest it to her."

Junot walked up and down the room much disturbed. "Will you allow me to speak to Mademoiselle Loulou about this alone?" he asked. "On the terms we now are there could be no impropriety."

"You don't know what you are talking about," replied Madame Permon. "As long as you are not Laura's husband you are a stranger to her, and what you are going to tell her won't make you very good friends either. Besides, what secret can there be about it? Why should you not wish me to hear?"

"Because it must be discussed with calmness," he replied. "But I can speak to her in the drawing-room, with the door into your room open."

Laura received his proposition with astonished indignation. To his representations that he could not appear, as Commandant of Paris, in uniform amongst the crowd that would collect round the church to see what was still so remarkable a spectacle, Laura replied that she saw no reason why he should object to be seen accomplishing a religious duty which nobody would think of neglecting, unless it were the Turks, whose example she hoped he did not propose to follow.

Junot tried to persuade her that the religious ceremony was unnecessary, and might cause him serious results, for while to her it was only a fancy, to him it meant a public profession of religion. Laura answered with spirit and decision that if it were so, she would ask him in what religion he had been brought up, and why, having been baptised, confirmed, received the Communion and confessed in the

Catholic faith, when it was a question of another sacrament, that of marriage, he should suddenly wish to act like an *infidel*; that she was too young to enter into controversy, but that of one thing he might rest assured, that their marriage would either be celebrated in church or not at all; and that she declined to discuss the matter any further; saying which, she got up and left the room, observing as she went out that she was sorry Junot could have thought her capable of accepting such a proposal.

Anyone who has had experience of family routs (and who has not?) can easily imagine the general consternation, in the midst of which a servant announced that Mademoiselle Olive and Mademoiselle de Beuvry had come with the *trousseau* and *corbeille*.

"Junot, Junot! will you hold your tongue?" cried Madame Permon, as Junot stamped his foot with an oath; and Albert went to Laura's room, where he found her much distressed, but declaring that about this matter she would decide for herself. It appeared that all this commotion had been caused by the First Consul, who, having a few days before narrowly escaped assassination by a fanatic, who accused him of attempting to destroy the republican institutions, had privately requested Junot not to be married in a church by day, lest that public profession of religion should confirm the suspicions of its enemies. He had added that "in case the family insisted on a religious marriage it could take place at night," and Junot, who regarded the First Consul as a god upon earth, had not only obeyed, but exceeded his instructions by never mentioning the alternative at all.

To this arrangement Madame Permon and Albert saw no objection, and Laura was persuaded to agree to it, though she did not like it because it reminded her of the Terror, when young people could only receive the priest's blessing on their marriage in haste and secrecy at the peril of their lives and his; also because she said they could not then have the usual Mass at the marriage, but this Junot arranged satisfactorily, saying that if the wedding took place at midnight the Mass could be celebrated after it. And with many apologies for having vexed her, Junot departed, and Laura went to look at her *trousseau* and *corbeille*.

The marriage took place as agreed upon. Laura wore a long dress of India muslin, high, with long sleeves, richly embroidered and trimmed with lace, and on her head a large lace veil which fell all, around her, fastened with orange flowers. She was very dark with masses of splendid dark hair, more attractive at that time than regularly pretty. (She soon developed into a beautiful woman.)

Junot was accompanied to the *mairie* by his own family and two or three of his brother officers; Laura by her brother, her uncle, Prince Demetrius Comnenus, who had emigrated and came from Munich on purpose, and by two or three old friends of her parents.

Crowds assembled to see the marriage of the Commandant of Paris, and the "*Dames de la Halle*" of evil renown, deputed four of their number to offer enormous bouquets to the bride. They were admitted into the *salon*, where they presented the bouquets to Laura and embraced her; and after the midnight marriage and Mass, she was conducted with music to the splendid *hôtel* which was to be her new home.

Chapter 7
A Mixed Party
1800

Junot had, in spite of the remonstrances of Madame Permon, insisted on giving a dinner the day after his wedding to several of his brother officers. Madame Permon was horrified at an idea so contrary to the usages of society, and assured him that it was like a carpenter's, apprentice celebrating his wedding festivities at La Courtille. As he would not listen, she, as a last resource, proposed to invite the guests to her own house instead. "But will they come, as they don't know me?"

"Without the least doubt," replied Junot. Invitations were therefore sent to Duroc, Bessières, Lannes, Eugène de Beauharnais, Rapp, and several others, renowned generals of Napoleon, but, with the exception of Eugène de Beauharnais, much more suited to a camp than a civilised drawing-room. Besides these were invited numbers of Madame Permon's old friends, who for the first time were seated at dinner with the Buonaparte family, nearly all of whom were present except Napoleon and Lucien; and afterwards the crowd of strangely assorted guests, looking askance at each other as they walked about the rooms, where they assuredly had never met before, composed altogether the most extraordinary and interesting assembly in which Laura had ever yet found herself.

For to her they were intensely interesting, all these young generals with famous reputations and dreadful manners, whose names she had so often heard, whom she had so much desired to see, and upon whom her mother's friends of the *faubourg St. Germain* looked with scarcely concealed disdain. It was bad enough, they thought, to meet the Buonapartes, but these rough, unmannerly fellows, with their loud voices, boisterous laughter and awkward movements! That Panoria Comnenus should have married Charles Permon had been—well—marrying out of her own set. Still, M. Permon was a thorough gentleman, a scholar, and a man of the world, and his friends were cultivated people of good position.

To marry Laurette to one of these unpolished *parvenus* was quite another matter. However, he was very rich, a gallant soldier, and as favourite of the First Consul had a great career before him; and he was Commandant of Paris. And for the sake of old friendship they came to this party given in Laurette's honour, but they treated the intruders with a politeness too exaggerated to be complimentary, and evidently due only to their deference for their hostess, while from time to time a significant glance, a mocking smile, or a contemptuous whisper was rapidly exchanged as some absurd speech or outrageous breach of good manners attracted their attention.

Madame Bacciochi, who went in for being literary and assumed the character of a *femme d'esprit*, had taken it into her head to institute a sort of club or society of women of cultivated tastes, all of whom should wear the same costume, which she devised and wore herself this evening. It proved, however, to be more a warning than an example. It consisted of a huge muslin turban embroidered with gold and a wreath of laurel over that, a long sleeveless tunic, and an immense shawl worn like a cloak. It was a *toilette*, as Laura remarked, partly resembling a Greek, a Roman, a Jewess—anything, in fact, but a well-dressed Frenchwoman, and she exclaimed—

"To see Madame Bacciochi dressed up in such a manner does not surprise me, for I am accustomed to it; but to hear her say that that is a costume for Christian women who fear God to wear is outrageous!"

One of the few members of the *faubourg St. Germain* who seemed prepared to enjoy himself that night was Monsieur de Caulaincourt, who came up to Laura with all the affection of an old friend and the courtesy of a well-bred Frenchman to offer his congratulations, after which, turning away into the crowd, he met Rapp, a stout, awkward-looking man about the age of Junot, whom he had often seen at the Tuileries, and who cried out—

"Why, what the devil are you doing here?"

"*Ma foi!*" he answered, "I have more right than you to ask that question, considering that I have known Madame Permon for five-and-twenty years and never seen you in her house before. How do you come to be dining here today?" And turning away, he went up to

Laura and asked her whether that fellow had called on them.

"No."

"Impossible."

"I assure you it is true."

"But at least he sent his cards?"

"No."

"Oh! come, my dear child, that is not possible. You have been too busy with your *trousseau* to see him, for it is incredible that a man who is received to dine at the table should take his place at that of *une femme comme il faut* as if it were a *table d'hôte* without first presenting himself to her and—"

Just then Rapp came up without being heard and cried out behind him—

"What are you saying there, dear father? Come, leave the place open for me. At wedding *fêtes* old people do penance." And seizing him in his arms, he carried him some paces off.

M. de Caulaincourt shook him off with a vigour very unexpected from an old man, and observing coldly, "Colonel! you and I are neither young enough nor old enough for such games," he turned to Laura and offered her his arm, saying, "Will you come and see what is going on in the next room?"

Junot found them sitting together, Laura in despair at the result of their first attempt to amalgamate old and new, trying to console M. de Caulaincourt, who indignantly declared that Rapp should give him satisfaction.

Junot, with many apologies, assured him that Rapp did not know how to behave in society, but was the best fellow in the world, and meant no harm.

"I will speak to him at once, and you will see."

"No, no, on no account. I don't want you to beg for excuses for me. Colonel Rapp has insulted me; he must understand and apologise, or else—"

But Junot hurried away, and presently returned with Rapp, who was ready to throw himself on his knees before M. de Caulaincourt, and full of apologies to him for his rudeness and to Laura, to whom he said Junot told him he had been wanting in respect in acting so in her presence.

Touched by his repentant simplicity, M. de Caulaincourt shook hands and declared they would be friends; but Madame Permon was not so forgiving She could not endure people with such manners, and when she heard the story she was so angry that she could scarcely be induced to receive Rapp with civility as long as she lived.

Laura looked with very different eyes upon her husband's friends. She had never known the old, stately, well-bred society so dear to her mother, and though a devout Catholic and sincerely attached to her mother's old friends, she was in most respects a child of the Revolution, or at any rate of the new order of things which had arisen out of it.

Without any sympathy for the Republic, whose bloodthirsty tyrants had been the terror of her childhood, she threw her whole heart and soul into the glories and excitements of the France of Napoleon.

The rough, unmannerly young soldiers, with their loud laughter, awkward movements, and conversation besprinkled with oaths, were heroes of romance to her. The *tri-colour*, held accursed by those who loved the lilies and the white banner, was to her the flag that led the French armies to victory, and the First Consul, so rapidly advancing towards empire, had changed from the sullen, discontented, poverty-stricken lad whom she played with and laughed at in the days when he used to be invited out of kindness to her parents' house, into a sort of demigod whom it was a crime to oppose, whose faults must be excused, his virtues magnified, and from whom the slightest notice was honour and distinction.

A few days after the party just described, M. de Caulaincourt was dining with Laura and her husband, when he noticed General Lannes, a great friend of Junot, who used to say that he was the bravest man in the French Army.

"That is the one of all your new friends whose appearance I like best," he said to Laura. "He is a very soldierlike fellow, and there is something taking about him. Will you introduce me?"

Laura took his arm, went with him to the other end of the room, where Lannes was talking to Junot, and introduced him as a distinguished officer, whereupon Lannes seized his hand, shook it violently, exclaiming, "Shake hands, old fellow! I like *les anciens*; there is always something to be learnt from them! In what regiment did you serve? Were you biped or quadruped? Ah! the devil!" as the astonished old gentleman was taken with a violent fit of coughing.

Junot said something in an undertone to Lannes, who continued, his sentences still full of oaths—

"Ah! you are the father of those two brave young fellows, one of them a colonel of *carabineers* in spite of his youth! You must be a brave man yourself. You have brought them up for their country instead of selling them to foreigners like so many others. You are an honest man, and I must embrace you."

So saying he threw his arms round M. de Caulaincourt and hugged him.

"Well," said Laura as they walked away, "what do you think of him?"

"Oh! a nice fellow—very nice; but somehow I expected rather a different sort of man. For instance, he swears like a renegade—it makes one shudder to hear him. But all that does not prevent his being a brave man and a good soldier."

"But how could you expect Lannes to be anything more than a brave man and a good soldier?"

"My dear child, it was his cursed powdered head that deceived me. I thought anyone who had his hair dressed in the old way would have the old manners too."

"What!" cried Laura; "do you mean to say you judged Lannes by his powdered head? It's very lucky you didn't meet Augereau; you would have made a much greater mistake with him."

Just then a tall man passed, and bowed in a much more gentleman-like manner.

"Who is that?" asked M. de Caulaincourt. "He is powdered, you see."

"That's Colonel Bessières. Shall I present him to you, *mon petit papa?*"

"No, no," he replied. "I have had enough for this time."

In vain Laura explained that Bessières never swore or used any barrack-room language; her old friend would not hear of any more of such introductions that evening. Shortly afterwards he met Augereau, and recollecting what Laura had said about him, was induced by curiosity to make his acquaintance, when the volley of oaths and foul language that poured from his lips so astonished and disgusted him that he almost took a dislike to the powdered hair and *queues* by which he had been so misled.

CHAPTER 8
Madame Person's Invitation
1800

The presentation of Laura, on her marriage, to the First Consul and his wife, had been arranged to take place after the opera.

There was at this time little or no ceremonial attending such occasions, for although Buonaparte was advancing with rapid steps towards supreme power, he had not as yet anything that could be called a court, and Joséphine had not even the *dames de compagnie*, who were shortly afterwards added to her household and before long developed into *dames du palais*.

Laura felt rather nervous as they drove up to the Tuileries, for she knew she would meet none of her old friends there, the only one possible, M. de Caulaincourt, being obliged to stay at home on account of his daughter's illness. As they went up the steps, they met Duroc and Rapp.

"How late you are!" cried Duroc. "Why, it's nearly eleven o'clock."

"Ah!" added Rapp, "Madame Junot is a *merveilleuse*, (female dandy), and is going to make a dandy of our good Junot?" And he roared with laughter.

"Madame Buonaparte told me to come after the opera," said Junot.

"Oh, well, that's a different thing," said Duroc; "if Madame Buonaparte named the time—"

Just then the folding doors of Madame Buonaparte's room opened and Eugène de Beauharnais ran down the staircase. His mother had sent him because, hearing a carriage stop, and seeing nobody announced, she feared they might have been told that they were too late. They went upstairs together, and Eugène, seeing that Laura was nervous, said in a reassuring voice, "Don't be afraid; my mother and sister are so kind."

His words at once restored her composure, for with all her new sympathies, Laura was Madame Permon's true daughter, and her early friends and associates were so far different from those she was likely to find in the *salon* of Joséphine and Hortense that the idea of being afraid of either of them shocked her, and throwing off the shyness, for which she suddenly felt a sort of contempt, she entered the great yellow drawing-room in which the stately magnificence of the court of the Bourbons was being so strangely travestied. The *salon*, which was of immense size, was half dark, except just round the fireplace, where masses of candles were surrounded with gauze to soften the light.

On one side of the fire sat Joséphine, doing some embroidery, on the other her daughter Hortense, a slight, graceful girl with blue eyes, fair, curly hair, and a gentle, rather languid manner. The First Consul was standing with his back to the fire, and as they entered, he watched Laura with critical looks. Joséphine rose, and coming forward to meet her, took her hands and kissed her, saying that she had been too long

EUGÈNE DE BEAUHARNAIS, VICEROY OF ITALY, SON OF JOSÉPHINE

a friend of Junot not to be also a friend of his wife, especially the one he had chosen.

"Oh! oh! Joséphine!" cried Napoleon, "you go too fast. How do you know that this little rascal is worth loving? Well, Mademoiselle Loulou, you see I don't forget the names of my old friends. Haven't you a word for me?" And taking her hand, he drew her nearer to him and looked earnestly at her.

"General," said Laura, smiling, "it is not for me to speak first."

"Well answered, very well. Ah! her mother's spirit. By the way, how is Madame Permon?"

"Ill, general; she suffers a great deal. For two years her health has been so bad that it makes us very uneasy."

"Really! I am sorry, very sorry indeed. Give her my kindest regards. She has a deuced hasty temper, but a kind heart and a generous spirit."

Laura withdrew her hand, which Napoleon had been holding all this time, and went and sat down by Joséphine. The conversation then became general. Duroc came in and began to talk to her, and on that evening began a friendship between them which was never broken.

Someone spoke of Count Louis de Cobentzel, who was expected at Paris, and Joséphine remarked that she had been told that he was wonderfully like Mirabeau.

"Who told you that?" asked Napoleon, turning round.

"I don't exactly remember, but I think it was Barras."

"And where did Barras see M. de Cobentzel? Mirabeau! He was ugly, and M. de Cobentzel is ugly, that's all. *Eh! pardieu!* you knew him, Junot. You were with me at the time of our famous treaty, and Duroc too. But neither of you ever saw Mirabeau. He was a scoundrel, but a clever scoundrel! He alone did more harm to the former masters of this house than all the States-General put together. But he was a scoundrel."

And the First Consul took a pinch of snuff, muttering, "He was a bad man, too tarnished to be a tribune of the people. Not that there are not some in my tribunal," he continued, smiling, "whose conduct is just as bad, and who don't possess his talents. As to Count Louis de Cobentzel—" But, probably remembering that as ambassador of another State he was not a subject for present criticism, he broke off his sentence, took another pinch of snuff, and turning to Laura, said—

"I hope we shall often see you here, Madame Junot. I intend to form a numerous family around me, composed of my generals and their wives, who will be the friends of my wife and Hortense, as their husbands are mine. Will that please you? I warn you that you will be mistaken if you expect to find all your fine friends of the *faubourg St. Germain* here. I don't like them; they are my enemies, and they show it by abusing me. But, as your mother lives amongst them, tell them I am not afraid of them. I fear them no more than the rest."

"General," replied Laura, with spirit, "allow me to decline to do what is in no way a woman's business, and certainly not that of Junot's wife. And permit me to carry no message from you to my friends but one of peace and union, which is all they desire."

Madame Pennon had made up her mind to give a ball a week or two after her daughter's marriage in honour of that event. Accordingly, one evening when Laura and Junot, who had been married four or five days, were dining with her, she proposed that they should make out the list of invitations together. Society in those days was smaller, simpler, more intimate and more friendly than now, and Madame Permon, like all her friends who lived in small houses or small apartments, when they gave a large evening party or ball, threw open all or nearly all their rooms, including bedrooms, which they arranged for people to sit or walk about in.

To this ball were invited a hundred and ten people, of whom seventy were men.

"I want it to be the prettiest ball that has been given for some time," said Madame Permon, as she settled herself on the sofa after dinner. "The house is very small, but it shall be like a basket of flowers. Now, Madame Laurette, take your old place at the writing-table and let us make the list together, for I must invite all your husband's old friends."

Junot got up and kissed her hand.

"But certainly," she said, "your friends are mine now. Only some of them swear too much, Laurette tells me that when you are angry it is rather the same thing. You really must correct yourself of that horrid trick; it is odious in people who belong to society."

Junot laughed and held up his finger. Laura blushed.

"What! because she told me that you swore? But I hope that because she is called Madame Junot, she will not leave off confiding in me and telling me all her joys and sorrows. She has not been long enough acquainted with your ear for it to replace mine. And what ear can listen as well as a mother's. Besides, she told me that you loved her very much. But come, it is late, and we have not had the *loto*; let us make haste and write."

Now the *loto* which Madame Permon insisted on playing every evening was the *bête noire* of Albert, Laurette, and Junot, who concealed their dislike of it from their mother and always played unless there were enough people present to do without them, in which case, when the detested round table and green silk bag were brought in, Albert and Junot would go out to the theatre or elsewhere, the latter saying that he would come back and fetch Laura later.

"I will write the list," said Junot hastily, when he heard the word "*loto*." And he sat down at the writing-table. Having written the names of all the women, beginning with Madame Buonaparte and Mademoiselle de Beauharnais, Junot waited to put down those of the men.

"The First Consul of the French Republic, one and indivisible," began Madame Permon. "That is how you say it, isn't it?"

"The First Consul!" cried they all.

"Why, yes! the First Consul. What is there surprising in that? Do you think I am Corsican enough for a *vendetta*? In the first place, it annoys me to dislike people, and then—"

"And then," said Junot, laughing, "you think perhaps you were more to blame than he."

"No, no! that's another matter. It was he who was in the wrong, a thousand times wrong. How can you say so when you saw the whole thing? But I have been thinking that now Laurette will be so much mixed up with him perhaps the sort of quarrel that there is between us may have disagreeable consequences for her. But it is not enough to invite him; do you think he will come?"

"I am certain he will," replied Junot. "Ask Laurette how he spoke of you when he heard of your illness."

"And so, you told him I was ill," said Madame Permon, who had heard the story ten times at least. "So, he thinks I am dying, and will expect to see a spectre?" And looking at the great mirror before her sofa, she smoothed down the dark curls of her hair. She was still beautiful.

"Well, mamma, tell me what time will suit you best and I will come and fetch you," said Junot.

"Fetch me? To go where?"

"Why, to the Tuileries, of course, to invite the First Consul and Madame Buonaparte!"

"My dear Junot," said Madame Permon, looking at him seriously, "you must be quite entirely mad."

"I see nothing that is not quite reasonable and sensible in what I say, mamma," answered Junot.

"And I say that you are mad. Do you suppose I shall go myself and ask General Buonaparte to come to my house again after having told him never to do so?"

"But you are going to send him an invitation?"

Madame Permon tried to explain that that was a different thing; but Junot, in despair, inquired how she meant to invite him.

"Why, how should I invite him? Just like anyone else, only that I will write the invitation with my own hand. He knows my handwriting well enough. And I have not taken so much trouble for anyone for three years. Ask Loulou."

Junot walked up and down the room very much disturbed.

"It will never do," he persisted. "It would be better not to invite him at all. He will think you mean an impoliteness."

"Then he will be mistaken. How can it be an impoliteness? He will think nothing of the sort, and you will see that after receiving the invitation he will come and call like any other well-bred man, or at any rate will leave his card."

"What! Do you think he has visiting cards?"

"And why not? My dear child, because Buonaparte gains victories, is there any reason why he should not pay visits?"

Junot looked at her with an air of consternation, and Albert and

Laura gave way to the fits of laughter they could no longer suppress. Although at present no pretensions of royalty had been put forth by Napoleon, still for more than a year he had held supreme power in France.

Albert made a sign to the others not to oppose his mother, and they arranged to go together to take the invitations to the Tuileries, excusing Madame Permon on account of her health, not letting her know anything about it, and not presenting the notes she had written.

This they accordingly did next day. Joséphine accepted for herself and Hortense, but said that it would be of no use to ask Napoleon, as he scarcely ever went out. Joséphine, who knew of the old friendship of the First Consul for the Permons and his wish to marry Madame Permon, had an aversion to any renewal of intimacy, and had been supposed to disapprove of Laura's marriage to Junot. She was well aware that they were great friends of her husband's family, whom she could not bear, which perhaps was not surprising.

When Laura and her husband and brother, however, went up to Napoleon's room, he accepted the invitation without any difficulty.

"Of course, I will come to the ball," he said, taking both Laura's hands. "Why do you look as if you thought I should refuse? I will come with pleasure. And yet I shall be in the midst of my enemies, for your mother's *salon* is filled with them."

As the day of the ball drew near, Laura felt a certain uneasiness in the first place as to how her mother would receive the First Consul, and also because Madame Permon insisted on her dancing the *menuet de la cour*. In spite of Albert's age and Laura's marriage, they never opposed their mother's will, so Laura had to resign herself and dance the minuet she detested because Madame Permon declared it had always been the custom.

As to the rest, the ball was most successful. The staircase and rooms were beautifully decorated with plants and flowers, and about nine o'clock Joséphine arrived with her son and daughter, saying that the First Consul had been unavoidably detained, but would not fail to come, only he begged they would not wait for him to begin dancing. Laura and Junot therefore opened the ball with Eugène and Hortense de Beauharnais, and just before eleven the trampling of the horses of the escort of the First Consul was heard under the windows, and presently Napoleon entered.

Madame Permon, who was dressed in white crepe with jonquils and diamonds, came forward to meet him with a low curtsey, but he held out his hand, saying with a smile—

"Well, Madame Permon, is that the way you receive an old friend?" And they entered the ballroom together.

It was very crowded and hot, in spite of which Napoleon kept on his well-known grey overcoat all the time. Looking round the room, he noticed that some of the ladies did not rise when he came in, a thing which always annoyed him. He went on, with Madame Permon still upon his arm, to her bedroom, where Talleyrand and several others, were sitting, ordered the dancing, which had stopped on his arrival, to go on again, and turning to Madame Permon with a look of admiration, asked if she would not dance with him, but she declined, saying that she had not danced for thirty years.

All the Buonaparte family except Joseph were present. Madame Leclerc had seated herself as far as she could from her sister-in-law, of whose exquisite toilette she was furiously jealous.

"Really," she exclaimed, looking at the poppies and golden corn Joséphine wore on her dress and in her hair, "I cannot understand how a woman of forty can wear wreaths of flowers!"

And on Laura observing that Madame Permon, who was older, was also wearing flowers, she replied only—

"Oh! that's very different."

Laura, dressed in India muslin embroidered with silver, was occupying herself with everybody and looking after everything that concerned the success of the evening. Thinking that her mother, although perfectly polite, was not sufficiently cordial to the First Consul, who was evidently inclined to renew their old friendship, at any rate in some degree, she went to look for her and persuaded her to come out of her *boudoir*, where she was sitting, into her bedroom, where Napoleon was still talking to Talleyrand. Directly he saw her he came up to her, and in a friendly, almost affectionate, manner, reproached her with her forgetfulness of an old friend, refusing to accept her excuses and explanations, and at last asking her if they were indeed no longer friends.

"Dear Napoleon," she replied in Italian, "I can never forget that you are the son of my friend and the brother of my good Joseph, Lucien and Paulette."

"So," interrupted he, "if I am still anything at all to you, it is only thanks to my mother and brothers! Well, one might as well expect firmness from the shifting sand of the desert as friendship from a woman."

Laura felt very uncomfortable during this discussion. Her mother was leaning back against the cushion on the sofa tapping with her foot, as she always did when she was getting angry; whilst Napoleon walked up and down with disturbed looks, and when at that moment Albert came in and offered him an ice, he replied—

"I assure you, my dear fellow, that neither Madame Permon nor I require it. I really think we are frozen as it is. I knew that absence brought forgetfulness, but not to such an extent as this."

"Indeed!" retorted Madame Permon. "It is excusable to forget after years have passed, but you found it too difficult to remember for a few days a thing upon which a person's whole prospects depended."

Albert and Laura felt in despair at the old grievance of the stupid Stephanopoli, who was not worth the trouble he had caused, being so inopportunely raked up just when the friendship of Napoleon was of such infinite importance to them all; and the First Consul gave vent to an irritated exclamation, but apparently changing his mind, he sat down by Madame Permon, took her hand, and began to laugh at her for not having left off her old trick of biting her nails.

"Come, come," she said presently, "let everything stay as it was. It is only you. Napoleon, who must not do that. You have so many steps to mount to the top of your ladder of glory that to desire repose for you would be wishing evil for us."

"Do you really think what you say?"

"You know how sincere I am," she replied. "I don't always say all I think, but I never say what I don't think. Have you forgotten my candour?"

Napoleon took her hand, pressed it affectionately, and as two o'clock struck asked for his carriage, saying he could not possibly stay to supper, but would come again to see her. Before he left he told them that enormous bills had been sent to Bourrienne for things ordered by Jérôme Buonaparte, who, though only fifteen, had bought amongst other things a magnificent dressing-case fitted up with gold, ivory, and mother-of-pearl, filled with razors, combs for moustaches, &c., and costing eight or ten thousand *francs*.

CHAPTER 9

The Consular Court
1800

The consular court, in which Laura occupied so distinguished a position, was composed in great part of the generals of Napoleon, chiefly young men and their wives, most of whom were scarcely past their childhood. Some of them were of good blood, for the newly risen officers and functionaries were eager to marry the daughters of the old French families, whose ruined parents were sometimes like Madame Permon, willing enough to give their consent. For the most part, however, the *faubourg St. Germain* held aloof, to the intense annoyance and irritation of Napoleon. Some of the younger generation served in the army or the State, as, for instance, the two sons of M. de Caulaincourt, but on the whole the two societies were entirely separate, and regarded each other with something like hatred.

But in all divisions and classes of society the stern lessons of the Revolution, whose perils and sorrows were still so fresh in every one's mind, had changed the tone into one of colder, stricter morality than had formerly prevailed. The early court of Napoleon was much more correct in morals than in manners, and he himself was, for some reason or other, extremely anxious that it should be so, and remarkably particular about the conduct and reputation of, at any rate, the women of his court, although, being devoid of either religion or morality, he did not trouble himself to carry his restrictions and regulations into his own way of life. He was extremely jealous of Joséphine, to whom, however, he never dreamed of being faithful, and his brothers and sisters were always ready to make mischief between them.

One conspicuous object of his suspicions and the malignity of Madame Leclerc, was a certain M. Charles, (his surname was Charles), who belonged to a family of the small *bourgeoisie*, and was *aide-de-camp* to General Leclerc. When Napoleon and Joséphine were at Milan, where they held a sort of court in the Palazzo Serbelloni, M. Charles was presented to the latter, who took a fancy to him and singled him out in a way that was sure to attract attention and give rise to slanderous gossip. For it does not appear that there was anything but an intimate and sentimental friendship between them.

M. Charles was about eight-and-twenty, good-looking, but very small, in no way remarkable. Napoleon was frequently absent, and while he was at one or another of the Italian towns, M. Charles was constantly at the Palazzo Serbelloni.

Madame Leclerc occupied herself in spying upon her sister-in-law and repeating to Napoleon all the gossip she could collect about her. Shortly afterwards he found a pretext for arresting M. Charles, who was compelled to leave the army, much to the distress of Joséphine, who got him a place in Paris, where they resumed their friendship when Napoleon was gone to Egypt and she returned from Italy.

LA MALMAISON.

Joséphine was then established at La Malmaison, where she was to be seen wandering about the gardens by moonlight, dressed in white with a long veil, leaning on the arm of M. Charles, who was constantly at La Malmaison and seemed very much at home there.

Everyone gossiped about it, and M. Gohier warned Joséphine and tried to persuade her to break off the intimacy.

Joséphine, however, refused, declaring with tears that it was nothing but a harmless friendship.

"Then get a divorce," said Gohier. "You say that there is nothing but friendship between you and M. Charles; but if your friendship is so exclusive that it makes you break all the rules of society, I advise you to get a divorce just the same as if you were in love. If your friendship is all that signifies to you, it will make up for everything else. Believe me, all this will bring you trouble."

When Napoleon came back, he was furious at all he heard, and threatened to divorce Joséphine. The quarrel was made up, owing partly to the intercession of her children, Eugène and Hortense, but on condition that M. Charles should be dismissed, and that she would promise never to see him again. (Bourrienne accuses Junot of having made mischief in this matter, but Madame d'Abrantès, in her *Mémoires*, disproves his assertion. Junot was a friend of M. Charles.)

The year before Laura's wedding, Caroline Buonaparte had been married to Joachim Murat, another of Napoleon's officers, the son of an innkeeper, who had by a certain impetuous courage and brilliancy raised himself to a high position in the republican army. Murat was rash, vain, and weak, and Napoleon disapproved of his marriage with Caroline, whom he wanted to marry to Moreau. He had also a private grudge against him, which was this:—

Murat was a friend of Madame Tallien and of Madame Buonaparte (Joséphine), and was very fond of boasting of the fact. He gave a *déjeuner* to a number of his brother officers, at which, after drinking a great quantity of champagne, he proposed to make punch in a special way which he declared had been taught him by the prettiest and most charming woman in Paris.

His comrades, whom the punch had deprived of whatever good sense the champagne had spared, at once began to question him about the circumstances and the name of the person in question, and succeeded in extracting from him the history of a day he had spent in the Champs Elysées and of a *déjeuner*, dinner and supper, rendered much more compromising by the remarks and stories exaggerated by his own vanity and folly, and the license of his companions, one of whom, catching up a gilt lemon-squeezer, which Murat was using for the punch, saw a monogram upon it which did not appear to be that of his host, but "J. B.," which he began to spell out as Buonaparte. Frightened at this, Murat managed to put a stop to the discussion, but the matter was immediately reported to Napoleon, who was furious, and whose first intention was to demand an explanation from Murat. On second thoughts, however, he considered this would be beneath his dignity, but he never liked Murat afterwards.

The lemon-squeezer disappeared, and Murat declared that it had been stolen, also that the monogram was "J. M." and that the young man who had supposed it to be anything else was not in a condition to see clearly at the time.

Murat was tall and picturesque-looking, but with rather the appearance of having negro blood in his veins; he had also a deplorable love of finery. He fell violently in love with Caroline Buonaparte, who had just left school, and as she returned his passion. Napoleon was induced to give his consent to the marriage.

Caroline had a lovely complexion, and pretty teeth, hands, and feet, but her features and figure were bad, and her utter want of distinction and good breeding were made more conspicuous by the magnificence she afterwards assumed. The contrast between the simplicity, refinement, and grace in dress, manners, and appearance which characterised the *faubourg St. Germain*, and the vulgarity, ostentation, and unmannerliness of the new society and court especially struck all foreigners who now and again visited Paris. Laura, however, enjoyed herself thoroughly in her new life. She went to the parties of her mother's

JOACHIM MURAT, KING OF NAPLES

old friends in the *faubourg St. Germain* as well as to those of the new court, and she delighted in the grand parades and military spectacles.

These she generally saw from Duroc's windows, which were close to those of Joséphine, where the *corps diplomatique* or any other foreigners of distinction always went for the same purpose. The first time she went to see the parade, Junot, who had to ride with all his *aides-de-camp*, could not go with her.

Madame Permon was ill, and Albert could not be away, so she went with Junot's parents and brother. They got out of the carriage at the gate, and crossed the garden to get to Duroc's rooms. But the crowd was so great that they could hardly pass, and old M. Junot, who was as usual in a bad humour, kept grumbling about a yellow *cachemire* shawl Laura had on, declaring that it was extravagant folly to wear anything so costly in such a crowd, and that it would be certain to be stolen.

"I am not so careless," he said; "I take care to keep my hand upon my watch; here it is in my waistcoat pocket. I have no fear of pickpockets. As to your shawl, you will certainly have it stolen."

Just then Laura felt someone pull at her shawl. She gave a cry, and M. Junot turned to see who it was; but every face looked quite unconscious, and Laura drew her shawl closer round her.

"Didn't I tell you so?" exclaimed he, and he went on grumbling till they arrived at Duroc's, where they took possession of the window reserved for them. Presently, wishing to look at his watch, he felt in his waistcoat pocket. It was gone, the nearest pickpocket having been guided by his own words to it.

"Well," said his wife, without turning her head from the window to reply to the clamour he made, "they stole your watch while you were tormenting your daughter-in-law about her shawl, and it served you right."

It was Laura's custom to dine at four o'clock; at any rate, dinner was ordered for that hour every day, but she very often dined and spent the evening with her mother, especially when Junot was at any official dinner, for she never let a day pass without seeing her.

Lucien Buonaparte used to come in the evening sometimes to pour into Madame Permon's ears his grievances and differences with Napoleon, to whose rapidly-growing power Lucien's fanatical republicanism was opposed, so that there were constant disputes between them, ending in a serious quarrel in which their mother, the Signora Laetitia, as Napoleon called her, took Lucien's side.

Lucien had lost his wife, and now left Paris, taking with him his two little girls, indignantly rejecting Madame Permon's suggestion to leave them with Joseph's wife, *née* Mademoiselle Clary, who was very goodhearted, but was described in a letter written at that time by Colonel Nightingale to Lord Cornwallis as:

"A very short, very thin, very ugly, and very vulgar little woman, without anything to say for herself."

"At the opera, where used to be seen brilliant groups of all the young people of fashion, and all the fashionable *'filles'* or *demi-monde* who rivalled or surpassed them in appearance, was now the strangest collection of odd blackguard-looking people that could be conceived." (*Journal of Miss Berry*, vol. ii.)

One evening, at the Comédie Française, Junot pointed out to Laura a woman of two or three and twenty, but looking much younger, who returned his bow with an air of old acquaintanceship, saying that she was Pauline, "our sovereign in the East." Her history was as follows: She was the natural daughter of a gentleman at Carcassonne by a servant, and supported herself by needlework. A certain M. and Madame de Sales took her up, and as she had received some education and was well conducted and attractive, they showed her great kindness, and had her to sing and recite at their parties, where a rich man named Fourès, whose father had made a fortune in trade, fell in love and proposed to marry her. Pauline accepted him from motives of interest and ambition, and when soon afterwards there was a call for more troops to go to Egypt, M. Fourès, who was very fond of her, wanted her to go with him. She agreed, and arrived in Egypt disguised in man's clothes, delighted with the adventure, and eager for any amusement that might come in her way.

One day there was a sort of fair or *fête* near Cairo, to which she went with a number of officers and young people, riding donkeys. Suddenly a troop of cavalry rode up, at the head of which was the First Consul surrounded by his staff. He saw and admired Pauline, but apparently took no notice of her and rode on.

The next day Madame Fourès received an invitation to dine with General Dupuy, who had a wife, or someone supposed to be his wife, who received his guests.

M. Fourès, who was lieutenant in the 22nd Chasseurs, thought it strange that he was not included in the invitation, but allowed her to accept it.

The party was a small one, and nothing unusual passed until just as the coffee was brought in, Buonaparte was announced. He stayed a very short time, during the whole of which he looked at no one but Madame Fourès. However, he left without speaking to her, and a few days later Berthier sent for her husband, and told him that he had been chosen by the commander-in-chief to carry some despatches to Europe, and must set out immediately, but that it would be impossible to take his wife as the ship was small and inconvenient, and besides there was danger from the English, who were on the watch for every French vessel that sailed. All this was explained by Berthier with much pretended sympathy, and the deluded Fourès set off upon his voyage, which was soon interfered with by an English captain, who captured M. Fourès and his despatches.

Proceeding to investigate the latter, the English captain found nothing of any importance in them, and had heard quite enough of the affair to make him understand why M, Fourès was sent to Europe. He therefore consented to take him back to Cairo, where, arriving unexpectedly, he found his lodgings empty and his wife established in a house of her own close to that of the commander-in-chief.

Fourès, who was deeply attached to his wife, was beside himself with grief and anger, but it was of no use—she refused to return to him, and he was obliged to consent to a divorce. Pauline was passionately in love with Napoleon, and lived with him as his mistress as long as he remained in Egypt. When the time came for him to return to

France, he announced to her that they must part. There was, he said, a possibility of his being captured by the English, and it would not do for her to be found with him.

Therefore, she had to stay behind, much alarmed about her husband, against whom she had now no protector, for Kléber, from whom she had to get a passport, would not give it until another officer interfered and got it for her.

When she arrived in France, Pauline was no longer of much importance to Napoleon, who had just become reconciled to Joséphine after his quarrel about M. Charles, and was very anxious she should not find out at so inopportune a moment the difference between his precepts and his practice. Therefore, he would not allow Pauline to have a house in Paris, so she bought one near Saint-Gervais, where Junot used to go to see her. M. Fourès meanwhile returned with the army from Egypt, and wanted to make his wife come back to him. She appealed to the divorce pronounced in Egypt, but it appeared that, as it had not been confirmed within the proper time in France, it was not legal.

Napoleon, to put an end to the matter, ordered Pauline to marry again. There was a M. Ramchouppe who was in love with her, and to him the First Consul promised a consulate in some distant place if she married him, which she consented to do.

Junot advised her to see some lawyer and consult him about the divorce, so she applied to her old friend M. de Sales, who belonged to that profession, and who told her that the divorce pronounced in Egypt was not legal, and as she evidently could not live happily with her husband, they had better agree in demanding a fresh one.

But of this Napoleon would not hear. He was just then going to be crowned, and did not want his name to be dragged into a case like this. He was very angry with M. de Sales for opposing his wishes, and declared that he was not going to have the Parisians gossiping at his expense, but that the marriage, whether legal or not, should take place without any further divorce. So it did; but the strangest part of the story is that the woman whom Napoleon had treated in this manner many years afterwards, when he was imprisoned at St. Helena, realised part of her fortune, and was preparing to make some attempt, which of course would have failed, to deliver him, when his death put an end to her hopes.

One advantage that Laura thoroughly appreciated in her husband's being Commandant of Paris was that it gave them a right to a box at each of the theatres, to which Madame Permon, who had gone to a new doctor and was for the time much better, often accompanied them.

One evening they were at the opera—Madame Permon, Laura, Junot and her brother. The house was very full, the *toilettes* were brilliant, and Junot, who had just been dining with Berthier, then Minister of War, was in high spirits because of some very flattering remarks made about him by the First Consul and repeated by Berthier.

Suddenly there was a tremendous explosion with a noise like the firing of a cannon. Junot went out into the corridor, but saw nobody. He came for his hat, saying that he would go and find out what it was, and at that moment the First Consul entered his box with Joséphine, Hortense, and Madame Murat, accompanied by several officers. A few minutes afterwards Duroc came to Junot's box and told them that Napoleon had narrowly escaped being assassinated. Directly the news became known there was an immense sensation in the theatre, women shedding tears and everyone cheering the First Consul. Junot went to take his orders, and then left the theatre, telling the others not to wait for him.

In the next box to theirs was M. Diestrich, *aide-de-camp* to General Vandamme, with his mother and sister. He told them that the intention of the assassins had been to place the cart in which was the explosive machine against the entrance to the opera house. Fortunately, the official obeyed the orders he had received never to allow any vehicle to stand there on the night of a first representation, otherwise the theatre would have been blown up. He added that he had come back for his mother and sister, as none of the assassins were yet arrested, and there was no saying whether another attempt might not be made when the First Consul came out.

Madame Permon therefore hurried Laura off, and Junot, looking in as they were putting on their cloaks, told her to get away at once, drop her mother at her house, and go on to Madame Buonaparte's, where he would meet her.

She found they had just returned from the opera, Joséphine was crying and Napoleon engaged in conversation with several officers and officials. Junot, Fouché, and others thought that these attempts were organised in some foreign country; Napoleon was of opinion that they were the work of fanatical Republicans, amongst whom, he said, were a number of the *septembriseurs*.

"They are a lot of wretches," he added, "who have calumniated

Liberty by the crimes they have committed in her name."

Nine people were killed by the explosion and at least twenty more died afterwards of the injuries they had received. Junot had had a narrow escape. He had been to the Tuileries on his way to the opera, but had just missed the First Consul. If he had found him, his own carriage would have been just behind his, and would certainly have been blown up. The last man of the escort had his horse killed. A slight delay in changing her shawl, which Rapp observed did not suit her dress, saved Joséphine; as it was, the windows of her carriage were shattered, and the broken glass fell all over Hortense and cut her neck.

A day or two afterwards Junot, who was occupied from morning till night in the researches made after the conspirators, came home so tired and exhausted that instead of going, as he had promised, to fetch Laura from her mother's, he sent the carriage with a message and went to bed, though it was only ten o'clock. He was sleeping in a little camp-bed near hers, as she had been suffering from a slight attack of fever. She went up to wish him goodnight, and bending over him, said—

"What! asleep already?" when Junot, who was dreaming that the assassins were in the room, started up in his sleep and gave her a violent kick, which flung her to the other side of the room. At the cry she gave her maid rushed in with a light, and Junot awoke almost out of his senses with horror and fright, for Laura was very much hurt and spat blood, besides which she was supposed to be *enceinte*. When the doctor arrived and examined into the state of the case he declared that if Junot had been a very little further off, so as to give more force to the blow, he would have killed her.

Although accustomed from her earliest childhood to be constantly in society, Laura found the enormous number of people she was now obliged to see and receive both perplexing and fatiguing. They were always giving dinners of five-and-twenty or thirty people, followed by *soirées* of more than a hundred, who, instead of being old and intimate friends, such as formed the circle of Madame Permon, were many of them strangers to her, and sometimes persons she regarded with aversion, even horror. One morning when they were at *déjeuner* a tall man entered dressed in blue. Junot called him "general," but did not introduce him to her, and seemed constrained in his manner. When they went into the drawing-room, to her astonishment he pushed before her, nearly knocking her down. Junot offered him coffee, which he refused, saying—

"No, thank you, general; I never take a *demi-tasse* in the morning. A *petit-verre* perhaps, if *mam'selle* permits."

"It is my wife," remarked Junot coldly.

"Ah! it is the *citoyenne* Junot," said the fellow, staring at her. "The devil! you haven't done badly, *mon collègue!*"

He then engaged in conversation with one of Junot's *aides-de-camp*, and Laura listened with increasing disgust to the ungrammatical, brutal language and shameless allusions to the crimes which had disgraced the Republicans in Brittany and La Vendée, in which he had evidently borne a leading part. It was Santerre. (Santerre, brewer in the *faubourg St. Antoine*, commanded the National Guard, August, 1792, when the Royal Family were in the Temple. Infamous for his cruelties in the war of La Vendée.)

"*Ma foi!*" exclaimed Junot when he was gone, "I did not choose to introduce such a fellow to you. I don't like him to come to my house, and he very seldom does.... It is impossible for me, republican though I am, to give my hand to Santerre when I meet him in the Tuileries gardens, the *revolutionary general*, which means general of that army in which the guillotine was always ready, like a cannon with a lighted fuse. I cannot bear them; their conduct is all stained with blood: they are repugnant to me. I am republican in principles and taste, but I have a horror of the blood and massacres and confiscations and all that awful reign of terror under which France groaned for years. Santerre is a wretch, he is under a sort of police *surveillance*, and I daresay he says I am proud and disdainful because I don't fraternise with him; no, I should think not, for I despise him."

"Why, I thought he was dead four years ago!" exclaimed Napoleon, when Laura told him about it. "Well, what do you think of him? Isn't he handsome and amiable? Those are the sort of people who would like to see the happy days of '93 again! M. Santerre would be charmed to gain a lieutenant-general's epaulettes as he gained those of general of brigade—by sending better men than himself to the scaffold."

CHAPTER 10
Napoleon and Laura
1801

The *château* of La Malmaison, which had been bought by Joséphine, was her favourite and at this time her most habitual residence. There was then very little state or ceremony in the life there, which was in some ways a good deal like that of a house party in a country house.

Everyone got up when they chose in the morning, and breakfast was at eleven in a small *salon* looking on the courtyard. No men were ever present unless they were members of the family of Buonaparte, and not often even then. After breakfast they talked, read, or otherwise amused themselves, and Joséphine often gave audiences, though Napoleon disliked her doing so. However, she did it out of kindness, and received in this way presents of jewels, which did not occur to her, as they did to her enemies, in the light of bribes.

Many of her old friends of the *faubourg St. Germain,* and some who had not troubled themselves about her when she was only the wife of the unfortunate Vicomte de Beauharnais, gathered round her now that her husband was the ruler of France, and Joséphine, who was extremely kind-hearted, was always ready to use in their favour whatever power she possessed, and anxious that it should be supposed to be more rather than less than it really was.

One of these friends, Madame d'Houdetot, was desirous to push on her brother, M. de Ceré, a good-looking, feather-brained young fellow, whom his sister presented to Joséphine. She invited him constantly to La Malmaison, and managed to get him a commission through Savary. But M. de Ceré was so careless and foolish that protection was of very little use to him. He was sent on a mission to Bordeaux, with orders to be back within a certain day, instead of which he stayed a fortnight over the allotted time. The First Consul was very angry, and even Joséphine refused to interfere any further, saying that he should not have stayed when he was ordered to return, and as he chose to disobey, there was nothing more to be done.

Instead of being made *aide-de-camp* to Napoleon, therefore, he was told that the First Consul forbade him to come into his presence. He left Paris for some months, at the end of which he returned and persuaded his sister and Savary to induce Joséphine to give him another chance. To his great joy they told him that she consented to receive him the next day, and that he was to bring a petition clearly explaining what he wanted, which she would give to the First Consul.

Accordingly, he wrote his petition, and was just going downstairs with it in his pocket to start for La Malmaison at the appointed time, when he was stopped by his tailor with a bill. Explaining where he was going and promising to come back in a few days and pay the bill, he put it into his pocket and drove off.

Joséphine received him very graciously, saying that she had spoken to the First Consul, who was disposed to overlook his offence if he would promise to amend; and taking the petition told him to come for the answer in a few days.

De Ceré, in high spirits, went to his sister's house and to his friends to receive their congratulations, and finally to the hotel where he was staying. It was very late, and on retiring to his room he recollected the tailor's bill and took it out to see how much it was. "The devil!" he muttered as he opened it, "it's a long bill; there's no end to it. Why, it looks like a petition! Ah! *mon Dieu!*"

It was the petition he had written, and he had sent his tailor's bill to the First Consul!

What was to be done? He consulted two or three of his brother officers, who advised him to go the next morning and explain the matter to Madame Buonaparte. But just as he entered the hall Joséphine, who was coming out from breakfast, hastened up to him, and holding out her hand, exclaimed—

"I am so glad! I gave your petition to the First Consul; we read it together; it was excellent and made a great impression upon him. He told me he would speak to Berthier, and in another fortnight, it would be all arranged. I assure you that this success, for I regard it as settled, made me happy all yesterday."

De Ceré was confounded, but of course dared not explain. It was

LOUIS BUONAPARTE, KING OF HOLLAND.

evident that Joséphine either could not or would not meddle any further in the matter, and had put the tailor's bill into the fire without looking at it. There was nothing more to be done but to return to Paris a sadder and wiser man.

The First Consul worked all day and never appeared till dinner, which was at six o'clock, and in fine weather was often out of doors. Every Wednesday there was a dinner party, and in the evenings, they danced, played games, and acted. There were often hunting parties; every one amused themselves, and the summer passed away pleasantly enough.

Hortense de Beauharnais had just been married to Louis Buonaparte against the will of them both, for they cared nothing for each other, were absolutely unsuited, and Hortense was in love with Duroc. Joséphine, however, disapproved of him, and Napoleon then, in spite of the entreaties of his stepdaughter, insisted on her becoming the wife of Louis, who, although a straightforward, honourable, well-meaning man, was cold, stiff, dull, and uninteresting, while Hortense was affectionate, lively, impressionable, and fond of society. The marriage turned out unhappily, as might have been expected, and Duroc became the implacable enemy of Joséphine. (Joséphine, alarmed at the enmity of her husband's family, who hated her, was most anxious for this marriage, by which she expected to secure an ally in Louis.)

Laura and the other young wives of the chief officers, though they were happy enough at La Malmaison, where their husbands came nearly every day, still did not wish to be always there, but would have preferred to be able to go sometimes to their own homes. This they could not do without asking leave, which was not always granted; already the fetters of a court seemed to hang upon them.

Laura was getting anxious to be with her mother again and also to see a little *château* and estate which Junot had spent nearly all the *dot* given by the First Consul in buying for her, as she wished to have a place of her own.

However, it was a long time before she could obtain the desired permission, and then only in consequence of circumstances quite unforeseen and unusual.

The Château de la Malmaison was not large, and her apartment consisted only of bedroom, dressing-room, and her maid's room adjoining.

One morning she was awakened by a violent rapping close to her, and beheld the First Consul standing by her bed. She looked at him with astonishment and rubbed her eyes, hardly believing she was awake.

"Yes, it is I," said he; "why that astonished look?"

Laura pointed to the window, wide open on account of the heat, and to her watch. It was not yet five o'clock; the sun was hardly risen, and the trees outside looked like dark masses.

"Really," said Napoleon, "is it so early? Well, so much the better; we will talk." And drawing a large armchair to the foot of the bed, he sat down with an enormous packet of letters, which he proceeded to examine. They were addressed "To the First Consul, to him alone." ('*Au premier consul, à lui-même; à lui seul en personne.*')

Laura suggested that a trustworthy person might be selected to save him all this business, to which he replied—

"Perhaps later on; it is impossible now. I have to see to it all. I can't neglect any petition or anything else when order has only so lately been restored."

"But this, for instance," said Laura, pointing to a large, ill-directed, badly-sealed letter; "surely this contains nothing that could not be told you by a secretary?"

He opened the letter, which was of three large pages, badly written. He read it through, and then said—

"Well, this letter is a proof that I do well to see for myself. Here, read it."

It was from a woman whose son had been killed in Egypt. The poor mother, whose husband had died also from the effects of his military service, had written more than ten letters to the Minister of War, the First Consul, and his secretary, stating that she was deprived of all means of subsistence, and could get no answer. Napoleon got up, found a pen, and made a note upon the letter.

The next was enclosed in several envelopes, all perfumed with essence of roses. He read it and laughed.

"It's a declaration," he said, "not of war, but of love. A beautiful lady, who says she has loved me ever since she saw me present the treaty of peace of Campo-Formio to the Directory. And if I want to see her I have only to give orders to the porter at the Bougival gate to admit a woman dressed in white who will say 'Napoleon.' And, *ma foi!*" he added, looking at the date, "it is for this evening!"

"*Mon Dieu!*" cried Laura, "you won't do anything so imprudent?"

He looked at her for a moment in silence.

"What does it matter to you whether I go to the Bougival gate? What should happen to me?"

"What does it matter to me? What could happen to you? What strange questions. General! Don't you see that this woman is a wretch in the pay of your enemies? The snare is too evident. Anyhow, there is danger. And then you ask me what your imprudence matters to me!"

Napoleon laughed.

"I was only joking," he said. "Do you think I am so stupid or so simple as to swallow such a bait? Every day I get those sort of letters, with rendezvous here or at the Tuileries or Luxembourg, but the only answer I make and they deserve is this—" and he wrote a few lines, enclosing the letter to the minister of police.

"The devil! there's six o'clock!" he exclaimed, as a clock struck. And collecting his papers, he pinched her foot through the coverlet, smiled, and left the room singing to himself—

Non, non, z'il est impossible
D'avoir un plus aimable enfant,
Un plus aimable? Ah! si vraiment, &c.

Laura got up without thinking any more of this strange visit. In the evening, about nine o'clock, Napoleon came up to her and whispered, "I am going to the Bougival gate."

"I don't believe it," replied Laura, also in a whisper. "You know too well what harm your death would do to France; but if you say another word about it, I will tell Madame Hortense or Junot."

"You are a little madcap," he replied, pinching her ear and lifting up his finger. "If you say a word about what I have let you see I shall not only be displeased, but you will give me pain."

"The last consideration is enough, General."

He looked at her for a moment.

"The spirit of your mother," he said. "Absolutely the spirit of your mother."

She made no reply, and after waiting in silence for a few minutes he walked into the billiard-room. The next morning Laura was awakened by the same knocking at the door of her maid's room, and again the First Consul entered with a packet of letters and newspapers. He apologised for waking her, said she ought not to sleep with the windows open, or she would spoil her teeth, which were little pearls like her mother's, and having paid her this compliment he sat down and looked over his letters and papers, discussing the contents with her and departing after a time in the same way as before.

But Laura now began to feel uneasy about these visits. She did not believe Napoleon meant any harm to her, and had all her life been accustomed to look upon him, not perhaps as a brother—always a doubtful expression between young people who are not really related to each other—but as a cousin, a relationship of the widest comprehension. Still, even cousins do not come and sit in each other's bedrooms at five o'clock in the morning, and she knew perfectly well that if Napoleon were seen coming out of her room at such an hour nobody would suppose he went there to read the papers.

Already the notice he took of her was attracting comment, as she saw by the disagreeable manner of some and the exaggerated politeness and attentions which others were eager to show her. Although she was only sixteen, she had lived too much in the world not to know what that meant, and disliked it extremely, but could not think what to do. She was afraid to tell Junot, who was hasty, jealous, and very much in love with her, and she did not like to say anything to Napoleon himself. So, she forbade her maid, who had not been long with her, to open the door to anyone who knocked so early in the morning.

"But, *madame*, if it is the First Consul?"

"I will not be woke up so early by the First Consul any more than anybody else. Do as I tell you."

That day Napoleon was rather more civil and complimentary than usual, and Laura saw that she was not the only one to observe it. He announced that the day after tomorrow he was going to give a *déjeuner* and hunting party, and that they would meet at ten o'clock.

On retiring to her room that night Laura repeated her orders to her maid not to open the door, and then went to bed in unusually low spirits. She was getting tired of being at La Malmaison, where, though everyone was very kind to her, she was amongst strangers. She would much rather have been amongst her own friends, saw very little of her husband, and fretted for her mother, who was in bad health and from whom she had never before been separated. She lay in her bed thinking how to get away, and cried herself to sleep.

On awaking in the morning, she thought she would go and get the key of the outer door, and stealing softly through the ante-room where her maid was asleep, she found that the door was unlocked and the key outside. She locked it, took the key, went back to bed, and presently heard the steps of the First Consul in the corridor. He knocked much more softly than before, and she heard her maid tell him that she had taken the key. Then she heard him go away, and went to sleep again.

She was awakened by the door of her own room being pushed open, and the First Consul entered.

"Are you afraid of being murdered?" he asked angrily.

Laura hesitated, and said that she had taken the key of her maid's door because she preferred that people should come in by her own.

Napoleon looked at her in silence, and then said—

"Tomorrow we are going to hunt at Butard; you have not forgotten, have you? We shall start early, and I shall come and call you myself, so that you may be in time. And as you are not here amongst a horde of Tartars, don't barricade yourself as you did today. Besides, you see your precautions have not prevented an old friend coming to you. *Adieu*."

And he went away.

Laura looked at her watch. It was nine o'clock, just the time when Napoleon would be certain to be seen by some of the maids who were now about the passages going to their mistresses' rooms, so it would be known all over the *château*. She called her maid and asked how he had got in. The woman replied that he had entered with a pass-key, and she had not dared to prevent his going into her mistress's room.

While dressing Laura tried to think of someone she could consult. She could have spoken to Duroc, but he was away; she thought of Hortense, then the remembrance of Joséphine put an end to that idea.

"*Mon Dieu!* what shall I do?" she exclaimed, sinking back into a chair and leaning her face in her hands. At that moment two arms were put round her and a well-known voice said—

"My Laura! what is the matter? "

With a cry of joy Laura threw herself into her husband's arms, and after the first greeting and inquiries begged him to take her back to Paris.

"Of course, I will, directly Madame Buonaparte goes back."

"Why not now?"

"Now? My dear child, but it is impossible!"

Laura said no more then, but waited till the evening. Since the attempt on the life of the First Consul the *préfet* of police and Junot were forbidden to be absent from Paris a single night. When Junot came to La Malmaison he always left about eleven o'clock. On this occasion it was four days since his last visit, and when Bessières set out on his return and everyone else separated for the night, Laura told Junot that she wanted him to take a letter to her mother and that he must come to her room while she wrote it. When they got there, she renewed her entreaties that he would take her with him, which, of course, at such an hour and without notice or excuse was impossible. Junot began to suspect that someone had been annoying her, and eagerly asked who it was, that he might avenge her.

Finding that she must remain where she was, Laura begged her husband to stay with her, to which with some hesitation he consented, remarking that he should get a reprimand.

About half-past four in the morning the door opened and the First Consul came in.

"What! still asleep, Madame Junot," he cried, "on a hunting morning. I told you—"

And as he spoke he undrew the curtain of the bed. Junot sat up and looked at him in astonishment.

"Eh! *mon Dieu, Général!* what are you doing here at this hour?"

"I came to wake up Madame Junot for the *chasse,*" replied Napoleon. "But I see she has an earlier alarum. I might reprimand, for you are contraband here, Monsieur Junot."

"*Mon Général*" replied Junot, "if ever a fault were excusable it is mine. If you had seen this little syren last night, employing all her magic for more than an hour to seduce me, I am sure you would forgive me."

Napoleon smiled, but it was a forced smile.

"Well! I forgive you entirely. It is Madame Junot who must be punished. To prove that I am not angry you shall go out hunting with us. Did you ride here?"

"No, *mon Général*, I drove."

"Well, Jardin will give you a horse. *Adieu*, Madame Junot. Make haste and get up." And he left the room.

When they were all starting the First Consul got into a little *calèche* and said to Laura—

"Madame Junot, may I have the honour of your company?"

Laura got into the carriage in silence, for she did not like the expression of his face and smile. The door was shut, and when they had gone a little distance from the *château* Napoleon, crossing his arms, turned to her and said—

"You think you are very clever."

There was no answer.

"You think you are very clever, don't you?"

"I don't think myself cleverer than other people, but I don't think I am an *imbécile*;" she answered, seeing that she must say something.

"An *imbécile*, no; but you are a fool."

She was silent.

"Can you explain to me for what reason you made your husband stay here?"

"The explanation is simple and short, General. I love Junot; we are married, and I suppose there is no scandal in a husband being with his wife."

"You knew that I had forbidden it, and that my orders ought to be obeyed."

"They have nothing to do with me. When consuls have to decide on the degrees of intimacy allowed between married people and the length of their interviews, I shall think about submitting to them. Until then, General, I can only say that I shall do as I please."

"You had no other reason but your love for your husband when you made him stay?"

"No, General."

"That's a lie."

"General!"

"Yes, it is," he went on in a changed voice. "I guessed your reason. You had a distrust of me which you ought not to have felt. Ah! you have nothing to say!"

"And if I had another reason than the distrust you speak of, General; if I saw that your visits at such an hour to the room of a woman of my age would compromise me strangely in the eyes of everybody else in the house, and if I took this means of stopping them—"

Napoleon's face softened.

"If that was it," he said, "why did not you tell me what troubled you? Have not I shown you friendship enough, naughty child, for the last week to give you confidence in me?"

"Perhaps I was wrong, General," said Laura; and she went on to allude to the affection her family had always shown him and the loyal devotion of Junot, to whom he could not wish to give pain.

"It is almost a sermon that you are preaching me," said Napoleon. "Who wants to give Junot pain? Why didn't you speak to me?"

"How could I, General, when yesterday morning you employed means that might be called unworthy to get into my room although the measures I took ought to have shown you that I considered the early visits you were good enough to pay me to be compromising, which they are. You came in for a moment with an offended air which certainly did not invite confidence. Therefore, I had no one to appeal to but myself. I may have been mistaken."

"Were not you acting under your mother's advice?"

"My mother? How could she direct me? Poor mother! I have not seen her for a month."

"You can write."

"*Mon Général*, I have not written to my mother that I am not safe under your roof. It would have given her too much pain."

"Madame Junot, you have known me long enough to understand that you will not continue to retain my friendship by speaking in that way. The only thing wanting to the way you are acting is that you should have told Junot what you have been fancying."

"I shall not answer such a question," said Laura angrily. "If you don't think I have either sense or reason, at least give me credit for good-feeling enough not to make him unhappy."

"Again!" cried Napoleon, striking the side of the carriage with his hand—"Again! hold your tongue!"

"No, I shall not hold my tongue. I shall go on with what I wish to have the honour of telling you. I beg you to believe that neither my mother, my husband, nor any of my friends know what has happened. As I did not suppose you had any bad intentions, it would have been absurd to complain of a mark of friendship because it might compromise me, but I thought it best to stop it at any rate, and no doubt my youth and inexperience have caused me to manage badly, since I have displeased you. I am sorry, but that is all I can say."

They were approaching the meet; already the sound of horns and barking of dogs was heard. Napoleon's face softened.

"Will you give me your word of honour that your husband knows nothing of all this nonsense?"

"Good God, General! how can you think of such a thing, knowing Junot as you do? Why, if I had told him what has been going on for the last week neither he nor I would be here now."

Napoleon said nothing at first, but drummed with his fingers on the edge of the carriage. Then turning to her, he said—

"Then you will not believe I meant no harm to you?"

"I am so sure of it that the attachment and admiration I have always had for you are the same as ever."

She stretched out her hand to him, but he smiled and shook his head.

"Then we are to quarrel," she said, "because you chose to do what was entirely your own fault, and now because you have given me pain you are going to let your beard grow and hang your dagger to your side!" (The sign of *vendetta* in Corsica.)

He looked out of the carriage, and then, turning to her, said—

"Believe that really I feel for you a friendship which it only depended upon yourself to make still stronger. But early education remains. You have been taught to be hostile to me; you don't like me, and I am sure———"

"I take the liberty of interrupting you, General, and I beg of you not to talk in that way. You make me unhappy; and besides, it is entirely untrue. Tell me you don't really think so; it would be too painful to leave you so."

"You are going!"

Laura showed him a letter, received that morning from her mother, urging her immediate return, as she was ill and wanted her.

"And when will you come back?" he asked, with a sarcastic look that irritated Laura, who replied hastily—

"Whenever I am wanted for my part, General; but you can dispose of my apartment, for I shall not occupy it any more, I assure you."

"As you please. And after this stupid affair it would not be very pleasant for either of us to see each other. You are quite right. Jardin! my horse." And he opened the door, jumped out, and rode away.

Laura returned to Paris with Junot, and dined that evening with her mother.

The next time she went to La Malmaison Napoleon was all right again in his planner towards her. A year afterwards, when, after dining at La Malmaison, a storm came on and Joséphine was trying to persuade her not to return home that night as she persisted in doing, Napoleon, who was stirring the logs of the fire, said without turning round—

"Torment her no more, Joséphine. I know her; she will not stay."

Although Laura no longer lived at La Malmaison, she often went down there to act in the theatricals, of which they all, including the First Consul, were passionately fond.

One day at dinner the conversation turned upon the delights of private theatricals, in which Cambacérès, the Second Consul, a grave, solemn-looking personage, joined, when Napoleon observed that he must be judging from hearsay, as he certainly never acted.

"And why not, *citoyen premier consul?* Don't you think I look pleasant or amusing (*plaisant*) enough to act?"

"Well, *citoyen* Cambacérès," said Napoleon, "because, in fact, you don't look amusing at all" (*vous n'avez pas l'air plaisant du tout*),

"Well! I have often acted, not only at Montpellier, but at the house of a friend of mine at Béziers, where theatricals went on half the year, and one of the parts in which I had great success was that of Renaud d'Ast."

"What! you sang," cried Madame Buonaparte.

Everyone laughed, but Cambacérès went on gravely—

"And as any part suited me equally, I played just as well Montauciel in *The Deserter*."

There was a burst of laughter all round the table, but Cambacérès, without attending to it, continued to relate one theatrical anecdote after another, illustrating the intrigues, jealousies, and petty quarrels that prevail behind the scenes; while the First Consul, who was himself the chief manager of the theatre at La Malmaison and its amateur company, listened intently with his elbows on the table.

The First Consul told an amusing story of Count Louis de Cobentzel the Austrian ambassador to Russia, which happened in 1796, at the court of St. Petersburg.

The Count de Cobentzel was no longer young, and had always been extremely ugly, but he was exceedingly fond of private theatricals, and had had a small theatre built at the Austrian embassy, where plays were constantly acted and patronised by the Empress Catherine, who was equally devoted to that diversion, and often wrote plays herself which were acted there. One day there was to be a grand representation, in which the Count de Cobentzel was to act the part of the Comtesse d'Escarbagnas (an old lady) in the presence of the empress.

He dressed early, in order to be ready to go upon the stage directly the empress should arrive, and waited in his dressing-room meanwhile.

Just then a courier arrived from Vienna with important despatches which were to be delivered into the hands of the Ambassador himself, so he sent to request an audience.

It was seven o'clock, and the Comte de Cobentzel, dressed as an old lady, with high heels, powdered and puffed hair, rouge, *paniers*, &c., was standing before the glass practising fanning himself and arranging the patches on his face.

He sent word that he was engaged and would see the messenger the next morning.

But the messenger, who was a young man and zealous, a complete contrast to Joséphine's unlucky M. de Ceré had a perfect mania for doing his duty. He had been ordered to arrive at St. Petersburg on a certain day before midnight, and having carried out his instructions, declared that he must see the ambassador that night, and made such a noise and commotion that one of his secretaries went up to him again and told him.

"Ah! the devil's in the obstinate fellow!" cried Cobentzel.

"Well, let him come in."

Without recollecting the necessity of explaining matters to the messenger, the secretary introduced him into the room, saying—

"There is *M. l'Ambassadeur*," and shut the door.

An old lady advanced towards him, with one hand putting a patch upon her face and saying as she held out the other, "Well, *Monsieur*, let me see these famous despatches."

The messenger looked around him in amazement, but there was no one else in the room.

"I want to see the ambassador," he said.

"Well, here is the ambassador. I am the ambassador," cried the figure, snatching at the packet and pulling with all its might.

The messenger thought it was a maniac, and keeping firm hold of the packet, ran to the door, calling for help. The ambassador ran after him, trying to explain, and then, exclaiming, "Well, you shall see him, stupid, your ambassador," he rushed into his bedroom, tore off the dress, and came back in black breeches, which made the rest of his costume look still more ridiculous.

At that moment the secretary returned, saying that the empress had arrived. He explained the truth to the messenger and made him give up the despatches to the count, who, when he had read them, found them to be so important that they must be attended to at once. They referred to the progress of Napoleon in Italy, in order to check which, the treaty now being arranged between England, Russia, and Austria must be signed and carried into execution. Cobentzel therefore sent for Lord Whitworth, the English ambassador, a tall, handsome, stately personage, who received the communications made by Cobentzel in his extraordinary dress with perfect composure, pointing out that the empress must not be kept waiting.

He went to her at once and explained the cause of the delay, and it is believed that in her impatience to hear full particulars of what was indicated to her by the English ambassador she would not wait any longer, so the Austrian ambassador had to appear at the interview in the dress of the old Comtesse d'Escarbagnas.

CHAPTER 11
Laura's First Child
1801-1802

The theatricals at La Malmaison usually took place on Wednesdays, and there were generally forty or fifty people at dinner and about a hundred and fifty in the evening. The best actors of the company, or *troupe*, were Hortense and Eugène de Beauharnais, Bourrienne, Lauriston, Lallemand, and a young officer called Isabey. Lucien Buonaparte was also good.

The First Consul took the deepest interest in these performances, and was so critical and sarcastic that he terrified most of the actors.

General Lallemand, who was one of Junot's *aides-de-camp*, used to have lessons from a famous comic actor called Michau, a great favourite with the public.

"It is always useful to be able to make people laugh," observed Michau one day; and he proceeded to tell his hearers that on one occasion during the Terror he was stopped in the streets of Paris by one of those troops of ruffians who went about committing murders in the days of what even to this day many French and some other persons of radical opinions call *la belle Revolution*.

By these worthy patriots he was seized, and in spite of his entreaties and remonstrances they were proceeding to express their favourite principles of "liberty, equality, and fraternity" by hanging him to the pole of a lamp which they had taken down for that purpose, when a baker with a red, merry face rushed into the midst of them, caught him up as if he were a child, and carried him away from them, exclaiming, "What are you about, you fellows? Don't you know the *pourichinel* (*polichinelle*) of the Republic, then?" whereupon about two hundred ruffians made their excuses to him for trying to hang him, as if they had been apologising for treading on his foot. (The Comédie Française was then called Théâtre de la République.)

An unlucky adventure befell young Isabey, who happened, on going into a gallery at La Malmaison, to see a man wearing the uniform of the *chasseurs de la garde* whom he took for Eugène de Beauharnais (then colonel of that regiment) looking at a book of engravings lying on a table at the other end. He approached very softly, and when he had come close behind him without his being aware of it, he sprang with one bound on to his shoulders. The man raised himself up and shook him violently off. It was the First Consul!

"What is the meaning of this joke?" he asked in a severe voice.

"I thought it was Eugène—" stammered Isabey.

"And if it had been Eugène, was that any reason why you should break his shoulders?" returned the First Consul. And he walked out of the gallery.

The story got about by some indiscretion, and not long afterwards, for no ostensible reason, Isabey was obliged to leave La Malmaison.

The prosperity of the country was growing rapidly. The numerous balls, dinners, and other *fêtes*, with the increasing luxury of dress and living, gave an impetus to trade; everyone flocked to the theatre where Mademoiselle Mars and Talma were in their glory. There was an exceedingly good Italian opera, and the Louvre was filled with all the most splendid statues, bronzes, pictures, and other works of art, the plunder of Italy, and later on of Spain, Germany, and the rest of Europe, waiting until a few years later the victorious armies of the Allies should restore them to their lawful owners.

By the peace of Lunéville between France and Austria the left bank of the Rhine from Holland to Switzerland was made the boundary of France, the possession of Venice was confirmed to Austria, and that of Parma and her other Italian conquests to France, to whom also were ceded the Ionian Isles.

The joy and triumph of this successful treaty concluded in February, 1801, was, however, followed in March by the loss of Egypt.

The English general, the gallant Abercrombie, was killed in the Battle of Alexandria, but the French Army capitulated, and a treaty was concluded between the two nations, which put an end for ever to Napoleon's plans for making Egypt a steppingstone to the ruin of England.

News travelled slowly in those days; and it was a beautiful summer's morning when Laura and her husband, knowing nothing of what had happened, received a visit from Rapp, who said he had come to breakfast with them, as the First Consul had sent him from La Malmaison to say that he wished to see Junot and wanted Laura to come too and spend the day.

Rapp was in bad spirits, and said as they drove down that the First Consul had certainly received some bad news, he seemed so gloomy, scarcely ate anything, but pushed away his chair, threw down his serviette, and asked for three cups of coffee in one hour.

Laura laughed, and said that very likely he was only out of temper.

When they arrived Junot went at once to the First Consul and remained with him till dinner-time, either shut up in his study or walking in an avenue in the garden. Napoleon placed Laura next to him at dinner and began to talk to her on indifferent matters, but she saw at once that something was wrong. It was not, however, until they returned to Paris that Junot could tell her what Napoleon had communicated to him before it was made public—the disaster in Egypt.

He well knew all the dreams and aspirations of which Egypt and the East had been the subject in the mind of Napoleon, even in the early days when they had wandered about the boulevards of Paris together, planning their future; and understood what, amidst all the success and splendour of his present position, he must have felt when he said, "Junot, we have lost Egypt."

It was the first serious check to his victorious career, from the nation he always regarded as his most deadly enemy, and there appeared to be something almost prophetic in the depression and gloom with which it seemed to overshadow his spirits.

The invasion of England was always a favourite project of Napoleon, and Boulogne was the headquarters of the activity which now prevailed in the building and arming of numbers of vessels of different kinds, while camps were pitched on the coast of the channel at this and other places. One night as the French flotilla lay at anchor near the shore it was suddenly attacked by Nelson, whose intention was to cut it off by getting in between it and the land. Although, owing to the protection given to the French flotilla by the forts and batteries close at hand, this plan was frustrated and the English fleet sustained heavy losses. Nelson gained a victory, which still further exasperated Napoleon.

The autumn and early winter passed away; it was the 5th of January, and Laura was daily expecting the birth of her child. The weather was so cold and the streets so slippery that Madame Permon, who was now too great an invalid to come to her daughter, had forbidden her to go out; therefore, their only communications were the letters they wrote every day to each other. Junot's mother, who was very fond of Laura, had come to stay and take care of her, and on the evening of this day they were giving a supper-party to General Suchet and some other friends to celebrate the first days of the New Year.

Everyone drank Laura's health in champagne, and she rose to return the compliment with a glass of water in her hand; for it was a singular thing that while Laura could never bear to touch wine of any kind, Junot had a sort of aversion, which he could never explain, to seeing women drink it. So strong was this unreasonable fancy (for he always drank it himself) that he told Laura that if he had seen her drink wine, he should not have married her.

"Well, but," said she, laughing, when he told her this, "what about Madame M——, who used, I am told, to drink a bottle of champagne and half a bottle of Madeira at dinner and supper? It is said that you loved her."

"Oh! what does that matter?" replied he, laughing also. "A mistress counts for nothing in a man's life. What does he care for her faults or virtues, so long as she is pretty, which is all he wants?"

As Laura stood at the head of her table with her glass of water, amongst the laughter and compliments of the sixteen or seventeen people present, a sudden and terrible pain made her sink back with a cry into her seat, while the glass dropped from her hand and she closed her eyes. When she opened them again, she saw Junot, white with fear, his glass still in his hand, and everybody else looking at her in consternation. With the courage of Jeanne d'Albret at the birth of Henri IV. she tried to resume the talk and laughter that had been interrupted, but it was useless. There was an end of the supper-party. Her mother-in-law took her away into her own room, Junot hurried off to send for Marchais, a famous doctor of the day, and all night long she lay between life and death.

The next morning Junot became so frightened and miserable that he could not endure to stay in the house any longer. He seized his hat, ran downstairs into the street, and did not stop until he got to the Tuileries. He rushed upstairs into the ante-chamber of Napoleon, where several of his friends were standing, who exclaimed in astonishment, "Good God! Junot, what is the matter?"

Junot asked only for the First Consul, who received him with great kindness and sympathy. "My old friend," he said, pressing his hand, "you have done well to come to me at this time." He sent a messenger immediately to inquire for Madame Junot, walking up and down the gallery with Junot and trying to comfort him. until the news was brought that a daughter was born and that Laura's danger was over.

Junot returned home, enchanted with his child and at the favourable turn things had taken, the only drawback being that his father, old M. Junot, had made himself disagreeable as usual, and when he heard that the child was a girl, having set his mind on having a grandson, he made such a grumbling and became so ill-tempered that Laura was very nearly made ill, the doctor was furious and so was his wife, who drove him away in a torrent of indignation, and told Junot that she had "arranged" his father, and she did not think he would ever behave so again.

For some time, the First Consul had resolved to re-establish religion in France, and now, the *concordat* upon ecclesiastical affairs having been signed by the Pope and the consuls, he resolved that a grand service should be held to celebrate its promulgation. Accordingly, on Easter Sunday a great festival was organised at Notre Dame (1802).

For the first time the household of the First Consul wore liveries, and besides her four *dames de compagnie*, sixty or eighty wives of the chief officers and functionaries were chosen to accompany Joséphine, amongst whom, of course, was Laura.

At half-past ten an immense procession left the Tuileries the cathedral of Notre Dame was crowded with women in splendid *toilettes*, and men in uniform, and the gorgeousness of the newly restored ceremonial, the holy chants and sacred music mingling with salvos of artillery, tramp of cavalry, and clash of swords, made a strong impression upon the spectators who thronged the church and streets.

The fanatical Republicans and enemies of religion were furious, and one of them. General Delmas, when asked by the First Consul how he liked the ceremony, replied—

"It's a fine mummery enough. To make it better still you only want the million of men who gave their blood to destroy what you have just re-established."

Napoleon was very angry with this answer, in which he said there was as little sense as good taste, what so many men had given their lives to destroy not being religion at all, but the *ancien régime*, which was a very different thing; and although he now created nine archbishops and forty-seven bishops, of whom Laura's uncle was one, (Bishop of Metz), they only received small salaries instead of the magnificent property lost for ever in the Revolution.

A terrible calamity soon afterwards befell Laura and Albert in the death of the mother they both adored. Madame Permon's illness had so much increased latterly, and her sufferings were so great that when the end came their grief was mingled with feelings of relief that she was at rest.

Junot, who had been extremely attached to his mother-in-law, arranged the funeral with great splendour. Many accused him of ostentation and extravagance in this matter, but Laura only saw in the arms of the *Comneni*, richly embroidered and thrown over the coffin, the three hundred poor people dressed in mourning following with tears and prayers and all the pomp of the ceremonial, the respect and affection her husband had borne to her mother and his love for herself.

Albert, at the time of his mother's death, was at Marseilles, where he held the post of commissioner of police. Laura, knowing the grief he would suffer, was very anxious to go to him, as he could not leave his duties, but she had not sufficiently recovered from the effects of her confinement to be able to undertake the journey.

Chapter 12
Birth of Laura's Second Daughter
1801-1802

The First Consul was much affected by the death of Madame Permon, and sent Laura many kind messages by Junot. Joséphine came to see her, accompanied by Lucien, who had always been Madame Permon's favourite. He had just returned from Spain, and the sight of him seemed to renew Laura's grief

Madame Leclerc was no longer in France, Napoleon having insisted on her accompanying her husband to St. Domingo, some time before.

She had made a most ridiculous scene when Laura went to see her after her departure was decided upon, throwing herself into her arms and complaining of the cruelty of her brother, who was sending her

PAULINE BUONAPARTE, PRINCESS BORGHESE.

into exile amongst savages and serpents; crying and sobbing, declaring that she should die before she arrived there, and then, when Laura consoled her as one might a child or an idiot, by telling her what pretty clothes she would wear there and how she would be queen of the island, she rang for her maid and ordered her to bring all her scarfs and India muslins to look at and choose from.

Then she declared she would ask her brother to send Laura with her (although it was only about a month before her confinement), that Junot could go too and be governor there instead of Commandant of Paris, and that they would take Madame Permon (who was unable to leave her bed from illness). Just as Laura, disgusted by her selfish folly, had got up to take leave, thinking that perhaps she would not be able to help giving vent to her indignation, Junot was announced, and turning eagerly to him, Pauline poured forth her new plans, which he received with shouts of laughter, much to her surprise. Finding he would not treat the idea seriously, she began to cry again, saying she had always loved Lauretta like a sister (which, as Laura afterwards remarked, was not saying much), and ending with—

"Ah! you would not have made all those reflections when we were at Marseilles! You would not have coolly allowed me to go away to be eaten up, or whatever may become of me in that savage country. And I have told Laurette so often of your attachment to me!"

To reason with such a person was of course impossible. Junot and Laura could do nothing but laugh, and offer her whatever consolations they thought suitable. The First Consul, when they told him of it, laughed too, but knew his sister well enough not to be surprised. A day or two afterwards he said to Junot, "I am very sorry you want to go to St. Domingo, for you will not go. I want you here."

When she was in St. Domingo, however, Pauline behaved very well; she had plenty of courage, and there was a good deal of truth in her anticipations of danger. The rebellion of the negroes under the ferocious Christophe and Dessalines broke out, fearful atrocities were committed, and in September, 1802, a furious horde of twelve thousand blacks poured down to besiege Cap, the chief town, which was only defended by one thousand soldiers, many of whom were down with fever.

Pauline, her little son, and a number of ladies who had taken refuge with her, were in her house near the seashore, indifferently defended by a company of artillery under the command of a friend of her husband's. General Leclerc, considering the house unsafe, and feeling uncertain as to the result of the battle he was waging: against the negroes, sent orders to put his wife and child on board ship, the French fleet being near at hand. Nothing would induce her to fly, and when the terrified ladies about her urged her to escape, and described the horrible fate of women who fell into the hands of the negroes, she only said, "You can go if you like. You are not the sister of Buonaparte."

The danger increased every moment, and General Leclerc sent an *aide-de-camp* with orders to carry her away by force if she would not go. She was accordingly placed in an armchair and carried by four soldiers, a grenadier walking by her side carrying the child. The escort was attacked by the blacks, who were put to flight, but just as they were embarking the news came that the French were victorious.

"You see," said Pauline; as she was carried back to the house, "I was quite right in not wanting to go."

Napoleon was very much pleased when the story was told him. Pauline was his favourite sister, and he was perfectly blind to the intrigues she carried on, never believing that her diversions went beyond vanity and flirtation.

The fact was, however, that her love affairs were many and various. At the time of her departure for St. Domingo the object of her affections was supposed to be Lafon, an actor at the *Théâtre Français*, and it was said that Mademoiselle Duchesnes, the actress, on hearing Pauline's departure announced, indiscreetly exclaimed before a roomful of people, "Lafon will be inconsolable; it will kill him!"

Her way of going on made her husband's life miserable, and yet he was a man of kind and gentle disposition, devotedly in love with her, and she had married him for love, or what she understood by that expression. But she was an incarnation of the most astounding folly, vanity, and selfishness, without the capability of either love or affection for anyone but herself If she cared for anybody it was for Napoleon. As to her husband, she tormented him with her infidelities, caprices, and humours, and then, when he died in St. Domingo, she gave way to paroxysms of grief and cut off all her hair to show her sorrow. But Napoleon, when told of it, remarked that she knew well enough that her hair would grow again all the better in consequence.

To other people Napoleon was neither so blind nor so lenient. He persisted, in spite of the entreaties of Joséphine, in dismissing one of her maids, a young girl of whom she was very fond, because two of his *aides-de-camp* had fallen in love with her, although she had given no encouragement to their attentions. In reply to all remonstrances he only repeated: *"Je ne veux pas de scandale chez-moi; point de désordre."*

Having taken a violent fancy to a young married woman of his court, and being careful to conceal from Joséphine the intrigue he was carrying on with her, he used to wait until everyone in the *château* was asleep, and then go softly to her apartment without his shoes. His first *valet-de-chambre*, Constant, was always anxious lest the affair should be discovered, and on one occasion the day began to dawn and still Napoleon had not returned.

Constant awoke the maid and sent her to knock at her mistress's door and say what time it was, according to the directions given him by Napoleon should such a case arise. Napoleon appeared in a few minutes, greatly agitated, saying that he had seen one of Joséphine's maids watching him through a window that looked into the corridor. As Joséphine's suspicions and jealousy had already been aroused by this affair, he was very angry and sent Constant to the maid ordering her to be silent and never to spy any more after him, unless she wanted to be sent away immediately; after which he desired Constant to take a little house for him in which he and Madame —— could meet in safety.

In February, 1802, peace with England was signed, and the treaty of Amiens confirmed to France the possession of Flanders, Brabant, and Belgium, besides which she had seized all the German territory on the left bank of the Rhine, Avignon, Savoy, Geneva, Basel, and Nice. Lombardy, Genoa and Tuscany had submitted to her, and in America she had gained the colonies of Louisiana and Guiana.

With her whole heart and soul Laura shared in the delirium of joy and triumph which seemed to intoxicate the nation during those few brilliant years, and in the hatred of England, the most formidable enemy of France, whom she had beaten in India, in Egypt, and at sea, having since 1793 destroyed or captured six hundred and fifty French ships and seventy-five thousand sailors.

After peace was signed foreigners of all nations flocked to Paris, which soon became so full that the most indifferent hotels and lodgings commanded enormous prices.

Russians and English were the most numerous and distinguished amongst the arrivals, and as Commandant of Paris Junot entertained all those illustrious personages whose presence made the capital more prosperous and brilliant than before.

Laura's second daughter, Constance, was born in May of this year.

As the enmity of Junot and his wife against England was merely political and national, it did not enter much into their social life, nor prevent their making many intimate friendships with English, as well as other foreigners.

Amongst these were the Duchess of Gordon and her youngest daughter. Lady Georgina, Countess Diwoff, Prince George Galitzin, the Austrian Ambassador, Count Philippe de Cobentzel, the Marquis of Hertford (then Lord Yarmouth), Princess Demidoff, Countess Lisbeth von Blumenthal, and Mr. Fox, who, as the opponent of Pitt and friend of France and the Revolution, was regarded by that portion of French society with the same delighted approbation as was lately bestowed upon the pro-Boers by the enemies of England.

But on one occasion when he was dining with Junot the conversation turned upon recent events in Egypt, and some of those present began to indulge in reflections on England and abuse of Pitt, in which a certain Colonel Green, a great friend of Junot and a fanatical admirer of Napoleon, permitted himself to join.

At once Fox changed countenance, and, as Laura afterwards observed, it was no longer the Opposition leader, but the countryman and brother of Pitt, who defended him with all the force and fire of his eloquence, casting at the same time an indignant look upon Colonel Green.

Struck with shame, the latter was instantly silent, and rising from his seat, came round the table and shook hands warmly with Fox, whose conduct in this matter won the respect and admiration of those present.

A characteristic story was told of him at Paris at that time. A creditor of his had called repeatedly with a bill of three hundred guineas, which it seemed impossible to induce him to pay. One morning, after receiving the usual answer from his valet, that Mr. Fox had no money and could not see him, the creditor, who had lost patience, pushed past the servant, opened a door, and found himself in the presence of his debtor, who was sitting at a table counting out and making into *rouleaux* several hundred pounds.

"It seems to me, sir," began the creditor, "that there is no impossibility whatever in your paying your debt to me. I am delighted to see that your circumstances are so much better than I was given to understand by your valet?"

"You are mistaken," replied Fox; "I have not ten guineas at my disposal. You must wait till a better opportunity."

"You are joking, sir," said the man, pointing to the table.

"That money is not mine," answered Fox; "it must all go before midday to pay a debt of honour, which is sacred."

"Well, sir, I doubt whether this creditor of yours has a prior right to mine. Remember that I lent you this money without interest more than three years ago."

"Oh, no!" cried Fox, laughing, "his is not nearly such an old debt as yours; in fact, I only incurred it a few hours ago; but it is a debt of honour, which, you know, must always be paid within twenty-four hours."

Then, seeing that the man did not understand the meaning of a debt of honour, he proceeded to explain.

"Last night I lost eight hundred guineas to Sheridan, for which he has no guarantee but my word of honour. If anything happened to me before he got his money, what proof would he have? You, at least, hold my signature, which my family would not dispute."

The man's face fell.

"And so," he said, "it is because your name is upon the bill, I hold that you do not pay it? Very well," he continued, tearing it to pieces, "now my debt is a debt of honour too, for I have no guarantee but yours, and I have a prior claim over your creditor of last night."

Fox turned to the table, from which he took three hundred guineas, which he gave to the creditor, saying—

"Thank you for having trusted me. Here is your money. Sheridan must wait for the rest of his."

The First Consul disliked foreigners, and at this time was much irritated by the numerous flirtations they carried on with the wives and daughters of his generals.

The *fête* of the 14th July, celebrating the idiotic destruction of a curious and interesting historical building, being about to take place, he said to his wife, "Joséphine, I am going to desire you to do something you will like. I want you to be very magnificent. Make all your preparations. As for me, I shall wear my splendid dress of crimson silk embroidered with gold, that the city of Lyon gave me, and I shall be superb."

Laura laughed, for she recollected having thought Napoleon looked most absurd in that dress.

"Well, what do you mean by that mocking smile, Madame Junot? You think I shall not look so well as all your good-looking English and Russians who make love to you and turn your young heads? It's all prejudice. I assure you that I am just as agreeable as that puppy the English colonel. They say he is the handsomest man in England; to me he seems like the king of fops."

Speaking of another man whose part Joséphine was taking. Napoleon replied to her remark that he had talents.

"What talents? *De l'esprit?* Brrh! who has not—to that extent? He sings well! A fine quality for a soldier, whose profession always makes him hoarse! Ah! he is good-looking, that is what touches you women! Well, I don't see anything at all extraordinary about him; he is just like a field-spider with those everlasting legs. It is not natural—" and he looked at his own legs, while Laura could not control her merriment.

"Well, little pest, what is there to laugh at? You are laughing at my legs. You don't find them good enough to figure in a *contre-danse*, like those of your elegant friend. But, at any rate, one can sing and dance without being a puppy. Look here, Madame Junot, tell me if Talleyrand's nephew is not a nice fellow?"

Laura cordially agreed, for he spoke of Louis de Périgord, the son of her old friend, one of the *faubourg St. Germain*, who served with distinction in the armies of the Republic.

Since the *concordat*, several children to whom the First Consul had promised to be godfather were waiting to receive public baptism, and amongst them was Laura's little daughter. Napoleon never chose to have as *commère* anyone but his wife, his mother, or Madame Louis Buonaparte. On this occasion he and Joséphine were the sponsors of the child, who was named after the latter. Another of the children now to be christened at St. Cloud by the Cardinal Caprara was the son of General Lannes, who was to be named Napoleon. None of the mothers were twenty years old.

Laura stood holding in her arms her child, who was fifteen months old, very pretty, and very much frightened at the cardinal, the chapter, the crowd of people, and the whole scene. Napoleon turned when the right moment arrived, saying—

"Give me your daughter, Madame Junot."

But the baby cried, clung round her mother's neck, and refused to go to him.

"What a little devil!" exclaimed Napoleon. "Ah! *ça*, will you come to me, Mademoiselle Demon?"

"*Je ne veux pas!*" replied the baby, looking angrily at the First Consul; but just then, catching sight of the cardinal's *biretta*, she was so pleased with it that she left off crying, allowed Napoleon to take her, and sat contentedly in his arms with her eyes fixed upon the object of her admiration, only rubbing her face vigorously every time he kissed her. But when the cardinal approached nearer, she suddenly stretched out her arm, and with a shout of triumph snatched the *biretta* from his head, to the diversion and consternation of all present.

"Oh, *pour cela*, my child!" cried the First Consul as soon as he could restrain his laughter, "you must not do that. Give me that plaything; for it is a toy like many others," he added, turning to the cardinal.

It was only by force that the *biretta* was taken from the little Joséphine, who tried to put it on her own head, then on that of her godfather, and when it was returned to its lawful owner, burst into a passion of tears and cries.

"She is a real demon, your daughter," said Napoleon, as he gave her back to her mother; "but she is very pretty, very pretty indeed! She is my goddaughter, my daughter. I hope you will remember that, Junot," he added, as he shook hands with his old comrade.

The following day Laura received from Joséphine a splendid pearl necklace, and from Napoleon the title deeds of an *hôtel*, Rue des Champs-Elysées. It had cost 200,000 *francs*.

Chapter 13
Narrow Escape of Laura and Caroline Murat
1802-1804

In the spring of 1802, the Consulate of Napoleon had been by the *Sénatus-Consulte* prolonged for ten years beyond those originally decreed in 1799. It was the first step to the Consulship for life and the Empire.

Junot, like all the enthusiastic followers of the First Consul, was delighted at this, and proposed to his wife to celebrate the event by a *déjeuner* in their new house in the Champs-Elysées, to be given at once, without waiting to furnish it, and which the First Consul and Madame Buonaparte were to be asked to honour with their presence.

Laura accordingly went to the Tuileries to carry her invitation to Joséphine, who received it with her usual kindness.

"Have you spoken of it to Buonaparte?" she inquired; and on hearing that Junot had gone to the First Consul she added, "We must wait for his answer, for you know I cannot accept any *fête* or dinner without his express permission," for Napoleon, knowing that Joséphine, in the carelessness and kindness of her heart, would accept invitations in rather an indiscriminate manner, had forbidden any engagements to be made without his leave. Napoleon, however, promised to be at this *déjeuner*, but made the absurd stipulation that there should be present twenty-five women and no men at all except himself, Junot, and Duroc.

The party was composed almost entirely of the young wives of his generals, most of whom were good-looking. Joséphine was there, her daughter, and the two sisters of Napoleon, Elisa and Caroline, who were then in France. Besides the men allowed by the First Consul, they persuaded him to permit General Suchet and his brother to be amongst the guests.

The party was amusing enough, and after the *déjeuner* Madame Buonaparte went all over the house, insisting upon going into every room. She then proposed that they should go to the Bois de Boulogne, where accordingly they proceeded in a long procession of carriages, so that, as Laura remarked, if they had only had more men with them, they would have looked like a *bourgeois lendemain de noce*. She drove with Madame Buonaparte, who talked long and sympathetically with her, finishing by saying that the First Consul had observed that it was not sufficient to give them a house without making it habitable, and had desired her to tell Laura that the sum of 100,000 *francs* was placed at the disposition of Junot and herself to furnish it in a suitable manner.

The next *fête* given by Laura in her new house was a brilliant ball, at which Napoleon, with Joséphine and other members of his family, were present. He desired to be shown all the house from garrets to cellars, and remained at the ball until one o'clock, which for him was an unusually late hour.

Joséphine wore a dress embroidered with silver, vine leaves and grapes trailing over it and in her hair; necklace, earrings, and bracelets of pearls. Hortense, dressed in pink and silver and crowned with roses, was the life and soul of the ball, and seemed amidst the admiration and popularity with which she was surrounded to forget the unhappiness of the loveless marriage to which she had been condemned by the interest of her mother and the tyranny of her stepfather.

Laura entered with eager delight into this life of splendour and excitement. At an age at which we are accustomed to see young girls just set free from the schoolroom, she had already been for two years the wife of the Commandant of Paris and one of the leaders of French society. She was a special favourite of Napoleon and his family, and her *salon* was frequented by the most illustrious personages who visited the capital.

Laura was essentially a woman of the world. Brought up from earliest childhood in the *salon* of her mother, she had inherited from her not merely her social qualities, but also that boundless extravagance which far exceeded the lavish hospitality and magnificence with which the First Consul required the Commandant of Paris to entertain. Neither she nor Junot seem to have had any idea of the management of money; it flowed like water through their hands.

But these years of brilliant success and prosperity were very nearly brought to a sudden close during this very summer by an act of childish folly on Laura's part.

She and Junot possessed a small estate called Bièvre, about twelve miles from Paris, where she delighted to pass as much time as she could in the hot weather. The house was not large, but it stood in a green, shady valley amongst woods that seemed to join the park, which, though small, was well planted with forest trees.

Laura was devoted to this place, which she declared was like a Swiss valley, just as many people say that Amsterdam is like Venice because in both you see boats and water; and who cannot see a pretty view in England without comparing it to the Alps or the Bay of Naples, or something else equally preposterous. And her descriptions of it excited the wish of Caroline Buonaparte, then Madame Murat, to see the place. Laura and Caroline Murat were at that time extremely intimate, and it was arranged that she and Murat should go down to Bièvre, and, as Junot had leave to shoot as much as he liked in the woods around, they should start early on the morning of their arrival, Laura and Caroline following the *chasse* in a carriage, and that they should lunch and spend the whole day in the woods.

HORTENSE DE BEAUHARNAIS, DAUGHTER OF JOSÉPHINE, AND WIFE OF LOUIS BUONAPARTE, KING OF HOLLAND

At that time in France riding and driving were rather unusual accomplishments for a woman. Laura could neither ride nor drive, and Junot, terrified at the chance of any accident happening to her, refused to allow her to learn.

Her drives were nearly always, as was the general custom, in a closed carriage. Junot, however, possessed a certain vehicle called a *boghey*. It was very light, something in the style of a dogcart, and Laura cast longing eyes upon it. When she wished Caroline Murat goodnight on the day of her arrival, she said to her—

"If you like we can have the most delicious drive tomorrow. Are you afraid to go in a *boghey?*"

"No, certainly not; I should delight in it," replied Caroline. "Well, it is settled."

Very early the next morning the preparations for the day's sport began. Laura and Caroline, whose heads were full of their project, refused to get up until, amid the barking of dogs and general noise and commotion, Junot and his companions had left the courtyard and started for the woods.

Then Laura sent orders to the coachman to bring the *boghey*, and to make matters worse, the horse she chose to drive was a certain Coco which belonged to Junot, and was not safe to drive at all; at any rate, by an inexperienced person. Laura, however, had taken it into her head that it was perfectly easy to drive one horse without learning. So, disregarding the entreaties of the coachman, who was horrified when he saw who were going in the *boghey*, she assured Caroline that she could drive, and they both got into that vehicle and set off at a tremendous pace.

They went on well enough at first, until Laura foolishly gave Coco a cut with the whip, which, with the way she fidgeted and jerked the reins, naturally irritated a horse whose temper would not bear trifling with, so that he took the bit in his teeth and ran away.

"Laurette," said Caroline, "do you know how to drive?"

"No," replied Laura. And they both burst out laughing, as Caroline exclaimed—

"You don't know how to drive! Oh! how foolish. What will they all say? But I can drive; give me the reins. Which way must I turn?"

"To the right," said Laura, as she gave the reins and whip into the hands of Caroline, whose powers of driving were very little better than her own. They had left behind them the quiet sandy lane along which the first part of their way led, and were tearing madly along the high-road, where the risk of meeting carts and other vehicles was added to their other dangers. A sharp turn led from that into another lane by which they must enter the woods of Verrières, and the jerk of the reins by which Caroline tried to turn the horse caused him to give a bound that almost threw them both out, and as they rushed into the lane Caroline dropped the reins and whip. They were now just approaching a deep stone-quarry without a parapet, into which there seemed every chance of their being precipitated, when the noise of a horse galloping at full speed was heard behind them.

"It is Murat!" exclaimed Caroline, looking behind her.

It was indeed Murat, and he was only just in time. Something had delayed or made him leave the shooting party and return to the house, where the servants in the greatest alarm and distress told him of this idiotic escapade of their young mistress.

Murat, of course, knew that his wife could scarcely drive at all, and in consternation mounted his horse and rode after them as fast as he could. He managed to catch hold of Coco and force him backwards from the brink of the quarry. Then seizing Caroline in his arms, he embraced her with tears in his eyes, kissing her hands and grumbling at her folly, for he was still passionately in love with her. "As for you, Madame Junot," he cried, holding up his finger, "I hope Junot will make a scene about this. *Mon Dieu!*"

Junot was very angry, as well he might be, and it was some time before he could be appeased. However, a few days afterwards he gave a splendid *fête champêtre* at Bièvre in honour of Laura, whose *fête*, as has been before mentioned, was always celebrated on the 10th of August (St. Laurent).

Dinner for seventy people was laid upon a table surrounding the trunk of an enormous plane-tree, the spreading boughs of which formed a tent like a great hall of green foliage, amongst which were hung cages of singing birds, while the trunk was hung with garlands of flowers. Many complimentary verses were addressed to Laura, various songs were sung in her honour; in the grounds were illuminated transparencies, and over a pavilion in which Laura kept doves Junot had written the following lines:—

Quand ma Laure vient visiter
Ses amoureuses tourterelles,
C'est pour les apprendre d'aimer,
L'art charmant qu'elle sait mieux qu'elles.

These words appeared in an illumination. During the pauses of the dancing everyone rested and ate ices near a hermitage, in which a hermit made prophecies, if he did not tell fortunes. A magnificent display of fireworks crowned the entertainment.

Amongst all other topics the most absorbing and most interesting just at this time was that of the Consulate for life, which was now offered to Napoleon. Junot, who, in spite of his adoration for the First Consul, was an ardent Republican, regarded this proposal with disfavour, and was too little in the habit of concealing his thoughts not to let it be evident.

After he and Laura had dined one day at Saint Cloud, he had a private interview with Napoleon, who questioned him as to the opinion of society in Paris upon this point.

Junot replied that everyone seemed to be in favour of it, but his manner caused the First Consul to remark with displeasure—

"You announce that as if you were saying just the contrary. With the approbation of all France, am I to find censors in my dearest friends?"

When after a conversation of about half an hour they entered the drawing-room, Laura saw at once that something was the matter, and as they drove home her husband gave her an account of what had taken place. Between his ingrained Republicanism and his adoration of Napoleon he was certainly in an unfortunate position. He declared that, as an honest man, he should always speak the truth and give his opinion according to his conscience. The First Consul, on the other hand, hated to be opposed, and cared nothing about anybody's opinion unless it agreed with his own.

Junot told his wife that he perceived they were beginning to have a court, for it was no longer possible to speak the truth without giving offence, a state of things which can scarcely be considered peculiar to courts; but Junot fretted till he made himself ill, and when, a few days afterwards, Joséphine asked Laura to *déjeuner* at Saint Cloud, begging her to bring her child with her, Junot remained at home in bed.

As they left the room after *déjeuner* Napoleon appeared, and seeing the child, exclaimed—

"Ah! ah! Here is our god-daughter the Cardinalesse! *Bon jour, Mamselle*; come—look at me—there—open your eyes. The devil! do you know she is extremely pretty, this little girl? She is like her grandmother. *Ma foi*! yes—she is like poor Madame Permon. There indeed was a pretty woman—a beautiful woman—the most beautiful I ever saw." Meanwhile he was playing with the child, pulling her ears and nose, which she did not like. But Laura, foreseeing this, had told her daughter that if she did not cry once whilst they were at Saint Cloud, they should stop on their way home at a celebrated toy-shop, where she should have everything she wished for.

Although she was under two years old, the child was very precocious and understood this promise, of which her mother took every opportunity of reminding her, so that her formidable godfather expressed his approbation of her good temper, said she was just the sort of child he liked, and when Laura, on his inviting her to go out on the balcony with him, was about to give the baby to her nurse, he said—

"No, no, keep your daughter; a young mother is always interesting with her child in her arms. What is the matter with Junot?" he added, as they sat down on the circular balcony which surrounded the apartments of Joséphine.

"He has fever, General, so that he cannot get up."

"But this fever must have some name or other? Is it a putrid or malignant fever, or what?"

"Neither one nor the other, *citoyen Consul*; but you know Junot is very sensitive, and when anything wounds him it affects him in this way. And you know, General, that a doctor is very little use for that sort of thing."

"I see that Junot has told you of the sort of quarrel we had a few days ago. He was ridiculous."

"Allow me to disagree with you, General. I have no doubt you are joking, but I can only tell you that you have misunderstood Junot and given him great pain. Neither I nor this child can comfort him, and I don't believe he has told me all that passed."

Napoleon looked at Laura in silence, took her hand, then dropped it, embraced the child, rose hastily and disappeared.

Laura returned home and told Junot what had happened. He was weak and feverish, which, as he had not slept for three nights and had had on thirty leeches, was not surprising.

That evening she was sitting by him as he lay asleep upon a divan. It became dark, but she did not like to disturb him by ringing for lights, and after a time she too fell asleep in her chair. She was awakened by rapid steps on the stairs, and, starting up, went into the anteroom, into which the first *valet-de-chambre* of Junot came with a light, followed by Napoleon.

"Good evening, Madame Junot," he said; "you didn't expect me, did you? Well, where is your dying patient?" As he spoke he entered the little *salon* which led from Laura's rooms to Junot's, and in which he was lying.

"Well, Monsieur Junot, what's the matter, eh?" cried he. "What are you crying for, great baby? (*grand enfant*). Aha! I will attend to you." And he began to pull his ears, hair, and nose, according to the manner, more singular than refined, in which he was wont to show his affection for his friends. His visit, however, had the effect of restoring Junot to the health and happiness of which the displeasure of his idol had deprived him.

Junot was Napoleon's favourite *aide-de-camp*. A daring, brilliant soldier, his nickname in the army was "*La Tempête*." At the siege of Toulon, when the bursting of a shell scattered sand all over the despatches with which he was occupied, his cool remark, "Well, we wanted sand to dry the ink; here it is!" gained him the approval of Napoleon and the admiration of his comrades, but as governor and administrator he was not a success. Generous, affectionate, and loyal to his friends, his hasty, violent temper, extravagance, and dissipation were fatal to the conduct of affairs in any responsible post requiring calm judgment, foresight, and discretion. In spite of the undoubted affection with which both he and his wife were regarded by the First Consul, differences were now more and more frequently arising between them, in which, as generally happens, there were faults on both sides, but which tended more and more to estrange them from each other.

In the voluminous and interesting memoirs left by Laura an exaggerated worship of Napoleon is mingled with bitter complaints of his injustice, harshness, and ingratitude to his old and faithful friend and to herself. By comparing her statements with those of other biographers of the time, occasionally even by judging from her own remarks, one can form a tolerably decided idea of the grievances each attributed to the other.

Notwithstanding Laura's literary talents, social gifts and worldly experience, she does not appear to have had the advantage of a well-balanced mind or to have been at, all capable of an impartial judgment upon any matter nearly concerning herself, those she loved, or any question in which she was at all interested.

To take a single example—the seizure by Napoleon's troops of the pictures, statues, and other treasures of the different countries they overran. When the French carried off the most beautiful and valuable possessions of the Italians, Spaniards, and Germans, to fill the galleries of Paris, she gloried in the plunder, regarding it as perfectly legitimate and praiseworthy; but when the fortune of war changed, she called the restoration of these same treasures to their lawful owners an act of robbery, and no words were too strong to express her grief and indignation against the Allies for daring to give back their own property to those who had been despoiled of it by her countrymen!

The opinions of a person so ludicrously prejudiced must of course be received with due caution, and, in spite of her exculpation of and admiration for Junot, there can be no doubt that the displeasure of the First Consul was justifiable enough on several occasions, both now and afterwards. He was irritated by the mismanagement and extravagance of the Commandant of Paris, who, in spite of the generosity shown to Laura and himself, and the immense fortune accumulated so rapidly, was always in debt.

As to the accusations circulated against Junot of carelessness and incompetence in the business belonging to his exalted and responsible post, they were asserted by Laura to be slanders devised by his enemies in order to make mischief between him and the First Consul.

However, that might be, they had their effect to a certain extent; besides which, the persistent republicanism of Junot brought him on various occasions into opposition to Napoleon, who could not endure to be opposed.

Another and most unjust complaint made by Buonaparte against both Laura and her mother was that they received and frequented the society of persons who were his enemies.

Now it was undoubtedly true that the nearest relations and dearest friends of Madame Permon were of the *faubourg St. Germain*, and many of them *émigrés*. How could it be otherwise?

By her own birth, by her husband's principles, by every tie of gratitude, affection, and sympathy Madame Permon belonged to them, and Laura, although placed by her marriage amongst new surroundings, had no idea of giving up either her mother's old friends or her own at the dictation of anyone. She was perfectly loyal to Napoleon, and would never have dreamed of allowing any intrigues against him to be carried on at her house; but this he could never be induced really to believe, and his suspicious, tyrannical disposition was constantly discovering causes for blame where none existed. And when once any such idea had taken possession of him it was impossible to divest him of it; there remained always the same rankling distrust.

Junot was entirely in the right in the next difference that took place between him and Buonaparte It was on the occasion of the rupture with England, which Napoleon chose to represent as being caused by the perfidy of England in refusing to give up Malta as she had agreed to do, the real truth being that England, having expressly stipulated that the island should only be given up to the Knights of St. John conditionally on the entire restoration and re-establishment of the Order, had discovered that, owing to the intrigues of France, the Spanish priories had been destroyed, their revenues sequestrated, and there was no intention of carrying out the conditions of the treaty. The treaty having therefore become null and void, war was declared, and the English ambassador. Lord Whitworth, left Paris.

Before his departure he received positive assurances that the English subjects in France should be safe and unmolested, notwithstanding which Buonaparte, in a furious rage, ordered the seizure and imprisonment of all the English in the country.

Junot had been at work till four o'clock in the morning, and had only just gone to bed when a message came from the First Consul requiring his immediate presence at La Malmaison.

Napoleon was in a state of the greatest agitation and excitement, and, appealing to Junot as a friend upon whom he could absolutely depend, he desired him to take measures that every English man, woman and child in Paris should be arrested before the evening.

Junot was horrified at this project, which of course was quite contrary to international usages. He stood in silent consternation for some minutes, while Napoleon, reading his disapproval in his face, went on with his abuse of England and threats against his own officers who opposed his will.

"Are you going to repeat the scene of the other day?" he cried. "You and Lannes allow yourselves strange liberties. Even Duroc must needs come and preach to me in his quiet way! By God! *Messieurs*, I will show you that I can put my hat on the wrong way. (*Je sais mettre mon bonnet de travers.*) Lannes has had experience of that by this time. I don't suppose it amuses him much to eat oranges at Lisbon! As to you, Junot, don't trust too much to my friendship. On the day I doubt yours, mine will be destroyed."

Junot, who, with all his faults, was not a man to be brow-beaten, represented to Napoleon in the most forcible manner the outrageous character of the proposed measure and the discredit it would bring upon him and upon France, besides the cruelty and injustice it would entail; and made sundry uncomplimentary remarks upon those who were advising it.

Buonaparte, in reply, quoted a remark made by one of them:
"If the First Consul ordered me to kill my father, I would kill him."

"General," replied Junot, "I don't know how far it may be a proof of attachment to you to suppose you capable of ordering a son to kill his father. But it does not signify; if a man is unfortunate enough to think in that way, he had better not proclaim it."

Napoleon was struck with secret admiration of the courage of Junot, who certainly risked his future prospects by his resistance to the will of his chief Buonaparte himself related the history two years later to Laura, adding that he very nearly embraced the disinterested, brave officer as he stood before him.

However, he did not show any signs of relenting, but still insisted on the Temple, the Abbaye, La Force, and the other prisons of ill-omened reputation being filled with the helpless, unoffending English—mostly of the commercial class, as those of any social standing had left Paris in haste.

He thought, or pretended to think, that he was in danger from them, and gave Junot papers describing some ridiculous conspiracy, which, on being inquired into, resolved itself into an accusation against a single Englishman, said to have dined in a certain house, got drunk, and given vent to abuse of and threats against the First Consul. This was stated to have taken place on the 3rd of May, and the person accused was said to have been Junot's friend. Colonel Green, who, by the way, was a great admirer of Napoleon.

"You have a gilded tongue" (*la langue dorée*), said Napoleon, keeping to the familiar "*tu*" "and "*toz*," "but when all is said and done the conclusion I draw is that you and Madame Junot have a mania for receiving people who don't like me. If that were not well known they would not be made to speak in that fashion."

Junot replied by pointing out that even supposing Colonel Green to have been capable of the conduct of which he was accused in Paris on the 3rd of May, the thing was impossible, as he was not in France at that time, having returned to London on the 17th of April.

Convinced at last of the falsehoods he had been made to believe, Napoleon took Junot by the hand and spoke to him with all his old kindness and friendship. But after a long conference the only concession obtained was that as long as they remained quiet, the English should only be detained as prisoners within the towns in which they happened to be.

In the winter of 1803, the First Consul removed Junot from being Commandant of Paris—according to Laura, because he wished to give that post to Murat, and also because the change from the Republic to the Empire being now under discussion, he wanted Junot to be out of the way. Others, however, assert that dissatisfaction with his administration of affairs was the reason of his removal.

He was given another distinguished position, being sent to Arras to command the grenadiers of what was then called the "Army of England."

Laura went with her children to visit her father and mother-in-law in Burgundy, and joined her husband a few weeks later at Arras. It was then the spring of 1804.

CHAPTER 14
Junot and Laura at Arras
1804

The change from Paris to Arras could not, of course, have been a pleasant one to Laura; but she amused herself very well in the ancient capital of Artois, with the balls, dinners, hunting parties, and reviews which continually went on.

Junot threw himself heart and soul into his work, for which he was probably much better suited than he had been for his former post. The camp of Arras, of which he was now in command, was formed of twelve thousand grenadiers, intended for the advanced guard in the invasion of England, and he proceeded to reform and reorganise it in a manner that gained the highest approval of Napoleon.

Shortly after their departure from Paris the Chouan conspiracy was discovered, and the unfortunate leaders, Pichegru and Georges Cadoudal, met their death. This was soon followed by what is generally agreed to be the darkest stain upon the career of Buonaparte, the murder of the young Duc d'Enghien, last of the house of Condé.

This prince was treacherously seized outside the frontiers of France, hurried to Paris, accused of a conspiracy to regain the heritage of his family, of which he was, however, entirely innocent, and shot at Vincennes. Surely in Napoleon's sufferings on the barren rock of St. Helena this infamous assassination was justly avenged.

It called forth a cry of horror and indignation throughout the civilised world, and the nearest relations and most devoted friends and partisans of Buonaparte were for the most part filled with grief and consternation.

The news was brought to Junot in a despatch, which he read eagerly, with changing colour and looks of dismay; then, covering his face with his hands, he exclaimed—

"I am fortunate in being no longer Commandant of Paris!"

Joséphine's entreaties had been powerless to prevent the murder, which caused her the deepest distress, whilst the anger and grief of Buonaparte's mother were expressed in the bitter reproaches and tears with which she met him. In silence he listened while she overwhelmed him with her indignation, assuring him that the stain of so atrocious an action could never be washed away, and that in committing it he had only yielded to the counsels of his enemies, who rejoiced in tarnishing the history of his life by so horrible a page. She took charge of the faithful dog who had followed his unfortunate master to the last, and sent him, with the things she collected belonging to the Duc d'Enghien, to the woman he loved.

Joseph, the eldest and favourite brother of Napoleon, with whom he rarely had any disagreement, also strongly expressed his disapproval of this crime.

For some time longer, Junot and his wife remained at Arras. The presence of Madame Marmont, who was an intimate friend of Laura's, was a great pleasure to her. Marmont was perhaps Junot's favourite amongst all his comrades. Davoust was also at Arras, but was no acquisition in a social point of view, for although he was really a man of good birth, he had a hatred for the *ancien régime* which dated from the time when he had to endure a great deal of annoyance from his friends and acquaintances because he refused to emigrate, but took service under the republican generals. Carrying his new principles to an extreme, he was dirty, slovenly, and unmannerly.

The Empire was now proclaimed, and late in the summer the emperor visited Arras and Boulogne. There was a grand distribution of Crosses of the Legion of Honour at the latter, and a great review and other festivities at the former place, at all of which Laura was present. Junot was made *grand officier* and *grand'croix* of the order, and the emperor expressed the highest satisfaction with his grenadiers and showed especial favour and friendship to Junot himself

Laura was in a carriage with General Suchet and two or three friends, and when at the end of the review the troops were about to defile past, she got out and walked about in order to see them better. The emperor, who recognised her from a distance, sent an officer to invite her to come nearer to him that she might have a better view.

When the review was over. Napoleon, leaving the group in which he was, rode up to Laura, and, taking off his hat, asked her how she was, whether she was amusing herself at Arras, and if she wanted to go back to Paris. But she was so confused by this unexpected attention, and by suddenly remembering the necessity of addressing him as "Sire" or "*Votre Majesté*" that she was seized with an unwonted shyness, and replied with an embarrassment which irritated her whenever she recollected it. The emperor remained talking to her, and then, with a smile, took his leave and rode back.

Before leaving Arras, he gave Junot a pension of 30,000 *francs* for life, to date from his departure from Paris nine months before.

The *fête* at Boulogne was also magnificent, and in the evening Junot received orders from the emperor to go to Calais on business of importance as quickly as possible.

He proposed to Laura that they should start directly they left the ball, by which means they should arrive at Calais very early, have tea *à l'anglaise* at the famous *Hôtel Dessein*, and walk about Calais for an hour or two. They arrived accordingly at seven o'clock in the morning, and Laura, though she did not find much else to admire in Calais, was delighted with that celebrated establishment, which was now a scene of despair on account of the rupture of the treaty of Amiens, the English being its special supporters.

After these festivities Junot and his wife left Arras and returned to their *hôtel* in Paris in time to be present at the coronation of the emperor.

The formation of the new court was now the subject of universal interest, not only amongst the adherents of Napoleon but amongst many others who had hitherto held aloof, but now surrounded Joséphine eagerly petitioning for places as *dame du palais*, chamberlain, &c.

The principal posts were given to the friends and partisans of Buonaparte, although amongst them were to be found a few historic names welcomed by Napoleon, whose great wish to carry out what Laura called "his impossible system of fusion" now became more conspicuous.

The jealousy, rivalry, and heart-burnings that went on can easily be imagined. Besides the household of the empress, those of the sisters of Napoleon had to be formed. In that of the Princess Caroline were to be found a few names connected with the *faubourg St. Germain*, which owed her some gratitude for having on one occasion saved the life of the Marquis de la Riviere. In that of the Princess Elisa no such names appeared. She was the least pleasant and popular of the sisters, even in her own family, and with Napoleon she often disputed and quarrelled.

On one occasion they had an angry discussion about a play called *Wenceslas*. Napoleon ordered Talma to read the first act to him, at the end of which he said that Wenceslas was an old fool, and Ladislas an unnatural son, that the play was good for nothing, and they had much better read *Corneille*. The Princess Elisa contradicted him, and she and Napoleon so irritated each other in the course of their argument that they both lost their tempers, and Napoleon, exclaiming angrily, "It is intolerable! you are a caricature of the Duchesse du Maine," got up and left the room.

As for Pauline, she had been married some time before to Camillo, Prince Borghese, a remarkably handsome, stupid man, chosen for her by Napoleon not long after the death of General Leclerc.

Pauline's delight in being, as she said, "a real princess" knew no bounds.

Laura had been at Saint Cloud when that estimable person went to pay her wedding visit as *Princess* Borghese to *Madame* Buonaparte. It was in the evening in winter. She wore a dress of green velvet and was covered with the Borghese diamonds. She walked about, displaying her magnificent dress "like a peacock his tail," remarked Laura, by whom she sat down, saying—

"Do you see them, Laurette, *ma petite Laurette?* They are bursting with jealousy, *mon enfant!* I don't care. I am a princess, and a real princess!"

Pauline Buonaparte hated and envied Joséphine, and would often shed tears of spite caused by the grace, beauty, dress, and position of her sister-in-law. Her own happiness consisted in being more beautiful and more admired than anyone else. She was not only the first of her family to attain princely rank, but the only one to keep it.

Neither Lucien, Jérôme, nor their mother were present at the coronation of the emperor, owing to family dissensions of various kinds.

Jérôme Buonaparte, a spoilt, selfish lad of nineteen, the only one of Napoleon's brothers whose character was altogether contemptible, had chosen to marry in America, without the consent of Napoleon, the daughter of a certain Mr. Patterson, of Baltimore, In her *Mémoires* Laura observes that, although Jérôme was so young, yet, as he had obtained the consent of his mother and of Joseph, who was the head of his family, the marriage was perfectly legal.

ELISA BUONAPARTE, MADAME BACCIOCHI, GRAND DUCHESS OF TUSCANY.

Another biographer says that Madame Buonaparte had not given her consent, and that Mr. Patterson and his daughter resolved to risk the recognition of the marriage. But considering Laura's intimate friendship with the whole family, and the partial affection with which she regarded them, it seems probable that she knew the circumstances of the case. At any rate, Napoleon, whom she so indignantly declares undeserving of the name of tyrant, ordered all the ports of France, Holland, and Belgium to be closed against his brother and sister-in-law, who had sailed from America.

Jérôme, whose cowardly desertion of his wife and child took place the following year, at first refused to obey his brother, and returned with his wife to Baltimore.

Lucien was a man of a very different stamp. Although he had long since given up the fantastic follies of his youth, no longer called himself by absurd names or made himself in any way ridiculous, he remained consistently republican and independent. He made no attempt to conceal his disapproval of the disappearance of the republic and the despotic power to which Napoleon was so rapidly advancing; and was determined that he, at any rate, would not bow before the tyranny of his brother.

His first marriage had excited the displeasure of Napoleon, who was then in a much less powerful position, and he had recently made a second marriage with a widow, Madame Jouberthon, which had enraged the First Consul still more.

Madame Jouberthon was good-looking, fond of society, and had been a good deal talked about, with or without reason. Lucien was very much in love with her, and paid no attention to the interference and indignation of Napoleon, who was now eager to marry all the available members of his family to princes and royalties, and furious with Lucien's want of submission both in public and private matters, had exiled him. Lucien troubled himself little about this.

He had no ambition, but only wanted to live in peace with his wife and children amidst the scenes and pursuits he loved; for his pleasures and interests were in literary and artistic matters. So, he retired to Rome, where he was shortly joined by his mother, who vehemently took his part. After an angry interview with her second son, she left Paris; and although Napoleon caused her to be placed by David in the great picture of the coronation, she was really not present at it, being at that time in Rome, where she had neither title nor distinction of any kind.

The coronation was a magnificent sight. Laura had, of course, a place reserved for her in Notre-Dame, and Junot carried the Hand of Justice in the procession. It was apparently without emotion that Napoleon went through the imposing ceremony, and when the Pope was about to take the crown from the altar, he seized it and placed it upon his own head. When he came down from the altar to pass to his throne his eyes met Laura's, and as she read the triumph of his look, she remembered that drive with him in her father's carriage from Saint-Cyr long ago, and his exclamation, "Oh! if I were master!" A few days afterwards the emperor came up to her and said—

"Why did you wear a black velvet dress? Was it a sign of mourning?"

"Oh, sire!" cried Laura reproachfully; and tears came into her eyes.

"But why did you choose that gloomy, sinister colour?"

"Your Majesty could only see part of it. It was embroidered with gold. I wore my diamonds, and I thought this *toilette* was suitable, as I was not obliged to put on a court dress."

"Is that an indirect reproach because you are not made *dame du palais?*"

Laura explained that she was far from being offended, and in reply to Napoleon's persistent questions replied—

"Well, sire—but your Majesty will not believe me."

"Yes, I will. Come, speak."

"Then I am not sorry for it."

"Why?"

"Because my disposition is not submissive, and Your Majesty will be sure to arrange the etiquette of the *service d'honneur* of the empress like a military code."

He laughed.

"Well, perhaps so," he said. "Anyhow, I am pleased with you; you have given me a good answer, and I shall not forget it."

Joséphine looked magnificent. Her mantle was borne by her daughter, Caroline and Elisa, sisters of Napoleon, and Julie, wife of Joseph Buonaparte.

A few days afterwards Junot came to Laura with disturbed looks, saying that the emperor had chosen him as ambassador to Portugal.

"Well," said Laura, "and why are you not pleased?"

"Because I am not made for diplomacy, and Lannes says that the Court of Lisbon is like a mine of gunpowder. England is all-powerful there. Austria threatens; so, do Russia and Prussia, and you can easily imagine that with the sound of guns and cannon I shall not go and take a *siesta* in Portugal."

The commands of the emperor, however, could not be disobeyed, so Junot and Laura had to prepare for their journey, which, as the time approached for it, she disliked quite as much as he did.

She could not endure the idea of leaving Paris, which was gayer and more delightful than ever, especially just at this time when, after the coronation, one magnificent *fête* succeeded another. Also, she would be obliged to leave behind her second child, who was too young for the journey; and she did not like the account Madame Lannes gave her of society and life in Lisbon.

The emperor was well aware that the manners of many, perhaps most of those who composed his court, left much to be desired, and he was particularly sensitive as to the impression they produced upon foreigners. He knew that Laura was half *faubourg St. Germain*, had been brought up in the *salon* of such a mother as Madame Permon, was herself clever, amusing, and attractive, and possessed a knowledge of the world which he certainly would not find in most of the young wives of his generals.

He gave her minute directions for her behaviour in Portugal and in Spain, where Junot was also to go upon important but secret business.

"An ambassadress," he said, "is a much more important *pièce* in an embassy than people suppose; it is so everywhere, but more especially with us on account of the prejudice which exists against France. It is for you to give the Portuguese a proper idea of the Imperial Court. Don't be haughty or vain, still less touchy, but let your relations with the women of the Portuguese *noblesse* be reserved and dignified. You will meet at Lisbon several *émigrés* of the Court of Louis XVI.; be most scrupulously particular in your intercourse with them. It is in these circumstances that you must remember all the good you derived from the lessons of Madame Permon. Above all, take care not to ridicule the customs of the country when you don't understand them, nor yet those of the court....

"And be circumspect, you understand. The Queen of Spain will ask you about the empress, the Princess Louis, Princess Caroline, Princess Joseph. You must measure your words. The interior of my family can bear exposure, but it would not be agreeable to me that my sisters should be painted by a bad artist."

After other instructions he observed that very little French was spoken in Spain or Portugal, but a good deal of Italian, and desired her to speak to him in that language. She repeated some verses of Petrarca and Tasso with an accent so pure that he expressed his satisfaction, and then continued to talk of his family, of the caution to be observed in speaking of them, of the absolute necessity of never mentioning himself except as he was alluded to in the *Moniteur*; of never getting into any quarrels with the wives of the members of other legations, in which very often the husbands became involved, "so that two states may be brought to the verge of war by the quarrels of two silly women." Finally, he told her to entertain a great deal and to let her *salon* at Lisbon be as agreeable as it had been at Paris.

Before Laura set off on what she considered to be an honourable exile she took part in several splendid *fêtes* given by the army and by different societies and persons to the emperor. The most magnificent was that of the marshals of France, in which the decorations were all of silver gauze and fresh flowers, though it was in the heart of a severe winter.

A great deal of gossip was just then going on about a new love affair of the emperor's, the object of his attachment being this time a person of unblemished reputation. To attract the attention of Napoleon was a real misfortune for a woman. He bore her malice if she resisted him, and treated her with contempt if she did not.

He was extremely anxious that this new fancy should not be noticed, and Laura first observed it at a *fête* given for the coronation by the Minister of War. Now that there was an Empire and a court, there were naturally much stricter distinctions of rank.

The supper was at different tables, round which only women were seated. Laura took her place at that of the empress, thinking as she did so of those fraternal banquets only a few years since, when people were obliged to go out in rain or snow and eat with the pickpockets in the streets, unless they chose to risk losing their heads by refusing.

The emperor would not sit down, but walked about talking to the different ladies of the court amongst whom was Madame ——, the object of his present attention, who was sitting next Laura.

The manners of Napoleon that evening were so unusually polite and pleasant that they seemed to her unnatural, while everyone was comparing this *fête* to those brilliant *réunions* of the court of Louis XIV., whose traditional glories were the envy and admiration of the mushroom court.

Standing first by the empress, handing her plate, talking to her for a few minutes with the greatest courtesy, he presently arrived where Laura was seated, and, addressing himself to her, began to ask if she had been dancing much and if she were going to take many pretty things to Portugal, where, he observed, she would herself be an example of all that was graceful and charming. As he paid these unwonted compliments he was leaning partly on Laura's chair, partly on that of her neighbour, who just then tried to reach a dish of olives, which Napoleon, pushing between her chair and Laura's, handed her himself, remarking—

"You ought not to eat olives in the evening; you will do yourself harm. And you, Madame Junot, you don't eat olives; you are right, and doubly right, not to imitate Madame ——, for in everything she is inimitable."

The tone and look which accompanied these words almost startled Laura. Madame —— made no answer, but looked down and became crimson. The emperor stood by her in silence for a few moments, and then as he moved away, she raised her eyes, and Laura caught their expression as she looked after him, which augured ill for her future.

The empress was very much annoyed, and a day or two afterwards, when Laura was breakfasting at La Malmaison, she took her into her own room and, contriving to lead the conversation that way, asked her what the emperor had said to Madame ——, making severe observations upon those who were always trying to be the emperor's favourites, and declaring that their heads were all turned by a new novel called *Madame de la Vallière*, which everybody was reading.

It was at midnight on Shrove Tuesday, 1805, that Laura, with her husband and eldest child, started upon the journey she so dreaded.

Her grief was rather mitigated by the splendour with which they travelled, by order of the emperor, who desired that the first ambassador of the new empire should be surrounded with suitable magnificence. They travelled by Bordeaux to Bayonne, and then for thirteen weary days to Madrid, where they intended to pass five or six weeks.

Laura, who had studied during her journey a number of books upon Spain that she had collected and brought with her, passed all the time at her disposal in sight-seeing. She had, of course, to be presented at court, and to pay various visits of ceremony, and she formed a strong attachment to the charming but unfortunate princess of the Asturias, who died so soon afterwards under strong suspicions of poison, but who had then been only a short time married, and was the idol of her husband.

The only *hôtel* in Madrid, the Croix de Malte, being unfit to live in, Laura and her suite were lodged in a small house lent to them for the occasion by a French gentleman of their acquaintance.

When Junot had concluded his business at the Spanish Court, they proceeded to Lisbon, a more wearisome and dangerous journey than the first. Laura generally slept in the carriage, which was drawn by seven or eight mules. The inns were nearly always unfit to go into, and she had a comfortable bed in the roomy travelling-carriage, where she slumbered or read in comfort as they wound along through the dreary, half-cultivated plains or over the wild, open heaths, of which the fragrance filled the air.

One morning when they stopped for breakfast Junot came to the door of the carriage and called out—

"Laura! are you dressed? Make haste and come out."

"Yes, directly! But why are you so impatient? Your early journey seems to have made you hungry?"

"It is not I who am impatient, but an old friend who has come from Baltimore to breakfast with you."

When Laura opened the door and stepped out into the fresh morning air, she beheld Jérôme Buonaparte, whom she had not seen for years. Finding the ports of France, Holland, Belgium, Spain, Italy, and Portugal closed against his wife, who was now expecting the birth of her child, he had sent her to England, had landed himself, and was now on his way to his brother to try to soften his anger and induce him to relent in his persecution.

Jérôme breakfasted with Junot and Laura, and then walked about with them in a garden attached to the inn, before which the cavalcade was drawn up. For two hours Jérôme poured into their sympathising ears the grievances and difficulties of his position.

Opening a locket he wore, he showed them the portrait of his wife, a beautiful woman, very like Pauline Borghese, only with more expression and animation.

Junot began, as usual, by advising him not to oppose the emperor, but as Jérôme went on explaining the whole situation he felt that he could not possibly recommend any man to commit so dastardly an action as to desert his innocent wife and child from motives of simple self-interest. He therefore became more and more silent as the conversation went on, and Jérôme said that he would appeal to his brother the emperor, who was "good" and "just," and would listen to him. Jérôme declared that he would not yield, and quoted the case of Lucien and his first wife, to whom Napoleon made strong objections at first and became perfectly reconciled afterwards. Laura, however, knew well enough that it was not the goodness or justice of Napo-

JÉRÔME BUONAPARTE, KING OF WESTPHALIA

leon, but the difference between Lucien and Jérôme which decided these matters, and when the latter had started on his way to Paris, and they resumed their journey to Lisbon, she told Junot that she felt no confidence in Jérôme , but greatly feared for his young wife. Junot did not agree with her, but events soon proved that she was right.

CHAPTER 15
Illness of Laura
1805

They were now advancing towards Guadiana, and as they began to ascend the mountains of Santa Cruz the scenery grew more picturesque. Villages built on the slopes of the mountain, almond-trees flowering amongst the huge rocks and boulders, shady ilex trees and a richer vegetation enlivened their way until, after they left Meajadas, a town situated in a fertile plain, the landscape became more wild and gloomy than before. This part of the country was infested with robbers, and although their party was a large one, they were by no means safe from the attacks of the *banditti*, who were so numerous as to form a serious danger.

The cavalcade consisted of five carriages and two *fourgons* containing luggage, amongst which was a quantity of valuable plate and Laura's jewels. They had an escort of six men, and there were pistols and other arms in the carriages, in spite of which Laura, by no means timid, felt a certain amount of fear.

They had to go through a wood called the Confessional, because it was very rare for anyone to pass alone through it without being assassinated.

Whilst they were at Meajadas they were warned to keep their escort close to them, as the robbers were about. A priest of the place told them many stories of the crimes committed by them, and pointed out two men dressed in black velvet and leather, with belts full of pistols, knives, and daggers, who were just then crossing the little square of the town. He said they were well-known murderers, who lived at their ease in the town when they were not out with the band. The townspeople being poor, had nothing to tempt them; but travellers of distinction passing that way had better beware.

One of the stories he told related to the Count d'Aranjo, a friend of Laura's, who was Portuguese minister at Berlin, and was recalled to fill some important place at Lisbon.

Amongst other jewels, he had with him a very costly chain of pearls and diamonds, and a blue enamel watch with the hands and the hours of large diamonds, which he was taking from Madame de Talleyrand to the Duchess d'Ossuna. These and other jewels had been seen, and the count, who was brave even to rashness, had the further imprudence to separate himself from his escort, leaving them to join him at midday.

He was attacked by a gang of brigands, who plundered all the carriages of his suite, broke open his boxes, and dragged him and his secretary out, turning the latter into a ditch.

The count had hidden the watch and chain about him, and in answer to the threats of the brigands he only declared he would have them all hanged, while his secretary, who was an arrant coward, kept lifting his head out of the ditch and his voice in supplication to the brigands.

"*Monseigneur!*" he cried, when he heard his master refuse to tell where the money and the other jewels were, "what are you thinking of? *Mes bons messieurs*, I will tell you where it is. Look there, to the left, under the cushion, a little button in the panel. That's it, *mes bons messieurs*. Take it all, but don't kill us. The jewels are there too!"

And when the brigands were gone and he was again in the carriage and found that his master had saved the chain and watch, he almost wished to call the brigands back and give them up to them.

Laura was by no means reassured by the stories she heard, and when they passed into the wild forest, where on each side of the road they kept observing crosses with heaps of stones, marking the site of some murder, and when in the part called the Confessional an image of the Virgin was nailed to a tree to excite the last devotions of the traveller who was most likely to meet his death amongst those gloomy shadows, she turned pale, her heart beat faster, and Junot, though he pretended indifference, stopped the cavalcade, ordered the muleteers on no account to lose sight of each other, but to keep the carriages and *fourgons* close together, and carefully examined the arms of the escort.

They arrived, however, without any attack at the end of their day's journey, Junot walking a great part of the way by the side of Laura's carriage as a precaution, while she strained her eyes through the gloomy darkness as she gazed fearfully into the dark wood, expecting to see some sinister face appear out of the thickets. At last they drew up before a most miserable inn, or rather cabin. Laura preferred as usual to sleep in the carriage, but thinking perhaps a room might be better for the child, she chose the least squalid the place contained, ordered juniper to be burned and a brazier to be placed there, had Joséphine's little bed prepared, and soon the little one was asleep with her nurse in the room, and Madame Heldt, who was a sort of nursery governess and housekeeper, in the adjoining room.

During the night the nurse was alarmed by Madame Heldt opening her door and saying with terror-stricken looks—

"Madame Bergerot, there is a murdered man under my bed! Hush!" she added, as the other gave a cry of horror, "they will murder us all! And see, there is a great instrument of torture."

They looked under the bed and saw the feet of a man half covered with straw.

"*Mon Dieu!* but how are we to get out? And suppose it should not be a dead body?"

"What else should it be?" said the other; and opening the window, they looked out into the calm night.

Everyone seemed to be asleep; there was no sound but the trampling of the mules in the stalls close by. But just then, to their intense joy. Colonel Laborde, who accompanied Junot, came under the window. Not feeling at all convinced of the security of the place, he was making his rounds, and hearing the women call for help, he rushed into their room, where sure enough there was the dead body of a man lying under the bed. Opening the window looking into the forest, he called one of the escort, and they went down to find the landlord.

It appeared, however, that the man had not been murdered, but had died of pneumonia, and that the instrument of torture was an implement for threshing corn.

Everyone awoke. Junot was furious with the landlord, whom he seized and threatened to kill for putting two women and his child into the room with a corpse, but after a time peace was restored, and they continued their journey without any serious adventures, except that Joséphine's carriage was upset and she and her attendants had a narrow escape. Finally, they arrived safely at Lisbon.

As soon as she had been presented at court Laura opened her *salon*, and following the directions of the emperor, which thoroughly coincided with her own inclinations, she entertained lavishly.

She gave numbers of balls, and her parties, her dress, and everything about her displayed magnificence enough to satisfy the French *amour propre* and dazzle the different nations represented at the Portuguese Court.

Her position there was a particularly distinguished and brilliant one, as the other embassies did not attempt to vie with her in the splendour of her entertainments.

The wife of the English Ambassador was neither popular nor socially gifted in any way; the Spanish Ambassador was unmarried; the Russian Ambassador was not much liked and appeared reluctantly at the parties at the French Embassy, his sympathies being English and his powers of concealing them limited.

Holland was only represented by a consul-general. It was at the Austrian Embassy that Laura found her chief friends, and both she and Junot soon became very intimate with the Ambassador, Count von Lebzeltern, his wife and three daughters. Of course, she also made numerous friends of different nations, and was soon perfectly happy and a great favourite at the court of Lisbon. Passionately fond of dancing, and, as the Austrian Ambassadress said, "dancing like a fairy in the moonlight," she entered with delight into all the gaieties around her, which, however, did not prevent her taking the deepest interest in her new surroundings—the strange Oriental-looking town built on seven hills, the steep, narrow, crooked streets, so horribly dirty that they were only kept from being pestilential by the torrents of water which poured down them, rendering them impassable for some time after the violent and frequent storms.

Laura found the aspect of the streets of Lisbon much more lively than those of Madrid, where the amount of black in the costumes of the people gave them an imposing but sombre appearance. She sat usually in a little drawing-room looking over a kind of square, across which people were continually passing. The women wore red capes edged with black velvet, and handkerchiefs upon their heads; but no woman above the rank of a peasant or small shopkeeper ever walked in the streets. Laura therefore found herself condemned to go out only in a carriage drawn by four mules; for with two, as she said, it was impossible to pay several visits in a day, on account of the great distances.

The Portuguese theatre, *do Salitre,* was dark and dirty, the actors bad, and the costumes ridiculous; but the Italian Opera was at this time the most famous in Europe. Crescentini, Guaforini, Naldi, Monbelli, Matucchi, and, above all, Catalani in the height of her glory, formed a brilliant company, fully appreciated by Laura, who possessed all her mother's love of the theatre.

It being impossible to walk about in Lisbon, she used very often to drive out to some gardens in the suburbs and walk about there. In most of these gardens she was disappointed because, in spite of their splendid climate, the Portuguese, who neither knew nor cared anything about flowers or gardening, took no trouble about them. An immense piece of ground planted with olives, ilex, and broom was all the idea most of the great Portuguese families had of a garden; or, if they surrounded their villas and country houses with anything more choice, it was a shrubbery of laurels, orange-trees, and myrtles, with a pond.

But there was one garden called Bemfica, an exception to this state of things, in which Laura delighted to spend her time. It belonged to one of the Portuguese nobles, and was not very far from Lisbon. There were laurels five-and-twenty feet high, palms and bananas, groves of orange and lemon trees, enormous geraniums, magnolias, daturas, and many other delightful flowers.

Laura, who was passionately fond of them, had driven out there one lovely afternoon and stayed until late in the evening, spending most of the time in an avenue of magnolias in full flower. The air was faint and heavy with the scent of them, and the full moon was shining in all its southern radiance when she reluctantly got into her carriage and drove back to Lisbon, carrying an enormous bouquet given her by the gardener of magnolia, datura, orange and lemon blossoms, and other flowers. All the way home she kept inhaling their delicious fragrance and looking dreamily at the moonlight, contrasting it with that of her own cold, grey France, and feeling a delightful sort of languor stealing over her, which Junot remarked on when she got home, saying that she seemed very sleepy.

As she had walked about all day, however, she supposed she was only tired, and went to bed, placing the great bouquet close to her in water, and though at first, she felt unaccountably feverish, she fell asleep dreaming of her flowers.

It was her custom to get up very early, but the next morning her maid, finding that it was nine o'clock and she had not rung for her, came to her door and listened. Junot thought she must have overtired herself, and ordered her not to be disturbed; but when eleven o'clock came and still there was no sound, he went into her room himself and opened the shutters. Just as he did so he was startled by a loud cry from little Joséphine, who had climbed upon her mother's bed and found her lying pale and insensible.

Her maids rushed in, and Junot, seeing that she was asphyxiated, threw open the windows, which, according to the pernicious custom of the time and country, were closed,

Then, taking his wife in his arms, he carried her to the open window, and after some time, with much difficulty the doctor succeeded in arousing her. Slowly she came to herself, like one aroused from a heavy sleep, but if Junot had not happened to go into her room just then she would never have opened her eyes in this world again. As it was, she escaped with a headache only.

As the hot weather came on the Junots, like most of their friends, moved out of the town and took a villa in the delightful district of Cintra, whose mountains and valleys are covered with forests of oak, beech, poplar, orange, and lemon trees. Cascades fall from the rocks, and wander in streams through the meadows; here is to be seen a convent, there a ruined castle, whilst everywhere among the woods and on the mountain slopes are the villas and country houses of the inhabitants of Lisbon.

The house Junot had taken was in the most lovely valley of this enchanting region; and they found plenty of their friends near them, amongst whom were the Austrian Ambassador and his family, who had an apartment in the ancient royal *château* of Cintra. Often when the heat of the day had abated Laura and her husband would walk over there, spend the evening, and after having tea at eleven o'clock, return on foot through the fragrant woods, lighted by the moon or the torches carried by their servants.

As the summer wore on rumours of war came to disturb the tranquil life at Cintra. A coalition had again been formed against France, and Laura inveighed against the envious and unreasonable objections the other powers ventured to make to Napoleon's having—of course, entirely for the good of those duchies—seized upon Parma and Piacenza, and united them to France! Lucca was also "given" to the Princess Elisa.

With much pleasure they heard that to Madame Laetitia were at last granted the rank and titles proper for the mother of the emperor; and at the same time Laura received a *brevet de dame* as one of the ladies of her household.

Junot grew more and more uneasy lest he should be absent when battles were being fought, and he waited anxiously for the summons the emperor had promised him if war should break out.

At the end of the summer Laura became dangerously ill after a miscarriage, and for six weeks grew weaker and weaker. The Portuguese doctors in despair sent her to a miserable village called Caldas da Raynha, which possessed springs of such wonderful qualities that,

LAURE JUNOT (NÉE PERNON), DUCHESSE D'ABRANTÈS.

although she was carried there in a litter, at the end of a week she could walk, and was soon on the road to recovery.

Before she was well again Junot received his summons from the emperor. War was declared, and Duroc wrote to him to make haste, as he himself had a presentiment that the campaign would be a short one.

Junot accordingly hurried to Caldas, where he only spent a few hours with Laura, and then returned to Lisbon, whence he started immediately for Paris. The emperor had already left, so, after passing twenty-four hours there, he set off in a post-chaise to follow the army to Germany.

The troops marched so fast that he did not come up with them till he got to Brunn on the 1st of December. Napoleon was standing by a window with Berthier at about nine o'clock in the morning, looking out. The weather was foggy and gloomy, and it was scarcely light.

"What's that I see down there?" he exclaimed. "It's a post-chaise—and yet we don't expect any news this morning. Why, it's an *officier-général*. Really, if the thing were possible, I should say it was Junot. When did you write to him, Berthier?"

Berthier informed him.

"Then it can't be him," said the emperor. "He has twelve hundred leagues to travel after us, and with the best will in the world—"

At that moment the *aide-de-camp de service* announced General Junot.

Laura meanwhile returned to Lisbon, going in a boat up the Tagus, and being nearly drowned on the way, for a fearful storm came on, the sails were torn and the boat nearly swamped. Twenty men were rowing, but they could scarcely make way. At last Laura, dripping wet but congratulating herself that her child was not with her, was carried on shore through the water, and taken to a house where she got a fire and dry clothes; and that evening she found herself safe in her little yellow drawing-room at the French Embassy, with Joséphine on her knee, and several friends sitting with her, listening to the raging of the tempest outside.

Five days afterwards she was awakened in the morning by a cannonade so furious that the house shook with each volley. She sent at once to M. de Rayneral, *chargé d'affaires*, in Junot's absence, to know what had happened.

The news of Trafalgar had arrived in the night, and the English ships, of which the harbour was full, were celebrating the victory. But their triumph was mingled with mourning, for Nelson was dead.

The consternation with which the English victory had filled the French Embassy was, however, soon changed into rejoicing at the tidings of the Austrian defeat at Ulm and the surrender of General Mack and his army. The Battle of Austerlitz was the crowning success of the campaign; peace was signed with Austria, and Junot wrote to his wife from Munich that Napoleon was about to marry his stepson, Eugène de Beauharnais, to the daughter of the King of Bavaria.

Being now strong enough to travel, Laura prepared for her return to France. She went first to Madrid, and stayed there until February, amusing herself and going a great deal into society. Then she set off for Paris, her spirits rising higher and higher as she drew nearer to the frontier of France. She made these two journeys slowly but pleasantly with her child, under the escort of MM. de Cherval and Maignan, the gentlemen attached to her husband's suite, who took great care of them. Reading, walking, and botanising on the way, the time passed agreeably enough, and she arrived at Paris on Shrove Tuesday, 1806.

Chapter 16
Laura Remains at Paris
1806

The household of the emperor's mother, Signora Laetitia Buonaparte, now called Madame Mère, had not very long been formed when Laura, on her return from Portugal, began her attendance there. The emperor and his family had, in order to carry out their pretension to being French, changed their harmonious name of Buonaparte into "Bonaparte," pronounced like a French word.

Napoleon would even affect to have forgotten the soft, delicious language of Italy which was that of his early years, for Corsica had belonged to that country for six centuries and only been sold to France the year before he was born.

Madame Mère received Laura with great kindness and affection.

"Ah! you have no occasion to name Madame Junot to me. She is a child of my own. I love her as a daughter, and I hope her place with an old woman will be made as pleasant as possible to her. For it is dull for you—is it not?" she added.

Laura, however, made no objection to her post. She was very fond of Madame Mère, and always contradicted the prevailing reports of her stinginess. It was true that the emperor's mother exercised more economy than he approved of; the simple ascetic habits of her early life remained ingrained in her nature. She had no faith in the stability of the brilliant fortune of her family, and used to reply, when remonstrated with for saving money, that she was providing for a future day when she expected that all these kings and queens would be coming to her for help.

The extravagance of her daughters displeased her, though it satisfied Napoleon, who complained to his mother that she kept no state and spent no money, whereas her daughters all adapted themselves to their new position as if they had been born princesses, in which, however, he deceived himself Pauline was the best, but there was no real distinction or high breeding about that beautiful but surpassingly silly woman; Elisa was plain, disagreeable, and badly dressed; and Caroline, though she possessed a certain style of beauty, was awkward, highshouldered, and had a habit of giggling absolutely incompatible with the manners usual in society.

The emperor's mother was very glad to have the daughter of her old friend with her, and used to talk to Laura with confidence, asking her about the different people presented to her, whose names were mostly unfamiliar to her.

One day, on being told that someone whose name she asked was the Duchesse de Chevreuse, she observed, "She doesn't like us; and she detests the emperor; I am certain of that." And on Laura's asking her reason, she replied, "Her smile, and the disdainful movement of her head when I asked her if she were not happy to be so near the emperor, and then her silence when I inquired if her husband was attached to the emperor's household."

It was true enough; the new court and government were hated at the Hôtel de Luynes, and the Duchesse de Chevreuse was afterwards exiled by Napoleon.

Although surrounded with honours and riches, Madame Mère had no influence at court. The emperor had never forgiven her having taken the part of Lucien against himself. Her household was not a large one; it consisted of five ladies, an almoner, a *lectrice* (reader), two chamberlains, and four or five other gentlemen.

Festivities soon began in honour of the hereditary Prince of Baden, who came to Paris to marry Stephanie de Beauharnais, niece of Joséphine. It was a marriage of state, and as the prince was ugly, unattractive, looked sulky, and made himself disagreeable, everyone pitied his *fiancée*, a pretty, charming girl, sacrificed, like her cousin Hortense, to the ambition of the Buonapartes.

The emperor returned, but Junot remained for some time at Parma, of which he had been appointed governor. He kept writing to Laura, throwing out hints that he wished to be recalled; at any rate, that is how she interpreted his constant requests that she would ask the emperor when she and her children were to join him there, which she concluded to be an indirect way of inquiring whether his stay was to be long enough to make it worthwhile.

But Laura did not want to go to Italy. She was very happy at Paris, where she had only just returned, and the rumours she heard of Junot's proceedings at Parma convinced her that she was just as well away.

She looked with philosophic composure upon the frequent and passing flirtations and infidelities of her husband, which she never seems to have cared to imitate. Her children, her books, her friends and society, were interests sufficient for her happiness, and the love intrigues in which Junot, after his first passionate love for herself had subsided into a strong though unromantic affection and friendship, was constantly entangling himself, did not greatly trouble her. She knew perfectly well that they would not last, and that to Junot they were merely the amusements of the passing hour which in no way interfered with his affection for herself and his children.

★★★★★★

After the convention of Cintra . . . my father had orders to convey General Junot to La Rochelle. . . . Junot and my father became great friends. . . . Every evening Junot used to take out his wife's miniature and show it to my father and kiss it. She was a beautiful woman. (*Links with the Past*, Mrs. Charles Bagot).

★★★★★★

Of course, to many women of our own day, (1904), and especially of Anglo-Saxon race, such an union as this would be impossible. One of three things they would do either they would separate from their husbands, or they would amuse themselves in the same way, or if they did not choose to adopt the latter course and were deterred by important considerations, such as children or social reasons, from taking advantage of the former, their lives would be extremely unhappy.

Even at the time in question Joséphine's life was continually embittered by her jealousy of the numerous other women who were the objects of Napoleon's fancy, although, far from wishing to leave him, her one dread was lest he should leave her.

Laura, however, was quite a different sort of woman.

There had been no romance whatever in her marriage. Junot was ordered by Napoleon to find a wife at once. He thought Laura would be suitable in every way, and having convinced himself of that, allowed himself to fall in love with her.

She on her part was quite willing to marry anyone her mother chose, provided she felt no particular dislike to him. All she knew in Junot's favour was that he was rich, good-looking, and a brave soldier.

It is probable that she was entirely satisfied with the way her marriage turned out. Junot and she had no sort of ideal love for each other. Except their devotion to the emperor and their love of society and pleasure they had not a taste in common; their religious opinions were entirely different; and yet they got on very well together. Junot always treated Laura with the greatest kindness and consideration, and she looked with indulgence upon his flirtations, saying that he was "*très-beau garçon*, and must be excused."

She did not, however, under the circumstances feel inclined to leave Paris and take a long, tiresome journey to join her husband, who seemed so well able to amuse himself in her absence, and she told the emperor so when he made some remark on the subject. He replied by one of his usual speeches about women not interfering with their husbands' amusements, which was intended for the empress who ignored it, but taken up by his mother with an exclamation of disapproval and by the Princess Borghese, who, as she leaned back in her armchair arranging the drapery of her shawl, cried out indignantly, "*Quelle horreur!* I should just like to see Prince Camille taking it into his head to try and make me approve of—— ah! ah!——"

For Pauline, like Napoleon's true sister, had one code for herself and another for her husband. Her own love affairs were many and various. It was said that on one occasion when her mother reproached her for the scandal she caused, saying that her lover was actually seen going out of the door of her house in the morning, she replied—

"Well, how else should he go out? Would you have him go out of the window?"

One of her *liaisons* was with a young officer named De Canouville, very handsome, a brave soldier, but as thoughtless and indiscreet as herself, in consequence of which everybody talked about them. Pauline declared, as she always did on these occasions, that he was the only man she had ever loved. However, this lasted longer than most of her *liaisons*.

On one occasion the celebrated dentist. Bosquet, was sent for to her *hôtel* to do something to her teeth. On arriving he found in the room in which he was to perform the necessary operation a good-looking young man in a dressing-gown lying on a sofa, whom he supposed to be Prince Borghese, especially as he gave him earnest directions not to hurt the princess, but to take great care of her teeth, adding—

"I am most anxious about my Paulette's teeth, and I make you responsible for any accident."

"Don't be alarmed, *mon prince*," replied the dentist; "I assure your highness that there is no danger."

During the whole time the conversation went on in the same style; and M. Bosquet used afterwards to tell people of the affectionate anxiety of Prince Borghese for his wife, observing that it was delightful to see such touching attachment and conjugal devotion. Everyone laughed, and nobody undeceived him; but this was Colonel de Canouville: Prince Borghese was at that time in Italy. The end of the history of Pauline Borghese and Colonel de Canouville is as follows:—

When the Emperor Alexander visited Paris, he presented to Napoleon three magnificent fur pelisses. Napoleon gave one to his sister Pauline who gave it to Colonel de Canouville. That imprudent young officer had it made into a *dolman de hussard* and wore it at a review in the Place du Carrousel at which the Emperor Napoleon was present.

De Canouville was riding a restive horse which he could not manage, and this attracted the attention of the emperor, who called out in a voice of thunder, "Who is that officer?" and then recognising him and the fur he was wearing, he sent for Berthier and asked what he meant by having young fools hanging about who ought to be at the war. "It is just like you, Berthier," added the emperor angrily. "You see nothing—one has to tell you everything. I ought not to have had to send away that young man."

Berthier bowed, biting his nails, as he always did in any perplexity. The Princess Borghese had entreated him not to let De Canouville go, and he trembled at the thought of the emperor's anger if he should discover this.

"There are despatches to be taken to the Prince d'Essling," continued Napoleon; "let him take them and start for Spain this evening."

It was *Jeudi-gras*, there was a ball at the *hôtel* of Queen Hortense. De Canouville in despair rushed to Berthier, who cried out, "I can do nothing! I can do nothing! It is the emperor's order! Why the devil did you wear those things?" And he had to go.

Camillo Borghese was a great admirer of Laura's, but he was so dull and tiresome that no possible amusement could be obtained from his attentions, which she avoided as much as possible. He was always falling in love with and making declarations to the young wives of the generals and others who formed the emperor's court; and being, or fancying himself in love with Laura, he pursued and tormented her till she was half afraid of him.

One day when she was going to a ball a bouquet of flowers arrived from him, in which she discovered a note written on a piece of vellum in a sort of bad red ink, so faded and indistinct that she could not make it out. However, she took the flowers with her in the evening, and Prince Borghese, coming up to her with an air of mystery, asked in Italian if she had found the letter.

"What letter?" asked she.

"Hush! speak lower!" he exclaimed, looking with terror to where his wife was sitting, paying no attention at all to him. "It is written with my blood;" at which Laura went into such fits of laughter that some of her friends asked what was the matter, and on being told, so great was their merriment that Prince Borghese left the ball in disgust and went home to bed.

Another time a fancy *quadrille* was to be danced at a ball given by the Princess Caroline at the Palais de l'Elysée.

There were to be no men in this *quadrille*, and the women, of whom there were fifteen and of whom Laura was one, were to wear peasant costumes of Tyrol. It was arranged that they were to assemble at Laura's house, and then go together to the Elysée and wait for Caroline in a room opening into a gallery, where she could meet them.

When they were all assembled in the gallery of the ground floor in Laura's *hôtel*, a secretary of Junot's came and told her that someone wanted to speak to her alone. She went into a little *salon* which was dimly lighted, and there she saw a figure in an attitude of supplication, dressed in the Tyrolese costume of the *quadrille*. As she approached to see who it was, the figure came forward and looked so unlike a woman that she was frightened and turned towards the door, when the figure rapidly advanced, seized her in its arms and embraced her, whilst a well-known voice entreated her not to call for help, saying, "But it is I! What are you afraid of?"

It was Prince Borghese.

The emperor now began to make kings, queens, and sovereign princes of the different members of his family, a process which appeared to satisfy none of them. Joseph, who was perfectly happy at his beautiful country place, Mortefontaine, was, much against his own wishes, made King of Naples, and in spite of their entreaties and remonstrances he and his wife were obliged to depart to their new kingdom, which they were entirely unfitted to rule.

Lucien, the only one of the family who had the courage and spirit to defy Napoleon, was leading a tranquil, intellectual life away from his jurisdiction. Louis, who had submitted to be separated from the woman he really loved and married to one he disliked, was now preparing, against his will, to leave France and become King of Holland, a country both he and Hortense dreaded, and the climate of which disagreed with their health and is said to have caused the death of their son.

★★★★★★

Louis Buonaparte, when visiting his sister Caroline, then at

Madame Campan's school, fell in love with Emilie de Beauharnais, a schoolfellow of his sister's; but Napoleon would not hear of the marriage, and Louis gave way.

✶✶✶✶✶✶

The arrangements for the crown and the princess, chosen to reward Jérôme for his cowardly desertion of his wife and child, were not yet made.

As to his sisters, they were as eager as their brothers were reluctant to grasp the crowns and dignities bestowed upon them.

Napoleon had made Lucca into a sovereign principality for Elisa; and Caroline, insisting on having the same rank as her sister, was created Grande Duchesse de Berg. Then Pauline, not satisfied with being Princess Borghese, wanted sovereign rank too. The emperor made her Duchess of Guastalla, but when she discovered that it was only a miserable little place, she was very angry and began again her tears and complaints. Then Caroline wanted her grand-duchy made into a little kingdom, and Elisa declared that Lucca and Piombino were only a wretched little principality. The court was rent with their quarrels and clamours, which irritated Napoleon.

"Ah *ça!*" he exclaimed, "what is the meaning of all this? Why are they not satisfied? One would really think we were dividing the inheritance of the late king, our father."

July came, and Laura was making unwilling preparations to go to Parma with her two children. They had both been ill and the weather was very hot.

One evening, about two days before the one she had fixed on for the journey, she was at home very busy giving orders and making arrangements when General Bertrand was announced, and informed her that he came by *ordre supérieur*.

"Eh! *mon Dieu!*" exclaimed she, "what is an *ordre supérieur*, and what have I to do with it?"

"The emperor sends you word not to go."

"That is much less alarming. And do you know if Junot is to come back?"

"I know nothing at all."

"Nothing positive; but what is said?"

"Nothing. You know we are as secret as Venice was. Therefore, I know nothing; but I may guess."

"Well?"

"Well, I think I may say that there is nothing but good-fortune in whatever prevents your departure."

Delighted at this reprieve, Laura resumed her attendance on Madame Mère.

Soon afterwards, when she one day accompanied her to the Tuileries, the emperor sent for her to come into an inner room where he was sitting with some of his family.

As she made her curtsey, he said with an air of suppressed amusement—

"Well, Madame Junot, one learns a good deal in travelling! See how well you curtsey now! Does not she, Joséphine? Does not she look dignified? She is not a little girl any longer, she is *Madame l'Ambassadrice*—she is *Madame*——"

And he stopped short and looked at her with a smile.

"Well," he went on, "what would you like to be called? Do you know that there are not many names which are worthy to replace that of *Madame l'Ambassadrice?*"

And he rolled out the words in a sonorous voice.

She looked at him and smiled, and he continued—

"Oh! I know you want to hear why you did not go."

"That is true, sire, and I even wanted to ask Your Majesty whether we poor women are subject to military law? because if not—"

The emperor frowned.

"Well," he asked, "what would you do?"

"I should set off, sire."

His countenance cleared.

"*Ma foi!*" he exclaimed, "I have a great mind to let you start! No, no! stay quietly at home and look after your children. The Signora Laetitia tells me they are ill. The empress says my goddaughter is the prettiest little girl in Paris; however, she cannot be prettier than my niece Laetitia. You have not told me if you are pleased with Madame Junot, Signora Laetitia," he added, turning to his mother. "And you, are you glad to be with my mother?"

Laura replied by taking the hand of Madame Mère and pressing it to her lips.

Madame Mère drew her close to her and kissed her affectionately, saying—

"She is a good child and I shall try not to let her be too dull with me."

"Yes, yes," said the emperor, pinching Laura's ear; "and above all take care she doesn't fall asleep while she watches you play *that eternal reversis and stares till she is nearly blind at David's picture, which, however, is a striking lesson to those who shed their blood in battles, for it reminds them that sovereigns are always ungrateful."*

Laura was thunderstruck, for these incautious words had been spoken by her at a party two evenings before and repeated to the emperor, who, however, seeing her embarrassment, only said in a tone at once serious and affectionate—

"They are not *all.*"

A few days after this conversation Laura was spending the evening with one of her friends when a message was brought her that her husband had arrived. She had sent away her carriage, but set off to walk home, as it was a lovely summer's night. On the way she met the carriage with Junot in it, coming to fetch her, as he was impatient to see her after more than eight months' separation.

He had no idea why he was recalled, but after a few days of suspense the emperor made him Governor of Paris, in place of Louis Buonaparte, who was just setting off for his dreary exile in Holland.

It was the position Junot longed for above all others; it was a signal triumph over his enemies, and the emperor, when announcing his appointment to that exalted post, said he was certain that the people of Paris would receive with delight their former commandant, who would fulfil his duties as worthily as before.

Immediately afterwards peace was signed with Russia, to counterbalance which came the news of a battle won by the English over the French in Calabria—a defeat that seemed greatly to depress the emperor.

Chapter 17
The War
1806-1807

Although Junot had attained so brilliant a position, he was not long in becoming dissatisfied with it. Whenever France was at war with any other country, which appeared always likely to be the case, he could only be happy if he were fighting, and he had not been two months Governor of Paris before he wanted to throw up his appointment and join the army. When it was decided that the emperor should go, his excitement became almost uncontrollable and only yielded to the representations of his wife, who pointed out to him that the interests of the emperor would be much better advanced by his remaining Governor of Paris than by his seeking personal glory on the battlefield.

Napoleon left Paris on the night of September 25, 1806. Junot dined with him, and found him as friendly and affectionate in manner as in their earlier years.

A few days after his departure Junot said to Laura, "I want you to come and dine at Raincy and follow in your *calèche* the *chasse* Ouvrard has given me leave to give there."

Laura was ready enough; she was extremely fond of the country and her beloved Bièvre had been given up, as it was now too small for their requirements and too far from Paris. It was a lovely day early in October, and the place was enchanting. The village, the woods, the old *château*, of which, however, only part was standing, the rest having been pulled down with the vandalism of the day, the avenue, the gardens, the orangery, all delighted her. Junot showed her all over the *château*, and she was especially pleased with the immense *salon*, divided by columns and statues into three parts, of which one end was devoted to billiards, the other to music. The last room they entered was a bathroom worthy of ancient Rome.

Two immense baths of granite were enclosed between granite columns with blinds of white satin. The floor was paved with black and white marble and *giallo antico*. A circular sofa covered with green velvet went along the walls, and above it were the representations in *stucco* of mythological subjects; a lamp of costly workmanship hung from the ceiling, the chimney-piece was of *verde antico*.

"*Mon Dieu!*" cried Laura, "how happy one would be in a place like this!"

Junot looked at her with a smile.

"How do you like the *château* and park?" he asked.

"It is like fairyland."

"And suppose by the stroke of a wand you became its mistress?"

"I don't know. It certainly won't happen."

"Do you wish it very much? Well, it is yours," said Junot, putting his arms round Laura and kissing her.

It was one of the happiest days of her life, and she lost no time in establishing herself there with her family, in which was now included Madame Lallemand, whom Laura had known in Portugal and whom she had found living in a forlorn way at Versailles with a companion, having lost her mother and child, and her husband being with the army.

Laura, who loved her like a sister, invited her to live with her, and she continued to do so very happily for eight years.

Junot's mother also spent a great deal of time with them, and so did several of his relations. It was a pleasant life at Raincy. Junot could easily go to Paris and return to dinner, and Laura was as happy as possible, only disturbed by Junot's longings to be with the emperor, which were constantly being aroused by the news that arrived from the army. He kept a map of Germany in his library, with red and blue markers to show the position of the French and German troops.

The army invading Germany consisted of seven army corps, under Lefèvre, Bernadotte, Ney, Lannes, Davoust, Augereau, and Soult. The reserve on the borders of Westphalia was under Mortier, and the cavalry was commanded by Murat. It was a time of intense excitement. Scarcely ever did two days pass without a letter to Junot from Duroc, Berthier, or some other friend telling of the triumphs with which the victorious army was advancing towards Berlin. Auerbach, Jena, Leipsig, were added to the list of great battles won by Buonaparte, town after town fell into his hands, and on October 26th the French Army entered the Prussian capital.

Berthier might well write that it was like magic.

At the capitulation of Erfurt alone 14,000 Prussians, including five generals and the Prince of Orange, became prisoners of war, and a hundred and twenty pieces of artillery, besides an enormous quantity of military stores, fell into the hands of the French. As the winter came on Paris became very gay. The empress returned from Mayence, where she had gone with the emperor, and received as a sovereign at the Tuileries. The Grande Duchesse de Berg entertained at the Elysée, Cambacérès at his palace, and all the ministers at their *hôtels*.

Junot and Laura began a series of entertainments by a grand *déjeuner* given to Madame Mère, who came early and drove with Laura all about the place, with which she was delighted.

Laura presented her mother-in-law to Madame Mère, and observing that that simple, excellent woman seemed affected and almost tearful during *déjeuner*, she drew her aside afterwards and asked her what was the matter.

"For you were crying, dear mother," she said.

"Yes," she replied, "but it was with joy. When I saw myself at the table with the emperor's mother, when I saw my child, my dearest son, sitting by her, I said to myself that this house contained the two happiest mothers in France, and I cried."

Madame Mère, who was warming herself by the fire, now asked what they were talking of, and on hearing, spoke most kindly to Junot's mother, telling her that Junot was like a son of her own.

The following day a hunting party was given for the Grande Duchesse de Berg, with a dinner party and music afterwards. Then the empress came down and spent the day at Raincy, making herself as charming as she well knew how to do.

But very soon the excessive friendliness of the Grande Duchesse de Berg began to cause Laura very serious misgivings. It was evident that Junot was the object of her attentions, and Caroline was just then, except the empress, who was no longer young and did not dance, the head of society in Paris.

She opened the balls at which she was present with the Governor of Paris, she received him constantly alone, and Junot was soon as much in love with her as she wished him to be, greatly to the vexation and uneasiness of his wife, who saw the danger as well as the folly of this new intrigue.

For although Napoleon saw no objection to the *liaisons* of his officers with the wives and sisters of other men, his opinion was very different when any member of his own family was in question. This affair was certain to come to his ears, and Laura was well aware that Junot was endangering not only his future prospects but her own and her children's; and it was, in fact, from this foolish and unfortunate entanglement that she always dated the decline of his prosperous career and the beginning of the misfortunes with which it closed.

The death of her mother-in-law, which took place at Raincy, was a great sorrow both to her and Junot, who was devotedly attached to his mother.

He was now constantly engaged in inspecting the troops that were being poured into Germany, and only came to Raincy to dine and sleep, sometimes even returning to Paris after dinner to spend the evening with the Princess Caroline.

The appointments made by the emperor were more and more of members of the *ancien régime*, and Laura and Junot, reading over the list in the *Moniteur* one morning at breakfast, remarked that there were a hundred names, every one of which was to be found in Morèri.

The great question which was now the centre of the court intrigues was who, in the event of the emperor's death, was to be his successor! For it was of course very possible that one of the battles of which the tidings were constantly being brought to Paris might be fatal to Napoleon, as Trafalgar had been to Nelson.

All the different parties naturally tried to gain Junot to their interests. The empress spoke to him one evening on the subject, and having first assured him that it was partly owing to her influence that he was made Governor of Paris, she brought the conversation round to the point in question, asking what would happen in the event of the emperor being killed in battle.

"The case Your Majesty mentions has been provided for by the emperor and the Senate," replied he. "King Joseph would succeed the emperor, in default of him Prince Louis, his sons, and in default of them Prince Jérôme." (Lucien and his children were excluded from the succession. Joseph had no son.)

"Ah!" she exclaimed, "don't do the French the injustice of supposing them capable of accepting as their sovereign such a prince as Jérôme Buonaparte!"

"But; *Madame,* without defending Prince Jérôme Buonaparte, who is a mere boy, I will remind Your Majesty of her grandson, who would then occupy the throne of France. That is the order of succession."

"And do you think France, bleeding with internal wounds, would risk new dangers by a regency? I am certain that there would be great opposition to my grandson, but none at all to my son Eugène."

For Joséphine's great wish had always been that Napoleon should adopt her son, to whom he was deeply attached, and who was adored by the army.

Junot hesitated. Against the personal character of Eugène de Beauharnais there was nothing to be said, but it was a subject of too great importance to trifle with, and although the conversation was a long one, he took care not to commit himself in any way.

The Princess Caroline, on the other hand, was eager to get together a party strong enough to place her husband upon the throne in the event of its becoming vacant, though of course there was never any chance of success to so absurd a project as that of making Murat the successor of Napoleon. Junot, feeling a certain uneasiness after his conversation with the empress, confided it to Cambacérès.

"Well," he said, "and what did you understand?"

"I understood perfectly well that the empress was proposing to me to make Eugène Emperor and King of Italy if our master falls. That is what I heard with both my ears."

"And what have you decided?"

"What? Can there be two opinions about it? If the emperor should fall, which God forbid! is not there the King of Naples who would succeed? We could not have a better emperor. If an evil fate struck down Napoleon, King Joseph would be my emperor."

Cambacérès looked hard at Junot, and said something about the Princess Caroline Murat; then, seeing Junot was decided in his views, changed the conversation.

But the other generals would never have borne the elevation of Murat. After the battle of Eylau (January, 1807) there was even a quarrel between the emperor and Lannes, because Napoleon, in his bulletin announcing the victory, gave the chief credit of it to Murat.

"He is a puppet and a buffoon your —— brother-in-law," exclaimed Lannes, "with a face like a poodle and plumes like a dancing-dog. Come, come! you must be laughing at us! You say he is brave! Eh! and who is not in France? He would be pointed at if he were not. Augereau and I have done our duty, and we refuse the honour of this day to your brother-in-law *His Imperial and Royal Highness the Prince Murat!* It makes one shrug one's shoulders! And here is the mania for royalty gaining on him too. Is it to tack his mantle on to yours that you want to rob us of our glory? Oh! *mon Dieu!* take it then—we have plenty of it!"

"Yes," retorted Napoleon furiously, "I will take and give glory exactly as I choose, and you may understand that it is I, and I alone, who give you your glory and success.'"

Lannes turned pale, and looking fixedly at him, replied—

"Yes, yes! because we have waded in blood upon this battlefield! You think you are great because of this Battle of Eylau, and your feathered cock of a brother-in-law comes and crows out victory. And this victory, what is it? Twelve thousand corpses lying there for you . . . . . .and you deny to me, Lannes, the justice due to me."

Startled by the noise, Duroc hastily entered, and the scene was interrupted.

The absence of sons, brothers, husbands and fathers, and the anxiety felt for their safety, did not diminish the constant gaieties that went on at Paris during the winter. Laura was passionately fond of dancing, and Junot, however tired he might be, would always wait patiently and resignedly until she was ready to go home. In all respects he was courteous and considerate for her, except in the persistent folly of his infatuation for Caroline Murat, which Laura plainly saw was being encouraged and made use of in the hope of drawing him into the party who wished to place the Grand Duke de Berg on the throne of France, an idea which Junot assured her he should never entertain.

"Murat!" he exclaimed scornfully—"Murat Emperor of the French! *Allons donc!* Why not give it to Lannes, Masséna, Oudinot, or any other general in the army? They are equally brave." About her husband's imprudent flirtation with the emperor's sister Laura would have troubled herself very little, especially as he assured her and she believed that it was never carried to any criminal lengths. But dread of the consequences when Napoleon found out what was going on filled her mind and affected her health just at the time when she was again *enceinte*, and after having nothing but girls and miscarriages ardently hoped for a son. She was so slight and the condition of her health was so little evident that she could take part in all the gaieties that were going on; amongst them in the theatricals at Malmaison in honour of the empress's *fête*, in which she and Junot, the emperor's two sisters, and several other young people were to act.

Pauline Borghese and Caroline Murat gave a great deal of trouble about their dresses, their songs, their parts, and everything else. They disturbed Laura perpetually. The Grande Duchesse de Berg would send for her before she was dressed in the morning and the Princess Borghese would come to her room before she was up, spring upon the bed and sit there, preventing her from rising while she talked and chattered about the dresses and arrangements or told her that she ought not to allow the proceedings of Caroline and Junot.

Laura persuaded Mademoiselle Mars to come occasionally and give her a lesson during the fortnight of preparation, and the admiration she had always felt for that great actress grew into enthusiasm

CAROLINE BUONAPARTE, WIFE OF MURAT, KING OF NAPLES

under the fascination of a more intimate association with her.

The *fête* at La Malmaison began early in the day with a *déjeuner*, and in the course of the afternoon the Grande Duchesse de Berg had an attack of nerves, to which she was subject, and which ended in a fainting fit. While she was unconscious a letter fell out of the corsage of her dress and was picked up by the empress, who put it into her hand, which she kept closed in her own until the princess regained her senses. Directly she became aware of this the Princess Caroline, looking at the note, exclaimed, "It is from Murat!" but her confusion and uncalled-for explanation were not necessary to enlighten Laura, who knew perfectly well who was the writer of it.

The theatricals were a brilliant success, and it was very late when those who took part in them left La Malmaison. The Grande Duchesse de Berg insisted on Junot and his wife going in her carriage, much to the disgust of Laura, who would have been far more comfortable in her own, especially as the princess had another attack on the way which delayed them, so that they did not get to Paris till three o'clock in the morning, and then Junot went into the palace with her and Laura returned alone to her *hôtel*.

In the midst of all these gaieties came the disastrous news of the death from croup of Prince Louis, the eldest son of the King of Holland. It would seem as if the death of a child under seven years old, with two brothers to succeed him, could scarcely be an irreparable loss, except perhaps to his parents. But it is nevertheless true that the death of this boy was a very important matter.

The emperor had always been exceedingly fond of him, and as long as he lived seemed tolerably resigned to his being regarded as his heir. He was so like him in appearance as to give rise to the scandalous reports circulated about Napoleon and his stepdaughter, to which no weight was attached by anyone of importance. He was a handsome and clever child, of a charming disposition, and the emperor indulged and petted him, allowing him to touch and play with anything he liked, and watching with delight when, after a review, the child put on the plumed hat he had laid down, girded on his sword, and marched up and down imitating the sound of a drum.

He would take him on his knee and caress him, saying that he would grow up to be a brave and good soldier. But for his younger brothers he cared very little, and when the nephew who had been his special favourite was gone, his thoughts and wishes turned much more strongly towards the idea of a son of his own to succeed him. Joséphine knew this too well, and the fear of the threatened divorce mingled with her grief for her grandson's death and her daughter's sorrow.

It was late in July when Napoleon returned to Paris, after an absence of ten months. The peace of Tilsit was signed but the war still raged with England. He was received in Paris with a delirium of joy such as greeted him after Marengo.

Laura's fears were well founded. Before he left Poland, where he had spent some weeks in giving his army a little rest, he had received letters informing him of the proceedings of his sister and Junot, which made all the more impression as he was singularly blind to these sort of affairs which, however well known to others, were carefully concealed from him whenever it was possible, and when the objects of the preference of either Pauline or Caroline were persons whom it was nobody's interest to injure. But Junot had plenty of enemies, who were eager to represent his conduct in the worse possible light. Accordingly, the emperor received him with such coldness and constraint that Junot asked for a private audience and explanation. He had no trouble in obtaining either and the indignation of the emperor at once broke forth.

"Sire," replied Junot, in answer to his accusations, "at Marseille I was in love with the Princess Pauline, and you were on the point of giving her to me as my wife. I loved her devotedly, but yet my conduct was that of an honourable man. I have not changed since then; I am the same man, sire, with the same devotion to Your Majesty and your family. Sire, your suspicions pain me."

The emperor looked at him fixedly and then crossing his arms with a frown walked up and down the room. "I am willing to believe what you say," he replied at last, "but you are none the less guilty of imprudence, and in your position and my sister's, imprudences are faults, if they are not worse still. What is the meaning of this way of going on? Why does the Grande Duchesse de Berg go to your box at the opera? Why does she go in your carriage? Ah! ah! you are surprised, Monsieur Junot, that I know about your affairs and those of that little fool Madame Murat."

Junot was confounded, not supposing that his folly, which, however, was well known to the police and the public, had reached the emperor's ears.

"Yes," continued Napoleon; "I know that and many other things too in which I am willing to see nothing but imprudence, but which I consider seriously wrong on your part. What is this about a carriage with your livery? Your carriage and livery have no business to be seen in the courtyard of the Grande Duchesse de Berg at two o'clock in the morning. And that you, Junot, *you* should compromise my sister! ah!" And he threw himself into an armchair. "If Murat were to know of this," he went on, after a few moments' silence, "if he were to hear all these fine stories of *chasses* at Raincy and carriages with your livery at the theatres"—and again he began to walk up and down—"yes, if he knew all I have been saying, what would he do? you would have a terrible storm to meet."

"If Murat thinks he is injured," cried Junot, "it is not long since we were equal on the battlefield or anywhere else; and I will give him any satisfaction he likes. The Cossacks may be afraid of him, but it's not so easy to frighten me, and this time I will fight with pistols."

"*Eh! pardieu!*" cried Napoleon, "that's exactly what I feared. But I have arranged all that," he went on, in a milder tone. "I have spoken to him and it is all right."

"Sire," replied Junot, "I thank you, but I must remark to Your Majesty that I do not wish for any arrangement between the Grand Duc de Berg and myself. If he thinks himself injured, which I deny that he has any right to say, we are not far away from each other, my *hôtel* is very near the Elysée."

"Yes, yes!" said the emperor, "much too near, and apropos of that, what is the meaning of all these visits that my sister pays to your wife? They have been very intimate I know, but '*autre temps, autre coutume.*' That also has been remarked upon and made a subject of gossip."

"Sire, my wife is just now very unwell and cannot go out without the greatest care. Her Imperial Highness the Grande Duchesse de Berg has been kind enough to come and see her two or three times since the spring; that is what her numerous visits amount to."

"It is not true," replied the emperor taking a large letter out of a drawer and looking over it with a frown.

Junot recognised the handwriting and exclaimed hastily, "I beg Your Majesty's pardon, but if you judge and condemn your sister and your oldest friend on the accusations of the man who wrote that letter, I cannot believe in your impartiality. Why it is not a letter, it is a copy of a police report; well, he might have respected, at any rate, Your Majesty's sister. But there are ways and means of making people circumspect and polite, which I shall employ with him."

Much disturbed, the emperor forbade Junot to challenge either Murat or the writer of the accusations. Junot swore he would fight with him first, and if he came safe out of that duel would be ready for Murat. Napoleon, at last appealing to Junot's affection as an old friend, and telling him that he would speak to him again, closed the interview.

In spite of his protestations and attempts to throw the blame upon the treachery of his enemies, it is perfectly evident that Junot had no one, and nothing but himself to thank for the consequences of his obstinate folly.

The emperor put an end to his flirtation with the Grande Duchesse de Berg by exiling him from Paris, but softened the banishment by giving him command of the army then assembling on the Spanish frontier.

Junot came to Laura in a state of violent despair, and she, although seeing the exact fulfilment of her own predictions, was generous enough not to reproach him with the senseless vanity and disregard of her entreaties which had deprived them of their splendid position; but to calm and console him, as she had nearly always the power to do, and persuade him to submit with a good grace to what was now inevitable. In reading even Laura's one-sided account of this transaction, and comparing it with the statements of other writers, it is impossible to help seeing that Napoleon, however harshly, even cruelly, he treated Junot in after years, was in this case decidedly lenient. Besides his displeasure that Junot should have taken advantage of the brilliant position he had given him, to compromise his sister, Napoleon was irritated by the extravagance both of Junot and of Laura, who, as the emperor once remarked to her, was said to spend more money on her dress than any woman in Paris.

"You have not committed a crime but a fault," said Napoleon. "It is necessary that you should leave Paris for a time in order to put a stop to the gossip about my sister and yourself I defy any man to say any more about it, in view of the confidence with which I invest you. You will go to Lisbon with supreme authority, and correspond only with me. Come, my old friend, the *bâton de maréchal* lies there."

CHAPTER 18

Fontainebleau
1807

It was the 20th of August. Junot was to set out the following day but one. He had gone out to dinner, and Laura, tired with superintending the preparations for his departure, was just going to bed, though it was only nine o'clock, when a letter was brought from Duroc saying that the Princess Royal of Wurtemberg would arrive at Raincy at nine o'clock next morning, as the emperor wished her to breakfast there and remain until seven o'clock in the evening.

After unsuccessful attempts in other quarters the Emperor Napoleon had succeeded in inducing the King of Wurtemberg to sacrifice his daughter, who was to be given to Jérôme with the kingdom of Westphalia as a reward for his cowardly desertion of his wife and child.

The Empress Catherine of Russia indignantly refused to allow a Russian grand duchess to be given to a Buonaparte, even to the emperor himself It was reserved for the Emperor of Austria and the King of Wurtemberg so far to disregard the precepts of the Catholic Church as to give their daughters to men who were already married and whose wives were still living.

The Princess Catherine felt this acutely, and although she had reluctantly yielded to her father's entreaties, her pride revolted against the upstart Jérôme, and her religious scruples assured her that, as his real wife was alive, her marriage could not be a lawful one.

Laura sent for her chef, Réchaud, one of the most celebrated cooks in Europe, who replied, "*Madame* can start for Raincy when she pleases; everything shall be ready at the time she desires."

She set off at about ten o'clock, rejoicing in the brilliant moonlight which reminded her of Spain or Italy. When she got to Raincy some of the *fourgons* of provisions had already arrived, and all night along the road carts and different conveyances were coming and going with the things required at such short notice.

Laura slept in a room adjoining the bath-room, that her own might be given up to the princess, who at nine in the morning appeared before the *château*, where Laura, dressed in white *moirée* with a long train, and a white *toque* with feathers, stood waiting to receive her, thinking all the time of Jérôme's protestations and vows of fidelity to his wife and child that morning on the plains of Estramadura.

The Princess Catherine was between nineteen and twenty years old, with an air of distinction, but not to be compared in beauty to the lovely miniature of Jérôme's discarded wife. She looked cold and haughty, and Laura at first disliked her, but her courtesy of both speech and manner soon removed this impression. It was evident that she was suffering, and Laura pitied her with all her heart. She had been separated from her German attendants according to the custom and was surrounded by those chosen by the emperor with great care, for he was exceedingly delighted and proud of this alliance.

Bessières had married her by proxy for Jérôme, which did not appear to increase the favour with which she regarded him. Bessières was one of the most polished of Napoleon's Court, but when he made some joking remark to the Princess Catherine her reply was such as to put an end to any further attempts at the infraction of the strict etiquette of a German Court.

She placed Laura on her right hand, and conversed for a long time with her and Madame Lallemand, seeming to breathe more freely when her father's minister arrived. The *déjeuner* lasted till half-past eleven, after which they followed the *chasse* in a carriage till three, in spite of the great heat. The princess lost her constraint and became more cheerful, but when she had made her *toilette* in readiness to receive Prince Jérôme, Laura observed with regret that she was very badly dressed, reflecting that as she was obliged to marry Jérôme she might as well please him.

The princess dined in the library with Laura, Madame Lallemand, and three of her ladies, Junot entertaining Bessières and the rest. The dinner was a melancholy one, and the princess with some hesitation asked Laura if she could be told of the approach of Prince Jérôme a few minutes before his arrival. A man was accordingly posted at the end of the long avenue leading to the *château*.

The princess seemed nervous and absent during dinner, after which they retired to the great drawing-room, where coffee and ices were brought, and whence the sounds of laughter and mingled voices were heard from the dining-room. Presently it was announced that Prince Jérôme would arrive in five minutes. The princess thanked Laura with a half-smile, but she became crimson and seemed hardly able to speak. However, she made an attempt to calm her agitation, called her first lady of honour and gave orders for their departure immediately after the interview. Just then Madame Lallemand hastily whispered to Laura that she had recollected that the last time she saw Jérôme was at Baltimore with his wife whom she knew very well, and had certainly better not see him now.

"Ah! *mon Dieu*! I should think so!" cried Laura, and she pushed her through one door just as Jérôme Buonaparte entered by another, followed by the officers of his household.

Jérôme was the worst looking of all the brothers. Short, ill-made, high-shouldered without either grace or distinction, he could not have made a favourable impression upon the princess who turned from the fireplace where she was standing, to meet him, and after exchanging a few words pointed to an armchair by her side. They sat for a short time talking in a formal way, and then Jérôme rising said to her:

"My brother is expecting us. I don't wish to delay any longer the pleasure he will have in making the acquaintance of the new sister I am about to give him."

The princess rose with a smile, but when he had left the room her courage gave way and she sank back fainting. Laura and the others hurried in from the billiard-room beyond the columns where they were waiting, and with *eau-de-cologne* and fresh air she revived, and after a graceful and diplomatic farewell continued her journey to Paris, where she was welcomed with the greatest delight by the emperor and his family.

Junot left Paris a few days after for his distant command, in despair at being forced to go.

In spite of her approaching confinement, Laura continued to take part in all the festivities in honour of the marriage of the King and Queen of Westphalia.

She was now so identified with the Court of Napoleon, the family of Buonaparte, and the friends of her husband, that she was necessarily very much removed from her own and her mother's early connections of the *ancien régime*, with the exception of some very intimate friends such as the Comte de Narbonne, the De Caseaux, and a few more; and she complained of the airs given themselves by some of the *grandes dames* of the *faubourg St. Germain* and their open scorn for the new court.

The *faubourg St. Germain* dressed differently from the Imperial Court; their sleeves were longer, their waists longer, and they wore their hair lower over the forehead in imitation of the Duchesse de Chevreuse, who was the leader of fashion in that set.

The Duchesse de Chevreuse and Laura had been friends as young girls, but the marriage of one with the heir of a great house of the *faubourg St. Germain*, and the other with a conspicuous member of the court and army of Napoleon, had entirely separated them for many years, notwithstanding Laura's constant affection for the Comte de Narbonne, uncle of the duchess.

The Duchesse de Chevreuse was what in those days was called "*originale*." Nobody could imagine why she had not lost her reputation over and over again, so many and so strange were her escapades. She presented to her father-in-law, the Duc de Luynes, a Swedish gentleman covered with crosses and orders, whom she declared to be of high rank, and whom the duke received accordingly, but who turned out to be a well-known beggar of Saint Roch whom she had dressed up for the purpose.

She made a bet that she would stop one of her brothers at eleven o'clock at night in the Palais Royal, and carried out her intention, to his great indignation.

Another time, happening to hear that an old retired grocer was expecting his niece by the diligence from Rouen, she presented herself the day before in her place, making up some story to account for her early arrival, and so captivating her supposed uncle that he wanted to write and get a dispensation from Rome to marry her.

There was no real harm in the things she did, and for what was said of her she cared not at all, her motto which she had engraved upon everything was—

Bien faire et laisser dire.

One great cause for the enmity of Napoleon towards her is said to have been her refusal to become his mistress; and it seems hardly consistent with the political opinions she professed that she should have consented to be *dame du palais* to the empress. She was by far the most important person at the Hôtel de Luynes, where her husband was a nonentity in the house and her mother-in-law was entirely devoted to her. The Duchesse de Luynes who had been Mademoiselle de Laval Montmorency, was very pretty as a young girl, but her beauty having been destroyed by smallpox, she took no trouble nor interest in dress or the pursuits usual for women in those days; but made her chief happiness in horses and riding; galloping about the country, jumping hedges and ditches in a manner very unusual at that time in France.

Her husband, on the other hand, was always half asleep, in fact, so strange was the contrast between them that her brother, the Duc de Laval, on being told of the prospect of her first confinement exclaimed, "*Pardieu!* I am very glad to hear it; for that proves to me two things of which I was not sure: that my sister is a woman and my brother-in-law a man." The Duchesse de Luynes liked Laura, and at a great ball given at her *hôtel*, she said to her half reproachfully—

"You will see here many old faces that will recall to you the traditions in which you were brought up."

Later in the evening, as she walked about with her old friend the Comte de Narbonne, Laura, in speaking of Louis XVIII. called him "Comte de Lille," the name by which the Bonapartists designated that king.

The old count looked at her with a smile and observed, "I don't think you would have spoken of him so ten years ago."

After the departure of her husband, Laura was at Raincy, intending to stay there till her confinement was over, when she received an invitation which amounted to an order from the emperor to go to Fontainebleau for some days.

Not choosing to risk her child being born in the palace, she took a house in the town, and joined as well as she could in the amusements that were going on.

Nothing could be more magnificent than the court had now become. The luxury that surrounded the emperor, the splendour of the *fêtes* that perpetually took place, the excitement of the intrigues and love affairs for which Fontainebleau was so much better adapted than the Tuileries, would have been attractive and delightful enough to Laura at any other time. But just now her health of course prevented her enjoyment to a great extent, and Junot's letters from Portugal were full of complaints of the miseries of the part in which he now was; a horrible desert of which the delicious climate and scenery of Cintra and Estramadura could give no idea.

These autumn days at Fontainebleau being unusually warm and bright were generally spent by the court in the forest, where, after hunting or shooting, there was a *déjeuner*. Both men and women wore a uniform, with much more gold, silver, velvet, and feathers than could possibly be suitable for sporting purposes. Pauline Borghese and Caroline Murat were at the head of all this gaiety and dissipation.

A young Genoese *lectrice* in the household of the Grande Duchesse de Berg was just now the favourite mistress of the emperor, whom she had even persuaded to allow her to be presented at court, which no *lectrice* had ever thought of asking. He was also persecuting with his attentions another of the ladies of the household of one of his sisters, who was nearly always at the hunting parties and *déjeuners*; but who invariably declined his advances. So infatuated were many of the courtiers with regard to Napoleon, that it was remarked that she must be in love with someone else or she could not have resisted him.

The Buonaparte family encouraged these *liaisons* out of spite to Joséphine, who with all her efforts to appear happy and tranquil, could not conceal the anxiety and depression for which she had only too much cause. Besides all the other incidents which contributed to destroy her happiness, the air was full of rumours of the divorce she dreaded and which her husband's family were eager to accomplish.

"Madame Junot," she said one day to Laura, "they will not be satisfied until they have driven me from the throne of France. They are pitiless for me." It was of Pauline, Caroline, and Jérôme that she was speaking.

Duroc was also her enemy, but with more justice. On one occasion when Laura remonstrated with him on his hardheartedness, pointing out the sadness and melancholy of Joséphine, Duroc pointed to Hortense and his own wife who happened to be together at the end of the room, and said—

"Look there! it is heaven and hell! Who did it? Did not she? No! I have no pity!"

One morning everyone learnt with surprise that the emperor had left for Italy during the night, and it afterwards transpired that one of the objects of his journey was to meet Lucien, whom he had not seen since the marriage which had caused the quarrel between them some years since.

Napoleon was well aware that of all his brothers Lucien was the only one who possessed talents and character to understand and assist him, and being resolved to make another attempt to win him over, he had given him a rendezvous at Mantua.

Lucien arrived from Rome with two friends, to whom he remarked as he got out of the carriage that very likely he would go back that evening. Then he went into the long gallery where Napoleon was waiting for him, attended by Eugène de Beauharnais, Murat, Duroc, and several others. At a sign from the emperor they all left the gallery, and the brothers were alone.

"Well, Lucien," said Napoleon, after the first greetings were over; "what are your plans? Will you walk in my way now?"

"I have no plans," replied Lucien. "As to walking in Your Majesty's way, what does that mean? "

Napoleon took up a large map of Europe that lay upon a table, unrolled it, and threw it before his brother.

"Choose any kingdom you like," he exclaimed, "and on my word, as your brother and emperor, I will give it to you and keep you in it, for now I walk over the heads of all the kings in Europe. Do you hear?"

Then looking earnestly at Lucien, he continued—

"Lucien, you may share in my power. You have only to follow the path I point out to establish and maintain the most magnificent system a man has ever conceived. But to carry it out I must be seconded, and that I cannot be by my own family. You and Joseph are the only ones of my brothers who can be of any use to me. Louis is pig-headed and Jérôme a boy without any capacity. It is on you that all my hopes are fixed. Will you realise them?"

"Before we go any further," said Lucien, "I must warn you that I am not changed, my principles are the same as in 1799 and 1803. I am here with Napoleon the emperor what I was in my *curule* chair on the 18 *brumaire*. It is for you to say if you care to go on."

The interview was long and stormy. Neither would yield. In vain did Napoleon use entreaties, bribes, and threats to win over the only other member of his family whose talents and character rose above mediocrity.

The idea of separating from his wife Lucien rejected with scorn, to the offer of the grand-duchy of Tuscany or the kingdom of Italy he replied that, were he to accept either, he would rule according to his own ideas; the French troops must leave his territories, his government should be the blessing, not the curse of his people, and he ended by saying "I will not be your *prefect*."

Napoleon raged and stormed, but it was of no avail. Of all his family Lucien had always been the only one he could not bully or browbeat, and he valued him all the more for that reason. Consequently, the more clearly, he saw that this time he was not going to have his own way the more furious he became.

Flinging his watch on to the ground he stamped upon it exclaiming that thus he would break the wills of all who opposed him, and telling Lucien that he was the head of the family and he ought to obey

LUCIEN BUONAPARTE, PRINCE OF CANINO.

him as if he were his father.

"I am not your subject," exclaimed Lucien angrily; "and if you think you are going to impose your iron yoke upon me, you are mistaken, for I will never put my head under it. Remember what I told you at La Malmaison."

During a discussion at La Malmaison Lucien, who disapproved of the Empire then to be proclaimed, had said to Napoleon: "This Empire which you raise by force and maintain by violence will someday be destroyed by force and violence, and you with it."

There was a long silence, the two brothers stood opposite each other; between them was the table on which lay unrolled the map of Europe. Napoleon, pale with anger, regained his composure with an effort and said—

"Think of what I have said, Lucien. *La nuit porte conseil.* Tomorrow I hope in the interests of Europe and in your own that you will be more reasonable."

They shook hands and parted. Lucien went straight downstairs, got into the carriage where his friends waited for him, and returned to Rome. The next time the brothers met the prediction of Lucien had been fulfilled.

Laura's much desired son was born at Paris; the emperor and empress consented to be his godparents. It is needless to say that he was named Napoleon.

As soon as her health was sufficiently re-established Laura resumed her part in the whirl of gaieties which went on during the winter of 1807-8, and to which were now added numbers of children's parties. It was indeed a contrast to the secluded convent life of the little French girls of two generations since; this succession of balls, masquerades, &c., in which their mothers rivalled each other in the costly and picturesque costumes of the little ones. The heads of this childish society were the two little sons of the King of Holland and Achille Murat, a troublesome, spoilt boy, who thought himself a great personage and gave himself airs accordingly, which the events of a few years later probably caused him to relinquish.

Neither Junot nor Laura had changed their lavish expenditure and the emperor, irritated at the reports of extravagance he heard, sent for Laura to the Tuileries one morning, told her that he had decided to take Raincy off their hands, and desired her to write to Junot and tell him so. Struck with dismay, she represented that Junot did not wish to give it up, but Napoleon replied that it was all nonsense, Junot could hunt and shoot just as well in the forest of Saint-Germain, and the expense of keeping up Raincy was more than he could afford.

"Besides," he added, "I have given Neuilly to the Princess Pauline, and I want a place for myself close to Paris. Raincy will just suit me, so there is an end of it."

The emperor had by no means given up all hope of gaining Lucien, and between 1807 and 1809 various negotiations went on between them.

The first concerned a proposition of the emperor to marry the eldest daughter of Lucien to the Prince of the Asturias, who had requested Napoleon to find him a wife in his family. As the aim of the emperor was to place his relations upon all the thrones in Europe, the proposal to make his niece the future Queen of Spain suited him very well. Charlotte Buonaparte was a pretty, high-spirited girl of fifteen, the eldest daughter of Lucien by his first wife,

The emperor sent M. Campi, an old friend of the Buonaparte family, to Lucien with this proposal and the offer of the kingdom of Naples for himself, saying he had some other plan for Joseph. He went so far as to promise that if Lucien would accept the crown of Naples he should govern exactly as he chose without any interference, and this time the negotiations between the brothers might probably have been successful if Napoleon had not brought into the matter an unlucky instance of that petty malice which formed so incongruous a part of his disposition.

Whoever has studied the life and character of Buonaparte can hardly fail to be struck with the strange way in which the meanest and most contemptible suspicions, jealousies, and rancour were mingled with his great qualities, stupendous talents, and vast ambition. He carried his prying, suspicious tyranny into all kinds of little domestic details which might well have been considered beneath his notice; and in this case the disappointment of an ambitious plan for Lucien and the irritation caused by finding that he had one brother who refused to be his slave gave him a personal spite against that brother's wife and an obstinate resolution to separate them which seems as surprising as it was undignified. For there was no shadow of complaint against Lucien's wife. She made him perfectly happy, ruled her household and children admirably, shared all her husband's pursuits, entertained with hospitality and good taste.

Continuing his attempts to ruin Lucien's happiness as he had done that of Louis and Jérôme, he made the crown of Naples depend upon his brother's consenting to separate from his wife; to whom he offered the duchy of Parma and two of her daughters, the rest of the children to belong to Lucien! On this condition he would acknowledge her as his sister-in-law! It was certainly an improvement upon the pension of 60,000 *francs* he allowed Jérôme's discarded wife, but as she cared much more to be the wife of Lucien than the sister-in-law of Napoleon, and he regarded the offer as an insult, there was nothing more to be said. It is true that Madame Lucien, in a fit of morbid, overstrained generosity, sat up all night tormenting herself, and then went to her husband with a letter in her hand saying that for her children's sake she had written to the emperor to accept the sacrifice.

"Where is the letter?" asked Lucien, and when she gave it to him, he tore it up and threw it on the ground.

"*Mon ami! mon ami!*" exclaimed his wife with tears; "would you deprive your children of a crown?"

"Would I deprive them of their mother to give them a crown?" replied he, and after a few more observations on her part he declared again that nothing would induce him to separate from her, and ended by saying—

"If my brother wishes to give me back his friendship, let him do so without conditions, especially such cruel ones. We will be always together, *mon amie*, never separated."

The proposals were declined accordingly, except that one regarding Charlotte, which at first was accepted and preparations made for her departure. But at the last moment Lucien's heart failed him; he said that he could not send his child unprotected into a court of which he well knew the corruption and vice. Therefore, the marriage was broken off. Charlotte afterwards married Prince Gabrielli in whose great Roman palace her life was sufficiently splendid and probably much happier.

The time had now arrived when the emperor began to create a new *noblesse*, and not liking, for various reasons, to take old French titles, he named his new nobles after the victories and incidents in his wars—

One day when Laura was in the *pavilion de Flore* at the Tuileries, waiting for Madame Mère, she met Savary, who was greatly excited and asked her to embrace him, as he had great news for her. This she declined to do, observing when he told her that he was made a duke—

"That is indeed a surprising thing, but no reason at all why I should embrace you."

"And I am called Duc de Rovigo," he added, walking up and down the room, looking so puffed out with delight that he might have risen in the air like a balloon.

"Well, what have I to do with your title and your ridiculous name?" said Laura, who could not endure him; but at that moment Rapp came up and informed her that she was Duchesse d'Abrantès, "the prettiest name *of the troop*." At dinner she sat next Madame Lannes, whose husband had been created Duc de Montebello, and who remarked to her that they two had the prettiest of the new titles.

"Well, *Madame la Duchesse-gouverneuse*," said the emperor when he saw her, "how do you like your name of Abrantès? Junot will be pleased, for it is a mark of my approbation." (See note following.)

✶✶✶✶✶✶

Without money, without transport, without ammunition sufficient for a general action ... Junot led a raw army through the mountains of Portugal on the most difficult and dangerous line by which that country can be invaded.... Trusting to the rapidity of his movements and the renown of the French arms, he made his way through Lower Beira and suddenly appeared in the town of Abrantes ... pressed forward and reached Lisbon in time to see the fleet having the royal family on board clearing the mouth of the Tagus. (Napier's *Peninsular War*, vol. i.)

✶✶✶✶✶✶

"And what will they say in your *salons* of the *faubourg St. Germain*? They will be rather surprised at the reinforcement I send them."

Laura had still to fulfil the social duties belonging to the wife of the Governor of Paris, of which post Junot had not been deprived, and the various misunderstandings between him and the emperor involved interviews and discussions between herself and the latter.

"Do you know," said Caroline Murat one day after one of these long audiences; "that you are perhaps the only woman who can say she has been an hour and a half with the emperor?—unless there were reasons of quite a different kind," she added, laughing. "For I suppose there are not?"

"If there were," replied Laura, laughing too, "I should say nothing about it either way. I should keep silence. I should think that would be the best way to play that part, which, however, I imagine the emperor would make a very difficult one."

"What part?"

"That of favourite."

And Laura went on to relate to Caroline how a short time since at a masked ball she was standing close to the emperor and one of his favourites, both of whom she recognised and overheard.

"Prrrrr!" exclaimed Napoleon, in reply to some speech of his companion's, "there you are, like all the rest, with your imbecile reveries. The heart! What the devil do you think the heart is? A part of yourself through which a large vein carries the blood quickly when you run. Well! What is that? See what your romantic arrangements lead to. There is a poor girl who has believed the soft speeches of Murat and is probably ready to drown herself. What do you think of that, eh?" There was a low sound of sobs, and the emperor said impatiently—

"*Ma chère*, I do not like even to see Joséphine cry, and she is the woman I love above all others. Therefore, you are losing your time. *Adieu.* I came to the masked ball to amuse myself." And he walked away and joined Rapp and Duroc.

Junot sent his wife for her New Year's present a diamond clasp, a magnificent set of sapphires, another of rubies, and a third of aquamarines, a string of pearls, and a box of uncut diamonds which he advised her to have cut in Brussels, Antwerp, or Holland. For her uncle, the Abbé de Comnenus, he sent a box made of jasper with a cameo of the Pope.

He desired her to get another country house instead of Raincy, and as the summer approached, she took one at Neuilly with an orangery, theatre or *salle de spectacle*, conservatories, shady gardens and park, and a trellised walk along a canal. There she took up her abode for the hot weather with her children and Madame Lallemand. They drove into Paris after dinner to the theatres, rode in the mornings, had private theatricals, and amused themselves extremely.

Napoleon's attack upon Portugal, the friend of England, was only a preliminary to the French troops being poured into Spain. Ferdinand, Prince of the Asturias, whose young wife had died under strong suspicions of poison, ascribed her death to the machinations of his mother, who hated her, and to Manuel Godoy, the paramour of the queen, who had been raised to be Prime Minister of Spain. Ferdinand, who had been passionately attached to his wife, was for some time nearly mad with grief. His father, Charles IV., a weak old man, was governed by the queen and Godoy.

The court and royal family were rent by the dissensions between the king and queen and their son, who wrote secretly to Napoleon asking him to interfere and to give him a wife of the Buonaparte family. This was the beginning of the disastrous war between France and Spain, in which the English, having taken part, the victorious career of France began to be checked and the vast designs of Buonaparte defeated.

Early in September the emperor returned to Paris, after having spent most of the summer at Bayonne occupying himself with the affairs of what we are now accustomed to call the Peninsular War.

For the first time Laura observed a difference in the feeling of the Parisians for Napoleon, and a certain uneasiness caused by the fact of no news whatever having been received from the army in Portugal for two months. She herself was in great anxiety, and wrote to the emperor on his return, begging him to give her the assurance that Junot was alive.

Several days passed without any answer, and then Cambacérès came to tell her that she need have no fear for Junot, but that the emperor thought it strange that she should permit herself to question him on a political matter. Not in the least afraid of Napoleon, but not feeling reassured, Laura wrote to him again to ask for an audience.

There was going to be a great ball at the Hôtel-de-Ville in honour of Napoleon, and as wife of the governor she would be obliged to receive the guests. This she resolved not to do unless she were certain that nothing had happened to her husband.

The emperor appointed an audience at Saint-Cloud at nine in the evening. When she entered, he was standing at the open door leading from his room into the garden, looking absent and disturbed. He turned as she entered.

"Why cannot you believe what I tell you?" he began angrily. "Your husband is all right. What is the meaning of your *jérémiades de femmelette?*"

"Sire, I have felt reassured since Your Majesty was good enough to say I might be; but in the position I now hold I have come to ask Your Majesty to excuse me from appearing at the Hôtel-de-Ville tomorrow."

"Eh! what do you say? Not go to the Hôtel-de-Ville! And why not?"

"Because I am afraid something has happened to Junot, sire. I beg Your Majesty's pardon, but I have no news of Junot, and, I repeat, Your Majesty has none either. I will not risk receiving the news of his death in the middle of a ball."

The emperor looked angrily at her, but he restrained himself, shrugged his shoulders, and said—

"I have told you that your husband is quite well—why will you not believe me? I can't give you proofs, but I give you my word."

"Of course, that is enough for me, sire; but I cannot write it in a circular to the four thousand people who will be at the ball, and who will think it very strange to see me there when I have such cause for uneasiness."

"And why should four thousand people know you are uneasy?" exclaimed Napoleon in a terrible voice, coming forward impetuously. "There is the result of all your *conciliabules de salon* and gossiping with my enemies. You declaim against me and attack all that I do. There is the Prussian Minister, who is a friend of yours, and who was speaking lately in your house of my tyranny to his king. I am a very cruel tyrant, certainly!

"If their great Frederick that they make such a noise about had had to punish all the disloyalty I have, he would have done a good deal more; and, after all, Glogaw and Kustrin will be much better guarded by my troops than by the Prussians, who have no reason to be proud of the way they defended them."

It was about the tenth time since her return from Portugal that Napoleon had repeated to Laura things said in her *salon*, which had always been true until now. This, however, she felt certain to be incorrect, and she said so. Then, as she took her leave, he observed—

"I forbid you to repeat what I have said to you. Remember, and take care to obey me, or you will have to reckon with me!"

"I will obey you, sire, not from fear of your anger, but because I don't wish to blush before vanquished foreigners in betraying our internal dissensions," and she repeated her desire not to be present at the ball at the Hôtel-de-Ville, where her position would be immediately after the empress, considering the reports about the Army of Portugal.

"And what reports are there?" asked Napoleon in a voice that half frightened her, so that she replied in a low voice—

"They say the army is lost, that Junot has been forced to capitulate like Dupont, and that the English have carried him prisoner to Brazil."

"It is false—false, I tell you!" he exclaimed, swearing and striking the table with such violence that a heap of papers fell to the ground. "Junot capitulate like Dupont!—it is all a lie; but precisely *because* they say so you ought to go to the *Hôtel-de-Ville*. You *must* go there, even if you were ill—you understand. It is my will. Goodnight."

CHAPTER 19
Meeting With Junot
1808-1810

In obedience to the emperor Laura appeared at the Hôtel-de-Ville. The *fête*, although as magnificent as usual, was most melancholy, for the minds of all present were full of misgivings. A decree had already authorised the levy of 80,000 conscripts for the war, and it was proposed that 80,000 more—these being lads of eighteen, or even younger—should be raised to defend the coasts. The Parisians seemed under a kind of stupor. The emperor knew well that the absence of Laura would give confirmation to the reports circulating about the fate of Junot and his army; and probably that the Battle of Vimeiro had already been fought, in which Junot had been beaten and the army only escaped destruction by the victorious movements of Sir Arthur Wellesley having been checked by Sir Harry Burrard.

★★★★★★

Sir Harry Burrard was recalled and tried for his mistaken conduct in this matter. Junot's mismanagement of this campaign enraged Napoleon, who is said to have exclaimed, "I was going to send Junot before a Council of War, when fortunately, the English tried their generals and saved me the pain of punishing an old friend." (*Peninsular War,* Napier, vol. i.)

★★★★★★

With a sinking heart and an aching head Laura received the guests at the *Hôtel-de-Ville.* The empress, in deepest dejection, appeared only for a short time, and left before supper, at which Laura entertained the most distinguished of the French and foreign society in a separate room. The Treaty of Cintra, concluded by Junot with the English after the defeat of Vimeiro, caused great dissatisfaction in England as being too favourable to France, and did not mitigate the wrath of Napoleon.

The troops were to return to France and Junot with them. He had been leading his usual dissipated life in Portugal, and a paragraph in an English paper was shown to Laura which remarked that they had taken General Junot's *seraglio* again. About those affairs of her husband's, however, she did not trouble herself but made a hurried journey to La Rochelle to meet him, for the emperor would not allow him to come to Paris.

Taking with her the wife of Junot's first *aide-de-camp*, two maids, and three well-armed men, for Poitou was just then infested by a band of robbers, she travelled night and day, enjoying the journey with her usual light-hearted, adventurous spirits. The two maids, to one of whom, who had lived with her mother, she was much attached, were in the first carriage, with an armed *valet-de-chambre* riding in front of them; in the second she herself and her friend, Madame de Grandsaigne, with the other two men on the box.

On the second night they were travelling along the banks of the Loire between Blois and Tours, and Laura was lying back, dreamily watching the river glistening in the moonlight, when suddenly the carriage stopped. Putting her head out of the window she saw the postilion of the other carriage dead drunk in the road.

"*Mon Dieu!*" she exclaimed, "what has become of the other *calèche?*"

There was a general commotion.

"Instead of abusing your comrade, who cannot hear you," she said to one of the postilions, "take one of the horses and push on to see what has become of them." And ordering the other one to "arrange the drunken man as well as he could upon one of the horses," for she feared to leave him in the dangerous state of the country, they drove on, and soon arrived at the next stage, where before the inn door stood the *calèche* with the *valet-de-chambre* standing by it and the two women fast asleep inside—which, as she remarked, was fortunate for them, as if they had been awake they would certainly have screamed,, frightened the horses, and been upset into the Loire.

At eight o'clock in the morning they arrived at La Rochelle, where Laura found Junot waiting for her in a charming apartment which had been lent them, and her bath and breakfast prepared.

They sent for their three children at once. Junot had never seen the boy with whose birth he was so delighted, and they spent a month with their parents at La Rochelle, during which Junot made a hurried journey to meet the emperor at Angoulême, coming back depressed by his reception of him. Then he returned to Spain, and Laura, with her children, took the road back to Paris.

The passing love affairs of Junot in Spain had caused no estrangement between him and Laura, who told him of the newspaper report and laughed at him. "Did you love them all?" she asked.

"No, no; none of them."

"I don't believe a word of it."

"Yes, by my faith! Well, then, I swear it by yourself: I tell you truly, when I have been distracted from the straight path, my dear Laura, I deplore the cause more than I cared for the object."

To one of the ladies in question, the Countess da Ega, who had been very much talked of with Junot, Laura afterwards showed much attention and kindness in Paris to prove that the gossip and scandal of society did not affect her.

The emperor was now in Spain, and besides the hitherto unsuccessful campaign in that country there were disquieting rumours both from Italy and Germany. Napoleon had ordered Junot to take Saragossa, which he was accordingly besieging. His letters to Laura were tinged with melancholy and foreboding; the horrors of the siege he declared to be insupportable to anyone who had not a heart of stone. He had a friend in Saragossa for whose safety he feared; and the old wounds in his head, especially a scar which went along the left cheek close to the eye, were causing him great suffering.

On January 18th he wrote to her that only the thought of her and his children prevented his committing suicide. The coldness and displeasure of the emperor preyed upon his mind, and his good fortune seemed to have deserted him. When he entered Portugal, power, honour, fame, even a throne were within his view (*Peninsular War*, Napier, vol. i.)—but now—!

Laura was anxious and unhappy, her greatest consolation being the constant society of her brother, who was now in Paris, and to whose unchanging affection and friendship she always turned.

Society was as brilliant as ever this winter, but there was a difference; an undercurrent of depression and uncertainty seemed to be universally felt. The emperor had returned from Spain, and was again at the Tuileries. He sent Lannes to supersede Junot in the chief command at Saragossa, which naturally did not improve the spirits of the latter, and the exile of Madame Récamier, for whom Junot entertained an enthusiastic admiration, was a new grief to him.

Napoleon had disliked Madame de Stael, declared she was his enemy, and exiled her from France; but if he found her talents or intrigues in political matters troublesome, the same could not be said of Madame Récamier, whose popularity and celebrity arose from her extraordinary beauty and sweetness of temper, but who was content to amuse herself in a harmless way, doing all the good in her power, but possessing neither talents nor inclination for politics or conspiracies.

The ostensible reason for this act of tyranny was a visit she had paid to her unlucky friend Madame de Stael, at Coppet, on the Lake of Geneva; but in the opinion of Laura, Junot, and many others, it was to be attributed to the following cause. Fouché who, of all the villainous characters produced and fostered by the revolution, was one of the most cruel, remorseless, time-serving, and influential, and who was now Minister of Police, came to see Madame Récamier, and suggested to her that she should become one of the ladies of honour of the empress—a proposal which she declined, saying that the household of the empress was already filled up, and that she did not desire any post in it, preferring her liberty, and already possessing all she wanted.

For, as the wife of a rich banker much older than herself and eager to give her whatever she fancied, universally admired and respected, with numbers of friends and a blameless reputation, she was perfectly contented with her lot, and listened with reluctance to Fouché's assurances that the emperor was in need of a friend like herself, who would understand and sympathise with him, in whom he could confide, and with whom he could associate intimately, but as a friend only, without love, jealousy, or any agitating elements to disturb the calmness of their intercourse.

Madame Récamier heard all this with incredulity, for she knew

Madame Récamier

perfectly well that this was not at all the sort of friend the emperor ever wanted; but the insidious and frequent representations of Fouche, and his suggestions as to the untold good her influence might produce, began to take effect upon her mind.

One day, in the midst of all this, she was invited to *déjeuner* with one of the sisters of Napoleon, who, after leading the conversation on to the subject of the charm of a blameless friendship between a man and woman of good reputation, observed that such a friendship was what the emperor required but was impossible to find amongst the women with whom he was surrounded. She then asked Madame Récamier if she cared for the theatres, and which she preferred, and on being told the *Comédie Française*, exclaimed—

"Oh, well! then you must accept my box there. It is on the ground floor; you can go there without making any *toilette*; promise me you will."

Madame Récamier unsuspiciously promised, and the next morning, to her astonishment, received a letter from the Administration of the Comédie Française informing her that the princess had ordered free entry to be given to her into her box, and that whenever she, Madame Récamier, was there nobody else was to be admitted without the special permission of the said Madame Récamier.

This box from which everyone else was to be excluded was exactly opposite that of the emperor, and when Madame Récamier read this singular letter, she at once perceived the meaning of it all. She expressed her thanks for the offer, but took care never to avail herself of it.

It is difficult to see why Laura in after life, when speaking of Sir William Napier's *History of the Peninsular War*, should express such indignation at the remarks of that officer concerning Junot, for all he says of him is confirmed by her own writings. He describes him as by no means cruel, but sensual, dissipated, passionate, and extravagant, at the same time capricious and generous. Of considerable natural capacity, but lacking study and mental discipline, indolent in business, prompt and brave in action, arrogant and quick to give offence, but ready to forget an injury; at one moment a great man, the next below mediocrity.

He was, however, less greedy and rapacious than Lannes, Soult, and many of the other French generals, who stole the treasures even of convents, cut valuable pictures out of their frames and carried them off even when they did not allow them to be wantonly destroyed by their officers and men. (Peninsular War, Napier, vol. i.) Junot declared he bought and paid for all the jewels he sent Laura which caused so much gossip and commotion in Paris.

A new campaign was now beginning in Germany in which he was eager to join, and Laura, alarmed by his letters and anxious about his health, asked Duroc to obtain an audience for her with the emperor. Her intimate acquaintance with that general had excited the suspicions of Napoleon, who observed to him that he seemed to take a great interest in Madame Junot, and asked him upon his honour whether he were not in love with her.

Duroc explained that there was only a strong and sincere friendship between them, and the emperor, taking several pinches of snuff, looked at him fixedly and said, after a few moments' reflections. "Well, it is very singular!"

"It is his ideas that are very singular," observed Laura, to whom Duroc repeated this conversation; "and I believe he is always astonished when he finds any good in a woman." Duroc also told her that the emperor had said that he had had a great affection for Madame Permon, and took a paternal interest in herself, but that he wished she would not make her intimate friends amongst his enemies, or wear so many and such large diamonds. He promised, however, that Junot should be recalled in a fortnight, and Bessières sent in his place.

When he arrived, both he and Laura were shocked at the change in each other. Junot, however, after three weeks of a course of baths was much better, and ready to go to Germany, where the emperor had given him a secondary command. Before he started, he saw Laura set off for the Pyrenees, under the care of Madame Lallemand and M. de Cherval, two of her intimate friends.

She performed the journey lying at full length in the carriage, and was met at Bordeaux by her brother-in-law, M. de Geouffre, to whom she seemed at death's door. But after a week at Cauterêts she was much better, and spent the rest of her sojourn in that enchanting place, then so little known, in excursions amongst the mountains, upon which she was never tired of watching the sun setting over the ice and snow, and all those marvellous effects of which the ever-changing panorama only presents itself to us in scenery like this. With her intense love of beauty, Laura entered thoroughly into the fascination of the place, although her mind was disturbed by the letters from Germany, where the war raged more furiously than ever.

Victory after victory again attended the armies of Napoleon, but at last even the Parisians began to murmur at the fearful slaughter and the numbers of families thrown into mourning. The Battles of Essling and Wagram were especially remarkable for their horrible carnage, and the French troops overran Friulia, Styria, Istria, and the Vorarlberg.

Lannes was killed in the Battle of Essling, and in spite of their recent coolness Junot and Laura mourned for him sincerely. It was observed that the emperor only regretted the loss of the valuable general, and cared nothing about that of the old friend. Lannes had always been too little of a courtier and too much of an old comrade to please him.

The emperor returned in triumph to Paris, and Junot also; but a kind of depression and constraint seemed to pervade society. Politics were only talked of in whispers, but everyone's mind was secretly occupied with the prospect of the divorce of the emperor. His family for the most part were delighted, but the people murmured, for Joséphine was popular, and her evident unhappiness excited their compassion.

The manner in which Napoleon made public his intention was as heartless as usual.

There was to be a grand ball on the 2nd of December at the *Hôtel-de-Ville*, of which the courtyard was to be turned into an immense ballroom.

It was the business of Count Frochot to arrange everything, and Laura gave him the list of the ladies she had chosen to help her to receive the empress. She went to the *Hôtel-de-Ville* in good time, and found them waiting for her in the *salon*, leading on to the staircase. Presently the Count de Ségur came in, and taking her aside into a recess in a window, told her that they were not to wait for the empress, who would only be received by Count Frochot.

"Why is this?" asked Laura, looking thunderstruck.

"I don't know—or rather I *do* know, but I must not say"; and he proceeded to explain that Napoleon did not wish Laura to say that this order came from him.

"*Eh! bonté divine!*" exclaimed she; "then what am I to say? Am I to go and tell *ces dames* that it is a caprice of my own that prevents my going to meet the empress?"

"Why not? Pretty women may do as they like—"

Laura shrugged her shoulders angrily.

"If only M. de Narbonne were here—" she began, thinking aloud.

"Ah! *nous y voilà!* and why? Don't you think I can give you as good advice as Narbonne? What little good sense he possesses he got from me."

"Then that is why you have so little left," retorted she. "Come, try to help me a little, I don't know what to do."

He then explained that the empress would arrive alone with her ladies, and the Queen of Naples would accompany the emperor. While they were discussing the matter Junot and Count Frochot came in and were horrified to hear what was to be done. However, Junot observed that there was no time to be lost, if such were the emperor's orders Laura and the other ladies of the court must go at once to the *salle du Trône*; and immediately afterwards the sound of drums announced the arrival of the empress. Junot, in defiance of the emperor's anger, remained to receive her, and entered the *salle du Trône* with her and her ladies of honour.

Joséphine had never looked more graceful and charming than on this evening as she passed through the long gallery and anterooms, and entered the *salle du Trône*. With a melancholy smile, trembling lips, and eyes full of tears, she seated herself for the last time upon the throne, casting a piteous look at Laura, who could hardly restrain herself from throwing herself at her feet and expressing her sympathy.

Only a few days before, as they walked in the conservatory at La Malmaison, Joséphine had poured her grief and despair into Laura's ears, and Laura's child, who was playing about them, seeing her godmother in tears, had thrown her arms round her exclaiming, "*Je ne veux pas que tu pleures.*"

That evening was intolerable to Laura. The emperor arrived soon after and walked rapidly into the *salle du Trône* accompanied by Caroline and Jérôme. All the time he remained he was evidently trying to make himself agreeable, and to seem at ease, but there was an evident constraint about him, and the gloom and depression became more and more diffused as the hours went by. The heat was overpowering, and Laura, oppressed by that as well as by the agitation she could not overcome, fainted.

Junot, dreadfully alarmed, caught her in his arms, and carried her into Count Frochot's room, where he tore open her dress, cutting strings and laces wherever he found them to enable her to breathe. Then, wrapping her in a shawl, he put her into her carriage and took her home. Thus, ended this disastrous evening.

In his haste he left her diamonds behind, and forgot all about them. They were, however, safely returned next morning.

The divorce was declared soon afterwards, and the deepest compassion was felt for Joséphine. Laura went often to La Malmaison, which was thronged with the friends and sympathisers of Joséphine, many of whom, especially amongst the lower classes of the people, declared that Napoleon's star was on the wane.

His quarrel with Pius VII. was the next proceeding which caused still further indignation. He seized the States of the Church, and made the Pope prisoner; in which iniquitous acts he was vehemently opposed by Lucien who, utterly disgusted at the tyranny and oppression practised by his brother, resolved to abandon Europe for ever, and sailed for America with his family. But the vessel was taken by the English, and Lucien and his family carried prisoners to Malta, whence in the spring they were transferred to England. There he bought an estate near Worcester, and, installing himself and his family, he passed the time of his detention peacefully and happily enough with his studies, surrounded by a large circle of friends, both French and English.

Since the horrors of the Revolution had come to an end Paris had never been so *triste* as during the winter of 1810. The emperor wished it to be gay, but his orders and attempts were unsuccessful. There was no head to society; the Queen of Naples, who tried to assume that position, was disliked; people said that her parties were dull, the only amusement to be got at them being to see how ridiculous she made herself by her singing, which was atrocious.

All the royal and exalted personages, of whom there were many at Paris that year, went down to La Malmaison to pay their respects to Joséphine, to whom their visits, though partly painful, were at the same time a consolation.

Just after the carnival, Junot was ordered to Spain, and Laura resolved to accompany him.

It was bitterly cold when they left Paris and travelled straight to Bordeaux, where they only stopped for a few hours to see Laura's old friend, Madame de Caseaux.

When they were girls together Laura Permon was, after her father's death, left without fortune, whereas Laura de Caseaux was an heiress. But some years afterwards the de Caseaux had lost nearly everything, had left Paris, and were now living at Bordeaux. Laura de Caseaux, afterwards Madame de Castarèdi, was then in Paris, where she had gone to try to recover some part of their fortune, and Laura, now rich and influential, had received her early friend with affection, introduced her to persons in power, and helped her in every way she could. As her business could not be finished by the time Junot and his wife left, Laura de Caseaux was not able to travel with them, and they had not even the chance of letting Madame de Caseaux, who was now an invalid, know that they were coming.

As Laura knocked at her door, all the memories of her childhood, of her mother, of days gone by, seemed to rise to her heart; the exile and hardships before her increased her emotion, she entered her old friend's room in silence, and kneeling down by her, buried her face on her breast and began to cry. Madame de Caseaux was deeply affected; she kept Laura to dine and stay with her until nine o'clock, when Junot came to fetch her, as they had to start at two o'clock in the morning. Madame de Caseaux had not seen Junot since his wedding-day, and was touched by the gentleness and kindness with which he talked to her as he knelt down and kissed her hand, while Laura was sitting on a cushion at the feet of her old friend, who was playing with her hair as she used to do in days of old.

With blessings mingled with lamentations over the perils and hardships before Laura, Madame de Caseaux took leave of her, and she returned to her hotel.

She could not sleep, the wind was bitter and violent, she felt suffocated when the window was shut and frozen when it was open, and was thankful when at two o'clock the travelling carriage came to the door.

On the way to Bayonne they read in some newspapers, given them by their bankers at Bordeaux, the announcement of the coming marriage of the emperor with the Archduchess Marie-Louise of Austria. He had had some idea of an alliance with a Russian Grand duchess, but the Empress Catherine indignantly declared that she would rather throw her into the Neva than give her to Napoleon.

They reached Bayonne in twenty hours, and there began the real hardships of the new life Laura had chosen. It was four o'clock in the morning when they arrived there, and, exhausted with fatigue, she threw herself upon her bed and fell asleep in her riding-habit, for she had ridden the last part of the way.

Presently she was awakened by Junot standing by her, embracing her, and saying, "*Adieu.*"

"*Comment? adieu?*" she exclaimed.

"Yes, I have found orders here that I must be at Burgos by the 15th, so I have no time to lose, I must go. You will rejoin me by the next convoy, for which I shall leave an escort of 500 men of the Neufchâtel battalion; they are trusty men, don't be afraid."

"I don't want them. I did not come to Spain to travel comfortably with a convoy. I will go with you."

Junot looked at her with surprise and emotion.

"You will go with me now—without resting yourself?"

"At once."

"Then I will start later; lie down again and sleep for a few hours."

"Not a moment."

"But you are suffering, Laura."

"No."

"Your hands are burning. I cannot let you set off now. The advanced guard and the first division went yesterday; I can wait a few hours without failing in my duty; we will start at noon."

"I assure you that you distress me by all this; let us go now. Tell M. Prevôt to have my horse saddled, and understand that I *never* wish to cause you the least delay; that is settled."

Sometimes riding, sometimes driving in a *calèche* drawn by mules, sometimes walking, they journeyed along, the continual passing of the French troops having made the road tolerably safe.

One evening, about four days after they had entered Spain, Laura and Junot, tired with much walking, got into their *calèche*, where he fell asleep and she sat gazing out into the twilight as they wound up a mountain road, on each side of which were strewn fallen rocks half-covered with moss, and amongst them stunted oaks of weird, distorted shapes grew singly or in clumps and copses. Suddenly, struck by the singular form of one that hung over the road, she leaned out to look at it and her forehead came in contact with the foot of a corpse, which hung naked and bleeding, from its branches—there were four of them. Her cry of horror awoke Junot, who ordered the postilion to hurry forward, and assured Laura that the sight she had seen was inevitable in war.

"Child," he said, when she reproached him with his indifference, "if you cannot bear such sights, you should not go to the war."

CHAPTER 20

Continuing Hardships and Dangers
1811

Ney and the two Suchets were then in Spain; the elder Suchet had been made marshal, and had received other tokens of the approbation of the emperor, who was especially delighted at the taking of Taragona and other strong places, and most anxious for the submission of Spain to the rule of his brother Joseph, whom, much against his will, he had proclaimed king of that country.

Some of the officers gave a ball in honour of Laura, who, however, did not enjoy it, as the rooms were miserably small, the atmosphere suffocating, and the whole thing a failure.

The next day there was a *Te Deum* sung in the magnificent cathedral of Burgos, to which Laura went dressed in the Spanish costume which she often wore. Her knowledge of the language was the greatest advantage to her, and she exerted herself to mitigate in every way she could the horrors that went on around her; amongst others, she saved the lives of three young Spaniards whom the French were about to shoot for defending their old father when he was attacked by eleven French soldiers. It was a horrible war. The progress of the French armies was marked by plunder, destruction, and bloodshed, while the Spaniards, justly infuriated against the ruthless invaders of their country, retaliated with their proverbial cruelty, by deeds of savage ferocity.

The sombre picturesqueness of Burgos preyed upon Laura's spirits, and she was delighted when they were ordered to Valladolid, where they were lodged in the palace of Charles V., in the great square of the city. Shortly after their arrival, Junot received orders from Paris to go and take the town of Astorga, which filled him with delight. Just as he was starting an order came from Madrid that he should replace Marshal Ney at Salamanca; at which he threw himself into a violent passion, jumping up, and sitting down again, crumpling up the letter, dashing it upon the floor, and swearing vigorously all the time.

"What do you throw yourself into this state for?" asked Laura, taking hold of his hand. "You can't follow these contradictory orders. Write to Marshal Ney, you will see what he will say."

Junot, immediately pacified, seized her hands, kissed them again and again, received his answer in two days, and left Valladolid for Astorga on the 14th of April. He arrived there on the 17th, and narrowly escaped a shot aimed at him by some hidden foe as he approached the town. It capitulated on the 23rd, and Laura received a letter from him written on the 24th, telling her that during the siege he had another narrow escape, a ball having just missed his left eye. The attempted assassination reminded Laura of a similar attempt made in Portugal, when a man after persistently trying to force himself into Junot's presence, was arrested and found to be armed with a dagger and knife, with which he confessed his intention of murdering him.

Junot gave him twenty *piastres*, dismissing him, in spite of the remonstrances of his officers, with the remark, "Get away, and don't let your blood be on my head. Tell your companions I will give a hundred *piastres* to the one who will replace you."

On the day the prisoners from Astorga were to arrive M. Magnien invited Laura to drive with him to see them enter Valladolid. The day was lovely, and at first, she enjoyed herself, but presently she was startled by the sound of firing not far off, and inquired what it meant.

M. Magnien turned to the *chef de bataillon* in command of the convoy, who replied carelessly—

"Oh, it's nothing. Some of those rascals pretend they can't walk, but I have given orders to settle that. *Parbleu!* yes, lame indeed! If we listened to them, they would all be lame, and find their legs again to rejoin Don Julian when we had passed on."

Laura thought at first, she could not have understood rightly, but the *chef de bataillon* clearly explained that they were shooting all the prisoners who could not walk, lest they should join the guerilla chief, Don Julian. At that moment Laura saw two men fall.

"Let us go back! let us go back!" she cried. "*Mon Dieu! quelle horreur!*"

"Do you think our prisoners are better treated on the pontoons of Cadix, Madame?" asked the French officer scornfully. "My brother died there, poor fellow."

It was not safe to go outside the walls of Valladolid on account of the guerilla troops that were all over the country. Laura narrowly escaped being taken by a band of them, who approached in the disguise of peasants, while she was walking one day in a garden close to the gates—a favourite resort of hers, as it had both shade and water.

In the life of perils and privations to which she had condemned herself, and which she bore with the utmost courage and cheerfulness, Laura's greatest pleasures were the frequent letters she received from France, with the news of her children whom she had left under the care of a sister of Junot, and also of all that passed in the political and social world. The election of Bernadotte to be King of Sweden under the name of Charles XIII., the marriage of the Emperor Napoleon with the Archduchess Marie-Louise, with all the festivities and gossip attending those events, were of course intensely interesting to her.

Few cared much about the cold, ungifted, uninteresting girl who had taken Joséphine's place; except Buonaparte himself. Delighted at the success of his plans and immensely flattered by the alliance, he fell violently in love with her after his Oriental fashion, would allow her to receive no man but himself and her old music-master, objecting even to the man who came to wind up the clock, but in all other respects showing her boundless indulgence.

One of the few sympathetic anecdotes about that unsympathetic personage is this:—

Berthier, who had been made Prince de Neufchatel, was sent to Vienna to fetch her. After the ceremony of marriage by proxy, in which her uncle, the Archduke Charles, stood for Napoleon, the day for her departure arrived. Berthier went to her apartments, according to the usual etiquette, to accompany her to the carriage. When he entered the room where she was waiting for him he found her crying bitterly, and looking round, she explained, amidst tears and sobs, that it was not only that she had to part from her own family, but even to leave behind her the pets and favourite possessions of her girlhood—the drawings done by her sisters and uncle, the tapestry worked by her mother, the carpet given her by somebody else, her birds, her parrot, and worst of all her little dog, who, shut up in another room, was barking loudly.

Her father would not allow her to take them, as Buonaparte disliked Joséphine's pet dogs. Such a beginning of her married life certainly did not seem encouraging, and Berthier, telling the young empress that the journey was put off for two hours, retired, and after an interview with her father, the Emperor Francis II., returned to escort her on her way. Her progress through France was a succession of festivities and rejoicings. The emperor met her at Compiègne, the first days of her married life were passed at St. Cloud and then at Paris, where, Napoleon taking her by the hand, led her on to a balcony of the Tuileries and presented her to the people, while a thousand voices shouted, "*Vive l'Empereur! Vive l'Impératrice!*"

When they re-entered the room. Napoleon, telling her that he must pay her for the happiness she had given him, led her through a long, dark passage to a door, on the other side of which a dog was heard scratching. On opening it, the empress beheld her faithful dog, her parrot and other birds, and perceived that the room was furnished with all the familiar possessions she had left in Vienna—pictures, tapestry, armchairs, and everything else. She threw herself into the emperor's arms to thank him and the crowd, seeing this through the window, redoubled their cheers.

One day, after the courier from Paris had come in, Laura, noticing that Junot looked disturbed, asked what was the matter.

"We have a general commander-in-chief of the Army of Portugal," he replied, with a constrained smile. "The emperor does not think Ney or I are capable of leading our troops—"

"I hope it is not Davoust or Bessières!" said Laura.

"No," replied Junot, "I can't complain of the choice that has been made. It is Masséna. He is our senior. I only hope to God that Ney will get on with him as well as I shall."

Much as Junot disliked being under the orders of another in the country where he had been almost like a king, there was nothing to be done but to obey the commands of the emperor, and he went to receive Masséna, now Prince d'Essling, with due respect.

"*Monsieur le Maréchal*," he said, "my wife will be charmed to do the honours of the palace of Charles V., where we hope you will be comfortable."

"What! Madame Junot is at Valladolid!" exclaimed Masséna in evident perturbation.

"Certainly."

"But in that case," said Masséna, after an instant's reflection, "it will be *impossible* for me to live in the palace—*cela ne se peut pas!*"

"If you are afraid of not having room enough," replied Junot in a tone of pique, "it is for my wife and me to give place to you. Are you not our chief?"

"*Mon Dieu!* it is not that!" cried Masséna, "it is not that at all—it is because—"

There was, in fact, in the *calèche* of Masséna a young woman by whom, in spite of his age, he was accompanied, much to the derision of the other officers, one of whom, General Heblé, offered mingled complaints and apologies to Laura.

"*Mais que voulez-vous?* have not we all tried our utmost to prevent him, at his age, causing such a scandal? Nothing will persuade him! Oh! I could tell you the most extraordinary things about him!"

Masséna was, after Soult, one of the greatest of Napoleon's generals, but his courage and military talents were counterbalanced by the rapacity he sought to conceal under an apparent simplicity of manner, and the open immorality which even amongst his comrades was considered scandalous and ridiculous, especially as one of the young officers who witnessed it was his own son.

Matters were arranged somehow, and Masséna took up his abode in the palace, where he lived on very friendly terms with Junot and Laura. Often in the morning he would come in and sit with them, pouring out his complaints of the various persons who displeased him, but especially of Ney, whose vain, boastful nature rendered him furious at being placed under the orders of anyone.

One day Masséna brought a letter he had just received from the emperor, written with his own hand in those flattering terms which Napoleon knew so well how to use, and which were almost irresistible to his followers.

"But how do you suppose," grumbled Masséna, "that I can do any good work with a man like that Michel Ney, who treats me as if I were in my dotage and does not even listen when I speak to him? I tell you, Junot, that I have been on the point of giving him a blow in the face, and then, of course, offering him reparation with my sword—for the sword of the old soldier of Genoa is still sharp." (Masséna was Italian, being a native of Nice.)

In fact, much of the disaster which overtook the French army in the Peninsula may be attributed to the miserable jealousies and quarrels between the generals.

"You will see," exclaimed Masséna to Junot another time, "that that boaster will make all our operations fail by his obstinacy and idiotic vanity."

Masséna was very fond of Laura, and would often come to her rooms to sit and talk with her while she worked at the layette she was obliged to prepare, for she was again *enceinte*.

The old general took the greatest interest in the letters she received about her children, especially those written by Joséphine, her eldest daughter, whom he proposed to betroth to his eldest son. Junot

and Laura consented to this plan, but the marriage never took place, owing to the death of the *fiancé*.

A violent quarrel soon took place between Masséna and Ney, who wrote the former a letter of defiance from Salamanca, saying, among other things:

> I am a Duke and Marshal of the Empire as well as you. You say you are Commander of the Army of Portugal—I know it too well. Therefore, when you order Michel Ney to lead his troops against the enemy, you will see how he will obey you. But when it pleases you to upset the *état-major* of the army . . . . I shall no more attend to your orders than I fear your threats.

"You see it is impossible to do anything with that fellow!" cried Masséna as he walked up and down Laura's *salon* in a towering rage. The engineer officer whom he had twice sent to Ney with orders that he should conduct the siege of Ciudad-Rodrigo had twice been sent back by that general, and now declined to go again. "Am I Commander-in-chief *en peinture?*" he cried. "I say that this young man shall direct the siege, and, by the great devil in hell, Monsieur Ney shall bend his knee to my will, or my name is not Masséna." And he prepared to go himself to Ciudad-Rodrigo to enforce his orders, taking the officer in question with him.

Junot and his wife also went to Salamanca, where he too became involved in a dispute with Masséna, which, however, Laura succeeded in calming before both of them set out with the troops for Ciudad-Rodrigo, which the English under Wellington were coming up to succour.

Laura was left at Salamanca in no very pleasant position. The French were, of course, loathed by the inhabitants, who, after the departure of Masséna and his troops, thronged the churches to pray for their defeat and the victory of the English. Sometimes a peal of bells was heard, and on Laura's asking her landlady the reason, the Spaniard answered, with a flash of hatred in her eyes—

"For Ciudad-Rodrigo, *señora*, for Ciudad-Rodrigo! and for the English!"

After Junot had left, Laura wished to move from her lodgings near the gate of the city to a very pretty little house belonging to the Marquis de la Scala. On her asking whether he would let it to her, he replied that he should have pleasure in doing so if she would give him time to put some furniture into it, as nearly the whole of his had been stolen by a French general. Laura found on inquiring that the general in question had carried off a great deal of it to the siege of Ciudad-Rodrigo, including mattresses and all the kitchen apparatus, and had sent the rest in his *fourgons* to France! One day Laura was playing with the daughter of her landlady, a child of three years old, of whom she was very fond, when a chain round the baby's neck caught on something and jerked out a knife that was attached to it.

"Don't take it!" cried the child; "it is to kill a Frenchman with!"

About eleven o'clock one evening, as she was sitting with five or six other people, suddenly in a pause of the conversation Laura heard a feeble cry. She sent her *valet-de-chambre* to know what it was and he returned saying he could see nothing. Presently the cries recommenced, and Laura, calling for a light to be brought, and accompanied by the officers who were present, went into the courtyard and, guided by the cries, found on the cushions of her *calèche* a baby of about a week old, carefully dressed, with a note containing the following words:

"A mother in despair confides to Your Excellency what is most precious to her—her child—her daughter, who ought to be the support and consolation of her old age. It is known in Salamanca that your Excellency loves to do good and that you are about to become a mother. I dare to hope that you will adopt my poor child, and not abandon her. May her father feel the shame of the step he forces me to take."

This was in Spanish and well written, probably by some Spanish girl seduced and deserted by a Frenchman. Laura and her maid passed most of the night in feeding and looking after the child, and in the morning, she sent for a French *émigré* priest, who was now almost a naturalised Spaniard, to baptise it, giving it the names of Laura Juana Marie. She bought it everything necessary, and gave a sum of money to the *corregidor* to be paid for its maintenance until it was three years old, when it was to be sent to her in France.

"You see," she observed, "that we French are not so bad. I am saving the life of your countrywoman's child, which she deserted."

The *corregidor* looked at her with a glance of hostility.

"You may well save the life of one Spaniard when your husband kills so many," was his answer.

A few days afterwards she received the following letter from her husband:—

I have received your letter, dear Laura, and you may be sure that

I recognised *mon amie* in her good deed to the poor little orphan.... I send you letters from France. I think there are some with news of our children; write to me what they are doing. Here we have great heat, a great deal of firing, and very little to eat. Vegetables, above all, are scarce, which is very disagreeable. I can swallow as much dust as I like, and two sunstrokes have scorched my ears and face. I hope I shall be a little less ugly when I see you again, but colour does not matter. They say Notre Dame de Laurette was as black as the devil, but she inspired many passions. My Laura is dark, but she is as pretty as the prettiest *blondes*.

The walls of Ciudad-Rodrigo are falling *bien doucement*. We have enemies who disquiet us *bien doucement*. When we attack we do it *bien doucement*. Our soldiers, *par exemple*, do not sleep *bien doucement*; as to the provisions, they arrive *bien doucement*. I wish the *ordonnateur* (M. Michaud) did not arrive so *doucement*. When we dispute it is not always *bien doucement*. It would be all the same to me, my Laura, if I could *be bien doucement* with you, and after the fatigues of the day could rest *bien doucement* by your side. *Adieu*, my Laura; I embrace you a thousand times, and am going to the advanced posts to see the faces of the English nearer.

Ton ami &c. (The letter is, of course, in the second person singular.)

Ciudad-Rodrigo fell shortly afterwards, and Junot sent a hurried letter to Laura to be ready, as he would call for her at Salamanca; they were going on to Ledesma, which she heard with regret, as she found much to interest her at Salamanca besides being tolerably comfortable there, whereas Ledesma was an Arabic town perched on a sugarloaf-shaped rock surrounded by a burning, arid plain.

Before they left Salamanca, Laura had a narrow escape from being taken by the guerilla chief, Don Julian, who gave more trouble to the French than anyone in the Spanish Army. He had set his heart on taking Laura prisoner; and, having been warned of this, she discontinued her drives into the country, only going into an avenue just outside the gate of Zamora which led up a little hill so near the walls of the town that it was considered perfectly safe. One hot July evening Laura, whose health was, of course, now delicate, feeling unusually tired, went home early, while M. Magnien, who had been driving with her, walked on slowly to the top of the hill in question, from which he saw a man of suspicious appearance, with a red feather in his hat, mounted upon a mule, appear on the summit of a hill opposite. Presently another appeared, then a third, and when they numbered five M. Magnien turned and ran towards the town, pursued by the guerillas up to the gate, where, breathless and exhausted, he threw himself into the arms of the official who came out at that moment. Don Julian had been told the hour of Laura's drive, and made preparations accordingly, which were only frustrated by her going home early.

After being two months at Ledesma, Laura accompanied her husband to San-Felices-el-Grande, a much worse place of abode. At Ledesma she had lodged in the best house the place afforded, which she declared not to be nearly so good as a gardener's cottage in France; but it was a palace compared to her lodging at San-Felices-el-Grande.

The place was a miserable, ruined village among barren mountains many leagues from a town; the house she occupied was a damp, dark hole, in which she lay upon a bed of sickness in a room lighted only by a small window high up in the wall, and with a floor of beaten earth, on which was arranged the portable furniture she had in the *fourgon*, which alone made it habitable.

They had at first hoped that she would be able to get to Madrid if she could not return to France for her confinement. But the escort which would have been sufficient for her safety could not now be spared from Junot's *corps d'armée*, so that her only hope was that she might reach Lisbon, or even Coimbra, in time. The soldiers were dying of dysentery and nostalgia in alarming numbers. Junot and Ney, with whom he had an interview, both took a gloomy view of the present and future prospects of the war, and Laura grew worse and worse. Often when she awoke in the night from a feverish, troubled sleep she saw her husband standing by her bed crying or looking at her with mournful eyes.

"And I cannot get you out of this desert!" he would exclaim, kissing her hands and shedding tears of despair. "There is no possibility—none! I would rather send in my resignation and go with you myself than trust you to a miserable escort which would be defeated by the first band of guerillas posted in the woods of Matilla to lie in wait for you. But I cannot! I cannot without dishonour! for the guns will be at work again directly, and I cannot turn my back on the enemy."

The French were now besieging Almeida, which was the first fortress over the Portuguese border as Ciudad-Rodrigo was the last on the Spanish side.

Wellington was drawing on the army of Masséna into a country deserted and devastated by its inhabitants.

One evening after sunset there was a loud explosion, and the house shook violently. "What is it?" cried Laura in terror. "Is it an earthquake? Another danger in this dreadful country."

There was another detonation, and again the house rocked.

"It is the fortress!" was the general cry; and Junot with the rest rushed out to a ruined tower at the end of the village, on a rising ground. Presently he returned.

"Almeida is on fire!" he said; "it is a splendid sight! You must see it, Laura; they shall carry you."

Laura was accordingly carried up into the tower, from whence she looked out towards the beleaguered town.

The autumn wind howled among the mountains, the sky overhead was dark, but the horizon was a lurid mass of fire and from time to time sheets of flame shot up and despairing cries seemed to be borne upon the gale.

Almeida had been blown up—it appeared accidentally. A gunner leaving his post having fired his last shot at random towards the town, it fell into the open door of the arsenal of the *château* before which a hundred workmen were making cartridges. Besides this forty families were blown into the air, as the townspeople had crowded there for refuge. With the explosion the walls seemed to open, and the French troops poured in through the breaches.

Guns and mutilated bodies were flung out to an incredible distance, and when, the next day, Junot returned from visiting the scene of the catastrophe he was pale with horror at the frightful spectacle he had witnessed.

Meantime Laura's position, already terrible enough, became still more alarming as the day drew near on which her husband would be obliged to leave her.

Junot was nearly out of his mind at the idea of leaving his wife on the eve of her confinement alone, with an insufficient guard, and without the necessaries of life, in a hostile country. Masséna also declared it was out of the question. "Let us take the duchess with us," he said.

"It's impossible," replied Junot. "She will be confined in six weeks, and she is almost dying now."

"Well, then we must send her to Salamanca; that is the nearest and best place."

"No, no," said Junot gloomily, "I won't leave my wife at Salamanca; the town is not safe from a surprise. If she went there, Don Julian would be there too in three days."

"The devil! you are right, my poor Junot. But what are we to do?"

"It is horrible," said Junot at last, "but there is only one place where I can leave my wife without dying of anxiety, and that is Ciudad-Rodrigo."

"Ciudad-Rodrigo!"

"Yes! Ciudad-Rodrigo. Behind its ramparts at least she would be safe from Don Julian, and I should find her again and my child."

"But think, there is not a house in Ciudad-Rodrigo with a whole roof; the town is full of holes and ruins, and almost without inhabitants."

"Solitude is better than the society of the guerillas. The duchess shall go to Ciudad-Rodrigo, only I will ask of you as a favour to let her have one hundred and fifty men of the battalion of Neufchatel for her guard, and when she can join us, they will be her escort."

Masséna agreed, and two days afterwards the 8th Army Corps, with Junot in command, began its march into Portugal, and Laura, after a heart-breaking parting with her husband, set out with her escort for Ciudad-Rodrigo. One great consolation she had—the Baron Thomières, who had been *aide-de-camp* to Lannes and was now a general of brigade, had brought his wife with him to Spain. They were quartered three leagues off, but General Thomières found it difficult to take his wife with him, and Laura hearing of her, implored Junot to persuade Madame Thomières to stay with her, which he succeeded in doing, and Laura found in her a gentle, sympathetic friend, to whom she soon became deeply attached.

General Cacault was in command at Ciudad-Rodrigo, but his garrison consisted of sick or wounded soldiers left behind by Masséna, who as they wandered amongst the ruined streets, looked more fit to be in hospital than to defend a fortress.

As she entered this gloomy place, situated in the most dreary and desolate part of the Peninsula, Laura felt her heart sink. The dark, narrow streets, the deserted, half-demolished houses, the sickly, melancholy figures of her countrymen, and the not particularly friendly reception of General Cacault were not calculated to reassure her.

The general awaited her at the door of the house which had been prepared for her reception; that is to say, the roof had been made water-tight. It was the best in the town, and its rather out-of-the-way position had saved it from destruction. The canon to whom it belonged had fled with most of the townspeople.

Laura had a room arranged on the first floor—the ground floor was so dark as to be impossible—and made the house as comfortable as could be managed for herself and Madame Thomières. For the first month they received no news whatever of Junot or the army, and their days passed in dreary monotony and intense anxiety, aggravated by the conduct of General Cacault, from whom they received neither the courtesy of a gentleman nor yet the sympathy and consideration which would have been shown by a man with any kindness of heart for women in their terrible position.

Regardless of Laura's approaching confinement, he would enlarge in her presence upon the dangers which surrounded her, upon the plague or malignant fever which was expected to break out on account of the numbers of bodies buried nearly at the surface of the ground and continually disinterred by the half wild dogs about, and of the perils she ran from Don Julian, who knew of her presence there and was resolved on her capture. He complained of the additional risk to himself and his garrison; and when, with a contemptuous look, she retorted that the two hundred men she had brought were so much more fit to defend the place than his wretched garrison as to counterbalance any danger she might bring upon him, he altered his ground and said that so many additional mouths made him short of provisions.

Another great anxiety weighed upon Laura—what was she to do for a nurse for herself and the child about to be born? She had recently heard that the wife of a French officer who was confined during the absence of the doctor of the regiment had been obliged to have a Spanish midwife, who had murdered her and her infant. In the midst of her dilemma she heard with delight that her housekeeper, Madame Heldt, another maid, and the wet-nurse who had nursed her last child had arrived safely at Salamanca and were coming to her.

This nurse was a Burgundian, devotedly attached to Laura. She had been to inquire after her at her house in Paris, and on hearing that she was again *enceinte* had written begging to be allowed to come out to her, saying that she would be confined a little before her and would be ready to take Laura's baby, only stipulating that her husband should come with her; to which Laura joyfully agreed, ordering that no expense should be spared in making her journey easy and comfortable.

They arrived about the middle of October, and the faithful Rose shed tears when she saw the rooms and the food to which Laura was reduced. Rose gave birth to a daughter, who only lived a few weeks, about three weeks before the confinement of her mistress.

News arrived after a time of the defeat of the French at Busaco, to which, when he announced it. General Cacault added that Masséna's army was reported to be destroyed; but when Laura uttered a cry of horror, he assured her that the *corps d'armée* of the Duc d'Abrantès had not been engaged.

At last Laura was told that a ragged Portuguese wanted to speak to her, who on being admitted gave her a letter from Junot. He had written three letters and given them to three peasants, promising that she would give 1,200 *reals* for each that arrived safely.

Delighted with her letter, Laura was as gay and happy as a child for a day. Then it occurred to her that this letter was a month old and that many calamities might have happened since it was written. Also, that it was two months since she had heard from her children. Her fears and sorrows returned, with sleepless nights, anxious days with nothing to do but write and work at the clothes for the child so soon to be born, and a growing presentiment that it would not live or that she would not live or that she would not survive its birth amid so many perils and privations. For it was almost impossible to get food.

The French had ravaged and destroyed all the gardens, so that there were neither fruit nor vegetables, the meat was almost uneatable, poultry scarcely ever obtainable, eggs scarce and if procurable costing two *francs* each—nothing good but bread. Expecting to be at some civilised place for her confinement, Laura had foolishly brought none of the medicines required, and nothing could be brought into the town because the country was overrun by Don Julian and his bands.

There was another Frenchwoman at Ciudad-Rodrigo, the wife of an officer, and the three did their best to console one another.

At last Laura gave birth to a son after great danger and suffering, during which Madame Thomières nursed her with untiring devotion, The child was born on the 15th of November, and on the 24th General Cacault sent to say that he was so short of provisions that he must beg the Duchesse d'Abrantès and her escort to go on to Salamanca. Laura would have preferred to wait for three weeks after her confinement, but under these circumstances she at once consented to start, and decided to ride, which she said would be better than being shaken about on those horrible roads. She set forth accordingly with Madame Thomières, her child, her suite and guard, taking with them also a few invalids who were glad of the escort.

The recent passage of a large body of French troops had made the road rather safer, but still any who lagged behind the convoy were sure to be fired on. Joyfully she left Ciudad-Rodrigo, but the way lay through the notoriously dangerous forest of Matilla. As the convoy drew near the woods the road became so frightfully bad, owing to the roots and stumps of trees, holes, ruts, and other impediments, that the carts and light carriages were so violently shaken as to cause Laura to be seriously frightened about the safety of her child, especially as it was getting dark. She herself was on horseback and could not see where her horse trod, so she beheld with satisfaction the soldiers strike a light and make torches of a kind of dry fern which grew all over the ground they were traversing.

Not so General Coin, a friendly and excellent man, who had shown Laura much kindness, and who, indignant at the conduct of General Cacault, had volunteered to go with her to Salamanca, and now rode at the head of the convoy.

Before he could prevent it the whole convoy from one end to another was lighted up just as they were getting into the woods where the guerillas were likely to be concealed. Suddenly they heard the sound of horses galloping, there was a cry of "Halt!" and in a moment, they were surrounded by a troop of armed men. In the noise and tumult Laura believed they were lost, when the French tongue and the voice of a friend assured her of their safety.

General Thiebault, then commanding at Salamanca, had been told that the Duchesse d'Abrantès, with a very insufficient escort, was on her way to that city from Ciudad-Rodrigo, and had also received information that Don Julian, at the head of a formidable troop, intended to attack the convoy in the woods of Matilla. Therefore, he posted columns of soldiers along the road, and himself hurried forward to meet and protect her.

The rest of the journey was consequently performed in safety, and on the following day they arrived at Salamanca. General Thiebault had done his utmost to find suitable lodgings for the duchess and Madame Thomières, and Laura, after the horrors of the last few months, was thankful to find herself back in Salamanca and delighted with the apartments provided for herself and her suite in the house formerly occupied by Marshal Ney, where her *salon* soon became the resort of what French society was to be found in the place. They met in the evenings and amused themselves with chess, music, and conversation.

Laura received letters from her children and from Junot, for whom she waited contentedly in Salamanca, although warned that the town was not entirely safe and it might be necessary to retire into the fortress, as a great part of the garrison must be taken to reinforce Masséna, consequently she had better go to Valladolid, where Bessières commanded. General Thiebault, who greatly admired her courage and firmness, remarks in his *Memoirs* that this was another proof of those qualities in the duchess, for nearly all the officials were leaving.

In January, 1811, Junot received a severe wound in the face. The French Army was then at Rio Mayor, in full retreat before Wellington, from whom Junot received the following letter:—

Au Quartier-Général,
27 Janvier, 1811.

Monsieur,—J'ai appris avec grande peine que vous avez été blessè, et je vous prie de me faire savoir si je puis vous envoyer quelque chose qui puisse remédier à votre blessure ou accélérer votre rétablissement.

"Je ne sais pas si vous avez eu des nouvelles de Madame la Duchesse. Elle est accouchée a CiudadRodrigo et a été à Salamanque pour aller en France dans les premiers jours de ce mois.

J'ai l'honneur d'etre. Monsieur, votre très-obeissant serviteur,

Wellington.

À Monsieur,
Monsieur le Duc d'Abrantès.

Junot and his wife appreciated the courtesy of this letter and of a message sent by the Duke of Wellington to Don Julian that he was not in the habit of making war upon women, and was much displeased that the Duchesse d'Abrantès should have suffered any inconvenience or danger from him.

It was not until the end of April that Junot could return to Salamanca to fetch Laura and his son. He wished the child to be called Rodrigo, but the associations with that name were too terrible for Laura, and she named him Alfred.

They left Salamanca for Toro almost immediately, accompanied by Madame Thomières. When Laura found the inns impossible, she often used to ask to be taken in at some convent in the town, where she was always received with much hospitality. The Spanish nuns at that time had much more liberty than in most countries. They could receive strangers, and Laura remarks that they were only nominally cloistered, and that in Salamanca and Valladolid she knew convents from the *mi-*

rador (gallery or loggia round the top of the house), of which signals had been seen to be given and received.

On one occasion she was lodged at a convent, Junot remaining at the inn. She had a charming little room, the floor covered with Indian matting, a dado of Spanish leather round the walls, mirrors with silver frames, fine linen, mattresses of silk and wool, comfortable armchairs, curtained bed, and other comforts and luxuries.

The nuns came in, two or three at a time, to see her, and one very pretty young sister, contriving to speak to her alone, asked her in Spanish after Duroc. Laura told her that he was married, which seemed to interest but not to grieve her. Still it was evident that there had been some romance between them while Duroc was in Spain, and Laura afterwards discovered that the emperor had made love to the sister of this little nun.

Toro was, as Laura remarked, one of the most singular places she had occasion to inhabit during the whole campaign—a most picturesque old town in the province of Leon, perched upon a steep, conical hill like a sugar-loaf, with numbers of convents, but also a more lively, populous appearance than she expected. Around it stretched a fertile plain watered by the Douro.

The weather was delicious, and she longed to ride all over the country, which was out of the question because of the brigands. But by doubling the guard on the bridge and posting soldiers in a little wood or thicket not far off, it was considered to be safe enough to have a gallop within a certain distance.

Junot had gone away for a day or two when one morning Laura and Madame Thomières, having driven down the steep streets to the bottom of the town, mounted their horses and crossed the bridge over the river which flowed at the foot of the mountains. They were in high spirits and rode carelessly along talking and laughing without thinking where they were going until, after a rapid gallop, they pulled up close to the wood where the piquet was usually posted.

"How delicious this is!" exclaimed Madame Thomières; "what a pity we can't enjoy it without trembling with fear of the brigands!"

Laura started, for she recollected that that morning there was no piquet in the wood. She had forgotten to give the order.

On hearing this Madame Thomières said they had better go back, but Laura, looking longingly at the blue sky, the bright river, and the deep, shady wood, proposed to go on. At that moment one of the *piqueurs* who followed them rode up and said in a low voice, "Will

Madame look behind her?"

Out of the wood came a man on horseback, with a brown vest and a red feather, followed by several others. There was not a moment to lose; they turned and rode as hard as they could, with the brigands after them. Turning her head, Laura saw that their pursuers were not gaining upon them, and the *calèche* which they had left near the bridge was crossing it, and coming to meet them. Breathless, they pushed on till they got to it, the *valet-de-pied* was holding the door open.

Springing from their horses, and throwing the reins to the two *piqueurs*; they hurried into the *calèche*; the coachman whipped up his horses and the carriage being light, the horses fresh, and the riding horses relieved from their burden, the whole party fled at full speed in the direction of the bridge, when a crack was heard—the bar of the carriage had broken. The coachman swore, and the two friends began to think it was all over with them, but somehow or other by great exertions they got to the bridge in time, the guard came out, and the brigands rode back to the wood.

Masséna had been a failure in Spain, and was returning to France, being replaced by Marmont, and now a letter from the emperor informed Junot that he was appointed to a command in the north.

No words could express Laura's delight when he said to her—

"Laura, we are going back to France."

Throwing her arms round his neck, she cried and laughed with joy, and the preparations for their departure were begun at once.

Marmont came to see them before they left, and looking round at the long oak-panelled *salon*, out of which opened a small, dark bedroom, he exclaimed, "And you live here!"

"Oh! this is nothing," cried Laura. "If you had seen Ciudad-Rodrigo, Ledesma, or San-Felices-el-Grande—"

"And you laugh! you are merry!"

"I have not always been so, but we are going back to France!"

With a joyful heart Laura set out on her journey towards France, with her husband, her child, and her friend, Madame Thomières. They travelled peacefully enough to Valladolid and Burgos, after which the road became extremely dangerous. The notorious guerilla chief Mina, a man with all the daring of Don Julian, and without his good qualities, was the terror of that part of the country, and with his band had just fallen upon and massacred a convoy of French wounded, sick, and travellers on their way to France. This frightful catastrophe had happened in a narrow pass where the road ran between a deep river and precipitous rocks, and through which, not many days after the massacre, it was necessary for the Duc d'Abrantès and his escort to pass.

As they were very numerous, and as Mina had retired with his booty into the fastnesses of the mountains Junot thought it a favourable moment for the journey, but Laura's nerves were shaken by the horrors she had just heard, and when they entered the pass, in which the horrible remains of the carnage were still to be seen all round them, she turned pale and clasped her child shuddering in her arms, the faithful Rose growing still more terrified as they proceeded warily along, Junot on horseback riding now in front, now behind, now coming up to reassure his wife, and keeping a sharp look out upon the heights, which ever since daybreak had been patrolled by his men.

The journey was, however, performed in safety, and at length, after many alarms, they found themselves at the Bidassoa, the boundary of Spain. The bridge had been set on fire by the Spaniards, but the flames had been extinguished. In a transport of delight Laura insisted on walking over it, and again set her foot upon French ground.

CHAPTER 21
Laura Returns to Paris
1811-1812

At Bayonne they parted from Madame Thomières, who went on to Le Mans. As they stopped to change horses at a posting-house near Poitiers, they observed a crowd of people and a number of carriages before the door. A man came towards them, who proved to be Joseph, King of Spain, now on his way back from Paris, where he had been to attend the christening of his nephew, the King of Rome.

With all his old friendship Joseph Buonaparte got into the carriage, sat down opposite Laura, and answered her eager questions.

France was delirious with joy at the birth of the King of Rome, the emperor was well, but he was changed, said Joseph, who seemed melancholy, and repeated, "You will not find again the Napoleon of the army of Italy, my poor Junot! No! he is no longer the same."

Before entering Paris, they were met by a deputation of fifteen or twenty of the *dames de la Halle* bringing them magnificent bouquets of flowers, and demanding to see the child "born amongst the savage Spaniards." Laura showed them the baby, who was in the second carriage with his nurse, and assured them he should be a good Frenchman, and in a very short time found herself again in her own house with her children, after an absence of a year and a half.

They found society in Paris much changed. Although Joséphine had always favoured the *faubourg St. Germain*, her influence was not sufficiently powerful to counterbalance all the opposing elements which in the days of the Consulate and the earlier years of the Empire were so strong, and so numerous. But the marriage of the emperor with an Austrian archduchess at once gave preponderance to that party, which openly displayed its contempt for the new *noblesse*, without incurring the displeasure of the emperor, as would formerly have been the case.

The Duke and Duchess d'Abrantès were, on their return, presented to the empress, and Laura found amongst her *entourage* several of her old friends whom Napoleon had vainly wished her to give up on the plea of their enmity to himself Now the Comte de Narbonne, M. de Mouchy, the Comtesse Juste de Noailles, and others, were high in his favour, and on Laura finding herself seated near the emperor at a ball given by Queen Hortense, he observed, looking at M. de Narbonne—

"Well! are you satisfied? There is one of your friends with me."

"And how would it have been for me now, Sire, if I had obeyed your orders? How should I look now if I had done as you wished? for your Majesty recommended me more than twenty times to shut my doors on M. de Narbonne, Madame de Noailles, M. de Mouchy. I had the honour to tell you then that being my friends they could not be your enemies, and it appears I was right, since you have placed them near you."

The *fête St. Louis* was celebrated at Trianon to please the empress, who preferred it to all the other *châteaux* and palaces. For the first time all the men wore full court dress, except Marshal Ney, who could by no means be persuaded to put on anything but his uniform. But the costume, which was becoming enough to those who by birth, manners, habits, or appearance, were fitted to wear it, made some of those present, look so supremely ridiculous that, as Laura remarked, no caricature could equal their absurdity.

The new empress was not one to give *éclat* or brilliancy to the court festivities. She had no conversation, and no fascination or charm of manner. Neither had she the gift of beauty. A faultless complexion and pretty fair hair were the attractions which caught Napoleon's fancy; her figure, which was of medium height, was out of proportion, her bust and shoulders being much too large for the rest of her body. Thus, describing her, Laura adds that she had the glance of a Kalmuck and the mouth of an Austrian.

But the emperor was satisfied. She brought him a great alliance

"L'ESPOIR DE LA POSTÉRITÉ."
(The Emperor Napoleon, Empress Marie-Louise, and King of Rome.) (Rechu.)

and the heir he had longed for, and she submitted obediently or apathetically to his most unreasonable commands as long as his power and prosperity lasted. When his fortunes changed, she deserted him without an effort or a moment's hesitation, and transferred the passive submission that so highly pleased him to the emperor, her father.

Meanwhile, in spite of the disasters in the Peninsula, fortune still smiled upon Napoleon. The birth of his son had redoubled his popularity; the waiting multitude, listening breathlessly for that twenty-second gun, which would proclaim the fulfilment of their hearts' desire; the roar of triumph and delight which mingled with its thunder when it came had drawn tears from the emperor, hidden behind a curtain in the Tuileries watching and listening.

Marie-Louise was a cold, indifferent mother; but Napoleon adored his son, the one being he really loved devotedly. He would hold him in his arms for hours, and never tired of caressing and playing with him, though his manner of doing so was no more elegant than other ways in which he showed his affection or familiarity, one of his favourite tricks, besides pulling the child's ears and nose in his habitual fashion, being to smear his face with wine, gravy, or sauce.

Notwithstanding his countless *liaisons*, Napoleon had only two recognised illegitimate children, both sons. The mother of one was the young *lectrice* of his sister, Caroline Murat. Of her he very soon got tired, and was very angry when she came with her mother to Fontainebleau, and had herself announced in his apartments without his leave. He was, however, very fond of his son, and settled 30,000 *francs* a year upon him. This was one of the *liaisons* encouraged by his family in order to annoy Joséphine.

But whenever the emperor discovered or suspected any such plots he was exceedingly irritated, and on one occasion, it having come to his knowledge that certain persons were intriguing to make a young Irish girl, employed as *lectrice* by Joséphine, become his mistress, he ordered her to be immediately sent back to her family.

But with all the intrigues which were perfectly well known to his court and all his surroundings. Napoleon did not hesitate to assert that the worst quality a king could possess and the worst example he could set was that of immorality!

The strange hypocrisy of Buonaparte in such matters was exemplified a little later on in the following manner. General Dupont Derval having been killed during the Russian campaign, his widow applied for a pension. The emperor, however, discovering that the general had been divorced from his first wife, who was living and had one daughter—the present wife being an officer's widow with two daughters by her first husband—changed the destination of the brevet to the first wife, who was very well off, and did not require it.

The other, being poor and thinking it must be a mistake, appealed to the emperor, who replied, "I promised the pension and shall give it to the wife of General Dupont, that is, his real wife, the mother of his daughter," thus emphasising the respect he pretended to entertain for the marriage tie and his disapproval of divorce. At that very time, he had already divorced his own wife, forced Jérôme to desert his, and exiled Lucien because he refused to do the same.

A review of a recent life of Buonaparte speaks of Napoleon as "a cad," and in no way did this side of his character appear more distinctly than in the cynical materialism of his love intrigues. In their vices even more than in their virtues stands out sharply and strongly the difference between the kings and princes of Valois and Bourbon and the Corsican adventurer who sat upon their throne.

The courtly, magnificent gallantry of François I., the chivalrous, faithful, though lawless love of Henri II. and Diane de Poitiers, the romantic passion of Henri IV. and *La belle Gabrielle*, and the stately splendour of the licentious court and loves of Louis XIV. contrasted indeed with the coarse, brutal heartlessness which characterised the intrigues of Buonaparte.

To one only, to the woman who has been called the *La Vallière* of the Empire, can the slightest vestige of romance or sentiment be attached, and her disinterested love was worthy of a better object. She was a Pole, married by her family to a man old enough to be her grandfather, and she herself only two-and-twenty, when, at a great ball given to him by the Polish nobles in a palace at Warsaw, she first met Napoleon.

Struck with admiration of her fair, melancholy beauty, the emperor fell in love with her at once, and the next morning sent one of his chief officers to her with a letter containing proposals to which, indignant at this kind of love-making, she sent a peremptory refusal.

Napoleon, much taken aback, wrote her letter after letter, to which for some time he received no answer, but at length prevailed upon her to consent to an interview in his palace between ten and eleven one night. He sent the same personage with a carriage to fetch her from the place agreed upon, and waited, walking impatiently up and down the room until she arrived, pale, trembling, and tearful.

This was in January, 1807, and the first interview was followed by many others, which continued until the emperor left Warsaw. Two months after his departure he sent for her to Finkenstein, and leaving her old husband, who refused ever to see her again, she took possession of an apartment prepared for her by the emperor near his own. He was charmed with her, and spent all the time he could in her society, dining and breakfasting alone with her. Of a melancholy, romantic, passionate temperament, she was entirely devoted to him, cared nothing for society, but passed her time in reading when he was not with her.

In 1809, after the Battle of Wagram, he took a house for her in a *faubourg* of Vienna, and when the campaign was over, he arranged that she should come to Paris, escorted by her brother. He took a charming house for her in the Chaussée d'Antin, where she continued to lead a retired, studious life, seeing few people and caring only for the emperor. There her son was born and brought up in secret, being only taken by a private door into the *petits appartements* of the Tuileries to see his father, who was extremely fond of him, and created him Count Walewski. His mother gave the emperor a ring with this inscription,

"*Quand tu cesseras de m'aimer, n'oublies pas que je t'aime.*" She took her son to see Napoleon at Elba, where his extraordinary likeness to his father gave rise to a report that the King of Rome had arrived.

The Duke and Duchess d'Abrantès did not long remain with their children in Paris after their return from the hardships and dangers of their Spanish campaign. All over Europe the outlook was most threatening. From the Peninsula the accounts were chequered, the victories of Suchet in one part being counterbalanced by those of Wellington in another. In the north things looked worse still. Russia was growing more and more hostile, and Sweden had become her ally; for Bernadotte was not inclined to be the puppet of Napoleon. Louis Buonaparte had resigned the crown of Holland rather than submit to the tyranny of his brother.

When Junot had been restored to tolerable health by a course of the baths of Barèges, he entreated the emperor to give him an appointment, and was sent to Milan to take command of the troops in Italy, and to bring them north, for war with Russia was now about to begin. The emperor left for Germany, where the army was assembling for the invasion of Russia, the empress accompanying him as far as Dresden.

Paris at that time presented a singular and melancholy spectacle. In all ranks of society there was an enormous preponderance of women, whose husbands, fathers, sons, and brothers were with the army.

Most of Laura's friends were going either to some watering-place, to Italy, to Switzerland, or to their country places, and she, finding herself attacked by the same illness from which she had suffered before, resolved to go to Aix-les-Bains, leaving her little girls with their nurse and governess in the Abbaye-aux-Bois, her baby under the care of a friend, and taking her eldest boy, then three years old, with her. She was also accompanied by her brother-in-law, M. de Geouffre, and her friend, Madame Lallemand. They left Paris on the 12th of June, 1812, having taken the precaution of securing their rooms beforehand, which was fortunate, as the place was so crowded that it was almost impossible to find lodgings.

Those of the Queen of Spain, which were opposite Laura's, were not nearly so good, and the latter, who had agreed with about twenty friends to meet there, now complained that the enjoyment and freedom of the place was spoilt by its being so, overrun with queens and princesses, past, present, and future, that it was impossible to go anywhere without meeting them. The Empress Joséphine, the Queen of Spain, the future Queen of Sweden, the Princess Borghese, and Madame Mère were all there, besides Talma and other celebrities. Joséphine had lost none of the charm of manner and perfection of taste for which she had always been so celebrated. Laura observed that the best proof of her superiority in the art of dress was the contrast presented by Marie-Louise, who employed the same dressmakers, had an enormous allowance, and yet never looked well dressed.

On the morning of the 10th of August the Princess Borghese ordered an immense bouquet to send Laura in honour of her *fête*. This she gave to her little son Napoleon, who was very pretty and a great favourite of hers.

"Take it to your mother," she said, "and tell her that it is from the oldest friend she has at Aix; and tell her to look at the cord which ties it."

The cord was a chain of pearls and rubies.

A number of Laura's friends had invited her to a *fête* organised in her honour at Bonport, where they were to dine, and to which they were to go in boats up Lake Bourget.

Everyone who has seen Aix-les-Bains knows how enchanting is the scenery of that most lovely country, the splendour of the mountains, the beautiful lakes of Bourget and Annecy, the rich vegetation, the glowing colour.

The party consisted of twenty-three people, and a boat followed with a band of musicians. It was fine weather when they started, but, as often happens in those mountain lakes, a sudden storm came on which terrified many of the guests. Not Laura; she was deeply interested in listening to Talma, who, holding by the slender mast, recited the first act in *The Tempest*, his voice at times almost drowned by the noise around him. They arrived in safety, dried their clothes by a fire, dined, and then, the storm having cleared away, rambled about the ancient Château of Bonport and Abbey of Haute-Combe, gathering the wild flowers which grew in profusion, watching the moon rise, and enjoying the freedom from that court etiquette which, greatly to their vexation, had pursued and annoyed them in their summer wanderings.

The *fête* ended with a magnificent display of fireworks on the lake, after which they re-entered the boats and returned to Aix, where the next day Laura received a mild reprimand from Madame Mère for allowing fireworks in her own honour when the Imperial family were in the place.

Next the Princess Borghese gave a *fête* of the same kind on Lake Bourget, and a few days afterwards Laura and some of her friends drove to Geneva to be present at the *fête du lac*, and several water-parties given by different people upon the far-famed Lake Leman.

Laura met many acquaintances there and amused herself immensely, though she was considerably bored by a great dinner which the mayor gave in her honour.

One evening a ball was given by a Monsieur Saladin at his country house. Laura was still extremely fond of dancing, but on this occasion, she felt a strange presentiment of evil, which so weighed upon her spirits that she could not dance but went outside the ballroom and walked up and down in the garden which went down to the lake. Presently she saw groups of people standing about on the terrace talking anxiously to each other, and as she approached, she caught the words, "Spain"—"King Joseph"—"Marmont." There were pale faces, looks of consternation, and eager questions when the disastrous news became known.

There had been a great battle close to Salamanca. Marmont had been defeated by Wellington; the French had lost the whole of their artillery, 5,000 prisoners, and 8,000 killed and wounded, amongst the latter being Marmont himself There was an end to all festivities—Madame Marmont, who was at the ball, started for Spain, and Laura returned for the rest of September to Aix.

But the general uneasiness that began to be felt increased day by day, and put an end to the gay, careless amusements of that light-hearted society. From the north as well as the south came misgivings and evil rumours. The news intended for the public might be excellent, but private letters told a different story, and Laura had too many Russian friends not to possess sufficient sources of information to fill her mind with the gravest anxiety before the end of September saw her on her journey back to Paris.

She stayed at Lyon for a day or two to see Madame Récamier (who lived there in melancholy exile, from which the fall of her oppressor was before long to deliver her), and arrived in Paris early in October. That and the next months were full of uneasiness and alarms. Letters became scarcer and scarcer. After receiving one from Junot on the 29th of October, filled with affectionate inquiries and remarks about herself and his children, Laura heard no more for two months, during which she and everyone else were a prey to the most dreadful forebodings. In his fanatical infatuation for the emperor, Junot had persuaded him, through Laura's intercession, to have his infant son, Napoleon, enrolled among the Polish lancers of the Imperial Guard: and she had now caused a miniature of the child in that uniform to be painted and sent to his father in Russia.

The conspiracy of Malet, though it was promptly defeated and punished, disclosed serious internal perils, and it was evident that the nation, hitherto flattered and delighted by the victories and conquests which for more than fifteen years had attended its arms, was now becoming weary of the ceaseless warfare and horrible slaughter which many began to think too dear a price to pay either for glory or plunder.

Many of the best generals and officers of Buonaparte had been killed, and even amongst those who remained a large number shared the opinions of the soldiers and the people, and asked discontentedly what was the use of having riches and honours which they were allowed no time to enjoy, children who were torn from them to perish in the deserts of Spain or the snows of Russia, homes in which they were strangers, or to which they only returned crippled or invalided.

The despatches published could not be depended upon. Unable now, as always, from the days of the Hundred Years' War, till their last conflict with Germany, to bear a reverse with dignity and fortitude, the French adopted their invariable practice of publishing false successes to conceal their defeats, in the hope of pleasing the populace, who were all the more angry when they discovered the real truth.

But private letters brought the news of the burning of Moscow by the Russians and the retreat of the French army, filling Paris with consternation.

Furious at being baulked of his prey, Buonparte ordered the Kremlin to be blown up, a piece of useless spite worthy of a barbarian, and blamed even by his own fanatical supporters. The first courier bringing full news of the French disasters arrived on the 18th of December, and on the morning of the 20th the guns of the Invalides announced that the emperor had returned.

Many, both then and afterwards, have expressed the deepest indignation at the whole conduct of Buonaparte during, this crisis. His desertion of the unfortunate army, which he left to its fate while he pursued his own journey in safety, and the bulletin he issued; announcing that "his health had never been better," while to satisfy his vainglorious ambition thousands lay dead or dying upon the snows of Russia, seemed scarcely calculated to arouse the admiration of any one not blindly infatuated by him; while, on the other hand, his partisans maintained that his death would have been an irreparable loss to the army and the country, both of which would be much more benefited by his returning to Paris than by his remaining in Russia.

Accompanied by the Duke of Vicenza, he travelled day and night for a fortnight, narrowly escaping being captured by the Cossacks before reaching Wilna, changing from a sledge to a carriage at Erfurth and driving up to the gate of the Tuileries after the empress had retired to bed. In the morning the news that the emperor had returned spread through Paris.

Desperately anxious for news of Junot, but too ill to go herself, Laura sent her brother to the Tuileries, but he returned saying that it was impossible to get near the emperor owing to the immense crowds who were pressing round him for tidings of those dear to them who were with the army.

Laura, however, hoped that as the emperor had arrived his generals would soon follow, and Junot amongst them. But having waited a day or two and heard nothing she wrote to the emperor, who sent Duroc the next morning to say that she might be perfectly reassured, for Junot was quite well.

"I know it is not so," said Laura, looking at him steadily; "and you know it too, my dear duke."

Duroc looked down and said nothing.

"Duroc," continued Laura, taking his hand, "I am very ill, perhaps I shall never see those trees green again," and she pointed out into her garden. "Tell me the truth; what has happened between Junot and the emperor?"

"Nothing new," replied Duroc, who supposed that she was acquainted with what her friends had carefully concealed from her, and Junot, in his melancholy, despairing letters had not explained, namely, the two unfortunate bulletins in which Napoleon spoke with disapprobation of Junot: in one saying that he lost his way and made a false movement, in the other that he did not act with sufficient firmness.

The misrepresentations of Murat were partly the cause of this injustice; for in one case Junot had not received his orders, owing to the delay caused by the state of the roads; and in the other the dilatoriness and unpunctuality of one of his generals were in fault.

Junot wrote a letter of explanation to the emperor, who, after reading it attentively, remarked; "It is very unlucky, *for the bulletins are made!!*"

The state of gloomy despair and misery into which Junot was

plunged gave Laura serious apprehensions, only too fully justified as time went on.

The day after her interview with Duroc she received a letter from her husband, begging her to see the emperor and obtain leave for him to come to Paris as he was suffering dreadfully from his old wounds, which had always troubled him. He was also much alarmed about her health, and most anxious to see her, repeating always that she and his children were now all he cared for in the world. He wrote in one letter:

> My dear Laura, it is four o'clock in the morning; I cannot sleep, I am thinking of you and have got up to write to you. What a year you have spent, my dear angel! May this one begin better and go on better still! May I be able to come and take care of you, and that consolation at least lessen the sufferings so increased by my absence, and your anxiety for him who loves you so much.... If I do not get leave it will be impossible for me to get well enough to be fit for another campaign. Can the emperor refuse to let me come and see my Laura in the state she is now in, when I know my presence would be a comfort to her. This climate increases my pains, and yesterday I could not walk home, they were obliged to get me a carriage....

Chapter 22
Return of Junot
1812-1813

Besides her own shattered health and her great anxiety for her husband, Laura had another source of trouble regarding her brother, who, by the false accusations and machinations of Savary, Duc de Rovigo, always an enemy of Junot, Laura, and all her family, had been forced to resign his post at Marseille.

Alarmed by the increasing melancholy of Junot's letters, aware (although not knowing the full extent) of the harshness and injustice with which the emperor had now treated him, and understanding the circumstances of the intrigue to ruin her brother, she resolved to make an effort to help them both, and wrote to Duroc to procure her an audience of the emperor, saying that it must be in the evening, as she could not now get up until six or seven o'clock.

The emperor appointed nine o'clock on the following day. When the Duchesse d'Abrantès was announced he started in astonishment at her altered looks, exclaiming—

"*Mon Dieu!* Madame Junot, what is the matter with you? You are very ill! It is true! I see well enough that it is not *manières de vapeurs.*"

And he explained that he had been told she was pretending to be ill so that she might have an excuse for discontinuing her attendance on Madame Mère.

Laura raised her eyes, burning with fever, held out the thin hands on which her rings would no longer stay, and gave a contemptuous denial to these accusations, while Napoleon, seeing she was so weak she could hardly stand, took her hand, almost pushed her into an armchair, and seated himself by her side.

"*Ah, ça!* what do you want?" he asked. "It is for Junot, is it not? Well! he shall come back—but meanwhile he complains much of me, does he not? Come, speak the truth."

A vehement discussion followed, during which Laura pleaded Junot's faithful services, the dangerous state of his health, his deep attachment to the emperor, from whom harshness now would be a deathblow to him.

"He would not be in a bad humour like Lannes, who, though he loved you, sometimes treated you as he would not have treated an inferior; or be sulky, as you say yourself Ney is; nothing of the kind; it would be death to him." And, half-frightened at her own audacity, she sank back in her chair. Napoleon looked at her with a half-smile.

"It is inconceivable," he observed, "how like you are to your mother when you are angry. *Par Dieu!* you are as passionate as she was!"

"You are ungenerous, sire," replied Laura; "you know that I cannot go away—and yet I have long told Your Majesty that I will never listen to a word against my mother from your lips."

"Well! who detains you? what are you waiting for?" said he, rising as if to let her pass.

"Your answer, sire."

"What answer?"

"The one I came to ask you for—about Junot. I will not leave Your Majesty until I have it, whatever I may have to bear from you."

"You are a singular woman—a character of iron," said the emperor; and resuming the conversation, he reproached her with her visit to Madame Récamier, whose house and her father's had been the rendezvous of his enemies, pacing up and down the room in his usual way, absolutely refusing Laura's entreaty that she might return, but granting Junot four months' leave and listening with attention to her explanation of Albert's affair, which he received with favour and with evident regret. When Laura went so far as to say that he owed her brother some reparation, and asked for another appointment for him at Paris, Napoleon looked at her with a smile and inquired—

"Well! *Madame la Gouverneuse*, what are you waiting for? Do you think you are going to take the brevet with you?" and presently said, "Meanwhile, tell your brother I am very sorry for what has happened." Then, as she took leave—

"Well! do we part in anger? *Mauvaise tête, mauvaise tête!* Do you know you are very good to your friends, but I think you would be a real demon for your enemies." And with this and a few more friendly remarks the interview closed; the emperor turned again to his bureau, and Laura found Duroc and other friends waiting in the anteroom to escort her downstairs and to know the result of the audience.

It had been an exhausting one for Laura, but she had gained her point in both cases. Albert was already in Paris, and Junot lost no time in returning after he received the letter which, by the emperor's orders, she wrote to him announcing his recall.

Her nerves and health were, however, so seriously affected that she grew worse and worse. She would often have eight or ten fainting-fits in a day, to the great alarm of her brother, who, with Madame Lallemand, nursed her devotedly. One of these fainting-fits took place in her bath, and she would assuredly have been drowned if Madame Lallemand had not fortunately been present and saved her, lifting her with great exertion out of the bath and falling exhausted on the floor by her side, at the sacrifice, as Laura records, of a very charming pink *crêpe* dress she was wearing.

The meeting between her and Junot was terrible. They were both so changed that they looked at one another in despair. It was Laura, however, who was in the most immediate danger, and as the great doctor Corvisart had just returned to Paris, Junot called him in.

Corvisart, like many of the men about the court and household of Napoleon, was rough, almost brutal in manner, but extremely clever; and by his treatment, after a time of anxiety almost amounting to despair, she began to recover, and in spite of the severe cold of the winter, could be carried from one room to another and even go out a little in a carriage.

Junot watched over her with the tenderest care. He would not allow any of her women to sit or sleep in her room at night, but, in spite of his own sufferings, had a bed in her room and was always ready to give her the medicine and nourishment ordered during the night at short intervals. One night, when he thought she was asleep, Laura heard him sighing and groaning in such evident misery that, terror-stricken and distressed, she called out to know what was the matter, and as he did not hear her, she managed to get up and go to his bedside.

Bending over him, she found his face wet with tears, and throwing her arms round him she besought him to tell her the cause of his grief Seeing that any further concealment would do more harm than good, Junot poured into Laura's ears all the history of his misfortunes during the late campaign, the anger of the emperor, and the fatal bulletins. All night long she listened and sympathised and comforted him, glad that at any rate he had now the relief of being able to speak freely to her of what had been weighing so fearfully upon his mind; whilst he assured her repeatedly that she and his children were all he now cared for in the world, that she had always been his good angel, and that he had loved her just the same from the day he had first asked her mother's consent to their marriage.

After this conversation Junot seemed to a certain degree to recover his equanimity, although he still fretted and grieved over the change in the emperor.

Of the disasters in Russia he seldom spoke, except when they were alone together, and then with profound sadness, One day, at breakfast, he read out of the *Moniteur* a paragraph announcing the return to France of part of the troops from Russia, and threw down the paper with a contemptuous laugh and a muttered oath.

"Isn't it unworthy of the emperor's greatness," he said, "to try to hide from the nation the loss of its sons? And how can it be hidden? This paper speaks of the troops entering Mayence on their return from Russia! Of four hundred thousand men who crossed the Niemen, not fifty thousand have come back!"

All kinds of caricatures and epigrams were now circulated in Paris, greatly to the displeasure of the emperor.

In 1809, when the Kings of Bavaria, Saxony, and Wurtemberg, a number of princes and princesses, and the members of the Imperial family were all in Paris, an immense inscription appeared upon the Tuileries: "*Fonds à vendre—pas cher—fabrique de sires,*" at which Napoleon was much irritated, and the author of which he vainly tried to discover.

But in the disastrous days of 1813 they were doubly bitter to him, and were to be seen all about the streets. One said that he was "*mauvais* jardinier, car il avait laissé geler ses grenadiers et flétrir ses lauriers." (A bad gardener, for he had let his pomegranates—or grenadiers—freeze and his laurels wither.)

In another, a father says to his son, "*Venez ici, monsieur; allons, ne pleurez pas, qu'aves-vous fait de ces quatre cent mille petits soldats que je vous ai donnés pour vos étrennes, il n'y a pas encore un an? Où estelle, cette armée?*"

"*Je l'ai, papa, je l'ai (gelée).*"

******

"Come here, sir. Don't cry. What have you done with the four hundred thousand little soldiers I gave you less than a year ago for the New Year? Where is that army?"

"I have it, papa, I have it" (pronounced *gelée*, "frozen, papa, *rozen*.")

******

A third remarked, "*L'empereur a perdu tout son argenterie en Russie, mais en revenant en France il a été tout étonné de retrouver tous ses plats au Sénat.*"

******

"The emperor, having lost all his plate in Russia, was surprised on returning to France to find all his *dishes* at the Senate." (*Plat* means also a flunkey.)

******

A fourth was supposed to be a dialogue between two men crossing the Carrousel.

"*Monsieur, pourriez-vous me dire quelles sont les statues que je vois sur ces pilastres?*"

"*Oui, monsieur, ce sont des Victoires.*"

"*Monsieur, je vous demande pardon, les Victoires n'ont jamais cette tournure là—Des Victoires! que diable. Monsieur, venez-vous me conter là?*"

"*Mais tenez—vous voyez bien que ce sont des Victoires, elles tournent le dos à Napoléon!*"

******

"Can you tell me what statues those are on the pilasters?"
"Yes, *monsieur*, they are Victories."
"I beg your pardon, *monsieur*, Victories never look like that. Victories! What the devil are you telling me?"
"But look!—you can see they are Victories, they are turning their back on Napoleon."

******

A new campaign was now beginning in Germany, and Junot wrote to the emperor begging to be employed in it. About a week afterwards he came into his wife's room with looks of consternation, exclaiming, "Laura, I am going to leave you. I start at once. The emperor has just done me a great honour," he added sarcastically, as he threw upon her bed two brevets, one making him Governor of Venice, the other of Illyria.

The appointments were really important and distinguished, but they were not what Junot desired; and, in spite of the persuasions and representations of Laura, Duroc, and other friends, he was perfectly conscious that he had lost the favour of his idol. To him it was exile, and he was no longer Governor of Paris.

His farewell interview with the emperor, however, brought him some consolation, as he was received with all the kindness and graciousness which Napoleon so well knew how to assume, and he departed to his new post in better spirits, it having been arranged that he should stay first at Trieste and that Laura should join him at Venice as soon as she was able to travel, for she was again *enceinte*.

Although she assumed all the cheerfulness and confidence she possibly could under the circumstances, the state of her husband's health still caused her the gravest uneasiness. The many wounds he had in his head now appeared decidedly to be affecting his brain. Besides the frightful pains and headaches from which he suffered, he seemed to be half asleep all day and could not sleep at night; the hardships of the late campaigns, the state of anxiety and misery caused by the emperor's displeasure, added to the dissipation and excesses of his whole life, had all produced their fatal effect upon a violent, excitable temperament without the slightest self-control.

Early in May came the news of the victory of Lutzen and of the death of Bessières, who was killed in an engagement the day before. He was only forty-five, and was an irreparable loss to Napoleon, being one of the best of his generals. Bessières had always been a great friend of Junot and Laura, to whom his death was a fresh sorrow.

The empress was made regent during the absence of the emperor, with a council of which Cambacérès was president. A story circulated that one day, Napoleon, who was at this time much irritated against the Emperor of Austria and out of patience with Marie-Louise, who kept quoting her father, exclaimed angrily—

"*Votre père! votre père est une ganache!*" (old fool), and went out, banging the door after him.

Marie-Louise, having no idea what the word meant, asked the Duchesse de Montebello, saying that the emperor had applied it to her father, the Emperor of Austria.

"*Madame*," replied the lady-in-waiting, hesitating, "it means a brave and good man."

"It is strange," observed Marie-Louise, "for the emperor seemed angry when he said so."

Soon afterwards, wishing to make a civil speech to Cambacérès, she remarked—

"*Monsieur l'Archichancelier*, I am very glad the emperor has left me such a council as this, but especially of the choice of its president, and I hope that, advised by a *brave ganache* like you, I shall do nothing to displease the emperor."

Marie-Louise was no favourite with the French, and did not like them, which was natural enough, for she saw in them the murderers of her aunt.

Paris was just now deserted, only those remaining there who were obliged to do so. Laura was amongst the number, and she tried to distract herself by receiving every evening the friends who were left, and who came to amuse themselves with dancing, music, billiards, conversation, &c.

Next to Duroc, her great friend was Lavalette, and one evening he appeared in her *salon* with so melancholy a face that she thoughtlessly exclaimed—

"What is the matter? You look as if you had come from a funeral."

With a start which reminded her that the remark was unsuitable at this time, he gave her a letter. It was from Duroc, and with an exclamation of pleasure she opened it. It was written on the eve of the Battle of Bautzen, and she was soon buried in its contents. When she had finished it and looked up Lavalette was gone. The letter was as follows:—

> It is ten o'clock at night, and I am exhausted with fatigue, but I will not let the courier go without sending you news of me; it is so long since I have been able to write to you. But you will not blame me; you know all my friendship for you. I had a letter from Junot yesterday which I will answer as soon as I can. Meanwhile tell him that the emperor is pleased with him and loves him still. Poor Junot! he is like me, the affection of the emperor is our life. I cannot bear to see his grief. The death of Bessières has overwhelmed him. I think him happy to be so

mourned for, but if I thought I should be the same, it would cause me regret. Must we be the ones to give him new sorrows? Another victory! It is as if a fortunate presentiment had prevented my closing my letter. This victory is one of the most brilliant of the emperor's career. You may say so without doubt. *Adieu.* Let me hear from you. I am anxious about you.

Duroc.

At ten o'clock next morning M. de Lavalette was announced.

"What has happened to Junot?" cried Laura, hastening towards him.

"Nothing! Nothing!" he replied; and then, sitting down by her and taking her hands, he said, "My dear friend, a great misfortune has happened to you and all of us. Duroc is dead."

He had been killed by a cannon-ball, and the shock occasioned by his death was a severe one to Laura, whose grief for his loss mingled with forebodings as to what new misfortune might be her fate.

The calamity of Duroc's death just after that of Bessières' was a most serious one to Napoleon, who showed unusual feeling on this occasion. His best generals and most faithful friends seemed to be falling rapidly around him. A few days later came news of the death of General Thomières, the husband of Laura's friend, and very shortly after that the dread which had for some time hung over herself was realised.

She was lying one day on a sofa in her room, resting after a troubled, sleepless night, when she heard in the ante-room the voices of her brother and of her *bête noire*, Savary, Duc de Rovigo, who, in spite of Albert's remonstrances, insisted, in the name of the emperor, on seeing her, and announced that Junot was seriously ill; giving her a letter from the emperor, enclosing one which Junot, obviously in a moment of excitement approaching delirium, had written to him and sent by a special messenger. The emperor's letter was as follows:—

> Madame Junot, see what your husband writes me. I have been painfully affected in reading this letter. It gives you a just idea of his state, and you must take remedial measures at once. Set off without losing an hour. Junot must be very near France at this moment from what the viceroy writes me.

Laura read the letter and looked with a stupefied air at Savary, who; proceeded, in a manner brutal from its want of sympathy and feeling, to explain that the emperor's orders were that Junot should not be brought to Paris or its environs.

With an outburst of indignation Laura asked where she was to take her husband; whether the emperor supposed that he could go to the village where his father lived, and if it were likely she could find the advice and requirements for such an illness there. Had the emperor become an executioner—an assassin?

"Hush! hush!" cried Savary, going to the door to be sure no one was listening. "If such words were repeated to the emperor you would be lost."

But Laura did not care for that. She was ill and feverish already, and this overwhelming shock was too much for her. She declared that she did not believe the emperor had given any such order, and became almost delirious, to the great alarm of her brother, until a passion of tears seemed to restore her calmness to a certain extent, and she was able to enter into the question of what was to be done. Albert remarked that there was no time to lose, and Savary kept repeating, "But what can we do against the orders of the emperor?"

After a little consideration Laura decided that she would take a house on the Lake of Geneva, where she had many friends and there was an excellent doctor. She would start the following night, and all she asked of Savary was that he would send orders to Lyon that if the Duc d'Abrantès arrived that way he was to be sent to Geneva; if he came by the Simplon, she would be waiting for him herself.

Savary consented, and with many half-apologies and assurances of his sympathy and friendship, took his departure.

Left alone with his sister, Albert did all he could to help and comfort her. He sent for her children, who, seeing her tears, clung round her, asking if their father were ill. It was arranged that they were to be left in the care of Madame Lallemand, who was not well enough to go with Laura. She was to be accompanied by her brother and Madame Thomières but many of her friends, hearing of her trouble, hastened to see and console her. The old Abbe de Comnenus, her uncle, who lived with them, and of whom they were very fond, tried his best to calm her agitation, and succeeded to some degree, for he was a man of saintly life to whom she looked up with veneration as well as affection.

They left Paris at eleven o'clock on the night of the 17th July, and travelled without stopping to Geneva, where they arrived at ten on the morning of the 21st, dreadfully tired. They went to their usual hotel, and Laura sent at once for Dr. Butini, to whom she explained the state of the case, begging him to let no one know of her arrival. In the afternoon they drove along the shore of the lake till they found a suitable house, which they took, and having sent servants, linen, provisions, and everything necessary, Laura lay down to rest at about six o'clock in the evening, thinking that Junot would probably arrive in a few hours, and feeling more hopeful and satisfied.

Presently a letter was brought to her from Lyon. She turned pale and was afraid to open it, but Albert exclaimed, "What nonsense! Come! it is only to announce their arrival—perhaps tomorrow."

It was from Charles Maldan, son of Junot's sister, a weak, stupid young man, who had been for some time his uncle's secretary, and now wrote that, although they had found at Lyon an order of the Duc de Rovigo to proceed to Geneva, the officer who accompanied them had: decided to disregard it, having been told by the viceroy, Eugène Beauharnais, to take Junot to "his family"; that they were therefore going on to Montbard, where they hoped the duchess would join them.

Laura dropped the letter in despair. Who but herself and his children were "his family"? and what hope of recovery could there be for him in an out-of-the-way village? for Montbard was little more, where he could have neither proper medical advice nor many other things necessary in such a case. His father was very old, and in such bad health that, although she had passed through Montbard on her way to Geneva, she had not told him of the serious condition of his son.

Notwithstanding her fatigue from the long journey she had just made, Laura declared she would start for Montbard the next day, and Albert ordered everything to be ready for them to set off at four in the morning. But at one she was seized with violent pains, which resulted in the birth of a dead child, and nearly cost the mother's life.

Calling for her brother, she begged him to go to Montbard to look after her husband, and, unwilling as Albert was to leave her in such danger, it seemed the only thing to be done. Madame Thomières was with her, she had a maid who nursed her devotedly, and Dr. Butini, in whom they had all confidence; he therefore consented to set off at once.

On the following night (22nd-23rd July) Laura, awaking suddenly out of a troubled sleep, saw distinctly the form of her husband standing by her bed. He wore the same dark grey coat in which he had last left her, and he stood looking at her with a gentle, melancholy expression. She uttered a cry of terror, and in a moment Madame Thomières and her maid were at her side, entreating to be told what was the matter. They could not see the apparition, which moved slowly round her bed, and as she followed it with her eyes, she observed that it had one leg broken.

"Light up the room!" she cried. "Give me air! Give me light—more light!" and still the ghostly figure glided about the room, sometimes approaching her, sometimes going farther away, and beckoning her to follow it. It was not till the morning broke that it faded away into an indistinct cloud. Then Laura knew that Junot was dead.

When, a few days later, all was over, and Albert returned to her, she learned from him that it was at that very time that Junot, in a fit of madness, escaped from his bed; where he was lying, having broken his leg by a fall in a former frenzy, and, in the short absence of those who had been watching over him, succeeded in throwing himself out of a window.

It was a melancholy termination to a short and brilliant career, for Junot was only forty-one, and it was not more than twenty years since at the siege of Toulon he first won the favour of Napoleon, by which he rose from an obscure soldier, the son of a little country lawyer, to be General, Ambassador, Duc d'Abrantès, and the most powerful of Napoleon's Governors of Paris, for his authority stretched to Tours, and he commanded eighty thousand men. His death was probably owing to several causes: the dissipation of his life, the frightful wounds in his head, the hardships of the Russian campaign, followed by the heat of the climate in Illyria, and, added to all this, the excitement and agitation caused by the harshness of the emperor acting upon a violent and undisciplined nature and a brain already affected by the injuries to his head, all contributed to bring on what was generally pronounced to be madness, but asserted by Laura to be brain fever.

Although Montbard was not provided with the skill and comforts he would have had at Paris or Geneva, he had many friends there of whose kindness and attention to him Laura spoke with the warmest gratitude. He had recognised Albert, been delighted to see him, and talked to him of the emperor, for whom his adoration was still the same, and of his wife, for whom, in spite of his many passing infidelities, he always had great affection.

The emperor was at Dresden when the news was brought him, and at first, he appeared to be painfully affected by it. The letter fell from his hand, and, striking his forehead, he exclaimed in a tone of grief, "Junot! Junot! Oh! *mon Dieu!*" Then, picking it up and crumpling it in his hands as he clasped them together, he repeated, "Junot! *Voilà encore un de mes braves de moins!* Junot! Oh! *mon Dieu!*" and for a quarter of an hour he walked up and down, muttering to himself.

But his sorrow and compassion were alike short-lived.

When he had decided who was to replace Junot in Illyria, his thoughts went back to the letter which, although he was well aware it had been written almost in delirium, yet outweighed in his estimation twenty years of faithful service and devoted affection.

✶✶✶✶✶✶

The letter, except a few incoherent phrases, was as follows:—
"I who love you with the adoration of a savage for the sun—I who am all yours—well! this eternal war that has to be made for you, I want no more of it! I want peace! I want at last to rest my tired head and wounded limbs at home in my family, with my children, to have their affection, to be no longer a stranger to them. I want now to enjoy what I have bought with a price more precious than the treasures of India—with my blood, the blood of an honest man, a good Frenchman, and a true patriot. Well! I ask in fact for the tranquillity earned by twenty-two years of active service and seventeen wounds through which my blood has flowed, for my country first and for your glory afterwards."

✶✶✶✶✶✶

He sent orders to Laura that she was not to come within fifty leagues of Paris, and directed Savary to go to her *hôtel*, open the safe in which were Junot's papers, and bring away all his correspondence with the emperor and also the letters of the Queen of Naples.

The indignation of Laura, when this intelligence was brought by her brother-in-law, M. de Geouffre, may easily be imagined. She was still at Geneva, where for some weeks she had been carefully watched over by her brother, Madame Thomières, and her faithful maid, Blanche, comforted by constant letters from her children and numerous friends, and gradually recovering her strength.

She, however, merely gave M. de Geouffre a note for the Duc de Rovigo, in answer to his offers of service, saying that she counted upon his friendship to get her exile shortened.

When M. de Geouffre was gone, and Albert asked what she intended to do, she replied that she should return at once to Paris and live in her own house with her children, as she had a right to do.

Albert entirely agreed with her, and they immediately began to prepare for their journey.

Why "this infamy had been done," as they said, they could not understand—whether, as they supposed, it was the work of Savary and his clique, or some spiteful feeling on the part of Napoleon, which had destroyed his old friendship and affection for Laura, and made him treat her as he had done Madame de Stael, Madame Récamier, and the Duchesse de Chevreuse. But Laura had never been afraid of him, and neither Albert nor she thought it likely that Buonaparte, now that his prestige and popularity were declining, and the murmurs of his enemies growing louder both at home and abroad, would care to incur the odium of openly persecuting the widow of one of his bravest and most distinguished generals, whose terrible death was the subject of universal commiseration.

Laura sent for her children to meet her at Versailles, where she slept and remained till seven o'clock on the following evening, September 17th, when she drove to Paris and again entered her own house in the Champs Elysées. There she found a crowd of friends waiting to receive her, having come on purpose to show they were not afraid to offer this public mark of their sympathy and indignation.

When they were gone and Laura was just going to bed there was a thundering knock at the door, which had just been closed by the *Suisse*, a carriage drove into the courtyard, and the Duc de Rovigo appeared in a furious rage at her defiance of the order of the emperor transmitted through him.

After a discussion, in which he displayed even more than his usual insolence and brutality, Laura said—

"Now, Savary, you listen to me. I do not believe the emperor has exiled me, but if he has, I am sorry for him. What complaint has he against me? If he has so far forgotten himself, he has been set against Junot and me by our enemies. But, now hear what I wish you to tell the emperor. I will never ask anything of him either for myself or my children. I am the widow of Junot, the man who helped him out of his own slender means when he was at Paris without employment and often without food! I am the daughter of the woman who showed him kindness and care in his youth, almost in his childhood. Now, *Monsieur le Duc*, I am in the only shelter suitable for me, my own house, and I shall stay there."

Savary broke out into fury and threats, to which Laura only replied, as she rose from her chair—

"*Monsieur le Duc*, I must ask you to leave me to go to bed. If you want to arrest me, you know where to find me. Only I warn you of one thing, and that is that I shall not go out of this house without resisting—only force shall tear me from it. I will cling to the pieces of furniture, I will call on God and men to help me, and my cries will tell the Parisians that Junot's widow is carried from her own house by *gendarmes* only to offer one more victim to him who can no longer conquer nations. It will teach you that everyone will not allow themselves to be arrested without resistance."

Much taken aback, Savary changed his tone and left off trying to bully a woman who had certainly placed him in an awkward position. (Savary was one of those concerned in the arrest and murder of the Duc d'Enghien.) He knew perfectly well that such a scandal as would arise from the employment of violent measures was not to be thought of, and he began to protest that he had always liked Junot and Laura, and did not mean to make her angry.

She cut him short and begged him to go away, adding—

"I shall not change my mind. You know my intentions; it is for you to cause or to avoid a scandal. I shall not seek for one."

"Will you write to the emperor?"

"No."

"Why? You must have a reason."

"Of course. I will tell you what it is. The widow of Junot can never ask anything of him whom she regards as the cause of her husband's death. His being forbidden to come to Paris, where he could have had proper care and advice, was the finishing stroke. It is impossible for me to have anything do with the emperor. I will, in obedience to Junot's wishes, treat him with all due respect, . . . but if he tries any injustice or oppression on me, I will resist. That is my determination."

Savary went away without obtaining any other reply, and Laura was henceforth left unmolested.

CHAPTER 23

Abdication of Napoleon
1813

Although money had flowed like water through the hands both of Junot and Laura, he left his affairs in a most deplorable state. The little that remained was swallowed up by the debts with which they were always surrounded. Laura had still her *dot*, her dowry, and a claim on the fifth part of the *majorats* granted to her sons by Napoleon. She had also an immense quantity of jewels and other costly possessions, besides her *hôtel* at Paris; but she had no idea of managing money, and her quarrel with the emperor cut off any hope there might have been of his coming to her assistance.

She established herself again in her magnificent house with her four children, her brother, and two old uncles, and her friends gathered round her as usual.

Society in Paris appeared dead; the disastrous news that kept arriving from Spain and Germany seemed to paralyse everyone's spirits, and in her deep mourning Laura could not in any case have seen many people; but a small circle of her most intimate friends was to be found every evening in her *salon,* absorbed in the one subject of anxious discussion—the war.

Lavalette had in some measure taken the place of Duroc in Laura's friendship, and came constantly to bring her the latest news. The person about whom she now felt the greatest anxiety amongst those at the seat of war was Count Louis de Narbonne, who had always been to her like a second father.

One morning she was told that Lavalette was waiting to see her, and on entering the room was struck by his face of consternation.

"*Mon Dieu!*" he exclaimed; "how happy Junot is to be no longer here! We are lost! The emperor is completely crushed."

News had just come of the loss of a great battle. Napoleon had been beaten at Leipzig; the Saxons, Bavarians, and Wurtemburgers had deserted him and joined Blücher; the blowing up of the bridge over the Elster, intended to cover the retreat of the French army, had been prematurely carried out, ten thousand French soldiers being left on the other side to be killed or made prisoners.

The French Army was driven back across the Rhine, of three hundred thousand men only about fifty-five thousand returning to France. On the 3rd of November the emperor arrived at Mayence, for the second time re-entering his dominions as a fugitive. A few days later he received the news of the fall of Pampeluna, and that Wellington had driven Soult out of Spain, which was entirely cleared of the French troops. Spain and Portugal were now free, but at what a cost!

Laura felt a double pang as she remembered the bloodshed and suffering of the Spanish campaign, and the thousands of French soldiers whose bones were strewn over the battlefields of the Peninsula. For once she did not praise the benevolent intentions of the emperor towards those unfortunate countries or blame their resistance, but joined in the horror now expressed by so many at all the useless carnage and bloodshed for the will of one man, and all for nothing.

The Comte de Lavalette was devoted to Laura, and always at her service. One day she said to him—

"My dear, good friend, can you spare me a quarter of an hour?"

"Of course," he replied, sitting down by her.

"My dear count," she began, "you were a true friend to Junot; I like you for yourself first and then for that attachment, of which you gave him many proofs—amongst others these." And she took from a drawer of her bureau a packet of love-letters addressed to Junot, which she had found among his papers.

Lavalette looked confounded.

"I see by these letters," she continued, "that you knew of this intrigue of Junot's, for I won't call it a *liaison*, and that most of his letters passed through your hands to the person who wrote these."

"*Comment!*" exclaimed Lavalette; "Junot kept those letters. It is incredible!"

"Why should he destroy them?" asked Laura coolly. "They are very well written, and they express a sentiment which might be real and which he probably believed. But that is not what I want to talk to you about . . . listen to this."

Taking up one of the letters, she read it to him. It proved that the writer, besides carrying on with Junot an intrigue which had begun in Portugal and was continued in Paris, but had tried unsuccessfully to make mischief between him and herself. (This was a woman referred to in the English newspaper as belonging to Junot's *seraglio*.)

Laura had been perfectly aware of this affair, and on one occasion, when Junot was away, he had sent his letters by mistake to the wrong addresses, so that Laura received the one intended for Madame F——.

She read the letter, congratulated herself that that was not the way Junot had ever written to *her*, and when he came home, gave it to him, remarking—

"Of course, we have been too long married for me to think of being jealous; but it was a saying of the great Condé that a general might be defeated but never surprised. If a man is unfaithful to his wife, she ought not to know it."

Junot threw his arms round her, declaring that he loved her better than all the rest together, and when she asked for the letter which had miscarried, he exclaimed—

"Do you think I would give *you* a letter *she* has read?"

Laura now gave the letters and the portrait that was with them to Lavalette, requesting him to return them to Madame F——, as she was a friend of his.

The emperor was at Saint Cloud, taking measures for the defence of the country, which was threatened with immediate invasion.

He had sent word to Metternich that he was willing to accept the conditions of Frankfort, *i.e.,* the independence of Spain, Italy, Germany, and Holland, the boundaries of France to be the Rhine, the Alps, and the Pyrenees.

The *corps-legislatif* assembled on the 19th December and granted the emperor 300,000 conscripts; but many of those who would formerly have followed him with blind, unquestioning loyalty—Kléber, Duroc, Lannes, Junot, Bessières, and many more—were dead; Bernadotte was fighting for Sweden against France; the fidelity of Murat was wavering. Hundreds of thousands of his veteran soldiers lay dead on the battlefields of half the countries in Europe, whose place must now be filled by the new, boyish conscripts raised in haste to defend the country.

To Laura's other sorrows was added the loss of her second father, Count Louis de Narbonne, who died of the typhus fever now raging among the shattered remnants of the French troops in Germany. She had not seen him since Junot's death, but had received many letters from him, full of kindness and sympathy, and she felt his death acutely.

Slowly and steadily the hostile armies from all sides were closing upon France.

The English, Spaniards, and Portuguese under Wellington were approaching from the Pyrenees; the army of the North under Bernadotte, the German armies led by Blücher and Schwarzenberg, and countless reserves of Germans, Russians, Poles, and Dutch were pouring towards the frontiers of the country which all regarded as the common enemy of the rest of Europe.

Before the end of December, 1813, Blücher had crossed the Rhine; and the early weeks of 1814 saw the Russian troops at Nancy, the Austrians at Langres and Châlons, and Blücher established at Joinville.

The French Army was without money or proper provisions, and yet Napoleon, notwithstanding the general discontent and indignation, obstinately refused to sign conditions of peace, hoping against hope, perhaps for a more favourable result of the negotiations still going on at Frankfort, perhaps for a general rising in the country, which, drained of its strength and manhood, longed only for peace and rest.

To Laura and most of her compatriots of that generation, so accustomed from their childhood to a long succession of triumphs and victories that they had grown to fancy a sort of divine right in France to attack, meddle with, and rule over other countries, all this was like a kind of nightmare, which they could scarcely understand; but the warning words of Lucien to Napoleon were now being fulfilled: the Empire, built up with violence and bloodshed, was crumbling rapidly away.

At last the emperor set off, leaving the empress regent and Joseph Buonaparte Governor of Paris. He took leave of the National Guard, confiding his son to their protection with a visible emotion, which was declared by some to be a piece of acting, and deeply affected others. The Carrousel rang with shouts of "*Vive l'Empereur!*" "*Vive le Roi de Rome!*" and oaths of fidelity to be broken in a few weeks.

At first came tidings of successes. The emperor had driven back the Prussians beyond Saint Dizier, won battles at Brienne and Champ-Aubert, where he defeated the Russians, took two thousand prisoners, including a general, and thirty pieces of artillery. Laura went with Albert to see the spectacle of the last triumph of Napoleon, when ten banners taken from the enemy were brought into Paris.

It was Sunday, late in February, but the sun shone brilliantly. The quays, the Rue de Rivoli and the Place du Carrousel were crowded; there had been a review, and the troops filled the court of the Tuileries and the Carrousel. Joseph Buonaparte at their head looked so like the emperor that, as the procession approached with its banners and martial music, it recalled to their minds the remembrance of many a military triumph they had watched in the great days of the vanishing Empire. But it was only for a moment; the silence of the thronging multitudes and the gloom on the faces of the soldiers brought the

JOSEPH BUONAPARTE, KING OF SPAIN.

recollection that these banners had been taken within twenty leagues of Paris.

These short-lived successes only rendered the emperor more obstinate, and still he refused to sign any terms.

To those in Paris it was, of course, a time of alarm and consternation; the entrance of the Allies was now certain.

Besides the perils which might befall them, especially if the city were to be defended, Laura was aware that absolute ruin lay before her. The *majorats* granted by Napoleon as the inheritance of herself and her children were in foreign countries conquered by him, and would, of course, be lost now that those countries had shaken off the yoke of France. There were debts amounting to one million four hundred thousand *francs*, chiefly caused by the expense of living in their magnificent *hôtel* and the costly decorations and enlargements which Junot against his wife's advice, persisted in making.

Many of the marshals, generals, and members of the court of Napoleon remained rich even after the fall of the Empire; and Laura attributed the ruin of Junot's family with proud satisfaction to the fact that he had never been a rapacious robber like Soult, Masséna, and many others. But there can be no doubt that if it had not been for their own reckless extravagance, they could easily have saved from the lavish sums which they squandered in boundless luxury, pleasure and display, what would have amply secured the future of herself and her children. It was not only in selfish profusion that they had spent their fortune; they had shown great kindness and generosity to the members of both their families and to many others. Even now the Abbé de Comnenus and his younger brother, Prince George, both of whom were nearly seventy, lived with Laura and Albert, and regarded them almost as their own children.

The eldest brother. Prince Demetrius Comnenus, who was married and lived in Paris, came to see them, and pointed out that in this desperate state of affairs they must make use of his influence with the king who would soon be in the Tuileries.

Demetrius Comnenus was, as Louis XVIII. afterwards observed, one of the most loyal subjects he had in France. After his return from emigration he would never accept anything from the emperor; indeed, Laura, who was giving him a pension herself, dared not propose to him to accept the post of chamberlain offered by Napoleon. Everything which belonged to the Revolution or the Empire was abhorrent to him, and he would say to her reproachfully—

"You don't feel that as I do. Your mother—ah! your mother was a true Comnenus!"

Letters from Burgundy informed Laura of the death of her father-in-law, who had never recovered the loss of his son, and whose home at Montbard had been destroyed by the Germans and Cossacks, at the sight of whose uniforms he had been seized with paralysis.

The empress and her son left Paris for Blois on the 28th of March. Joseph Buonaparte remained in command, and the approach to Paris was guarded by Marshals Marmont and Mortier. As the enemy drew nearer and nearer, the greatest terror prevailed, the wildest reports were circulated. The emperor had sent orders to set fire to the powder magazine of Grenelle; Paris was to be blown up. These and other false rumours spread through the city, filling everyone with alarm.

Mindful of the late proceedings of her countrymen in like cases, Laura put her diamonds in a belt which she fastened round her waist, and concealed her other most valuable jewels about herself and her children's governess.

It was the 30th of March. The population of Paris were awakened at daybreak by the sound of firing, and the plain of St. Denis was covered with the allied troops.

All day long Marmont, with about eight thousand men, defended the heights of Belleville and Romainville.

Joseph Buonaparte authorised Marmont about noon to capitulate, and himself left Paris by the Bois de Boulogne to join the emperor at Fontainebleau.

Laura waited in great anxiety, surrounded by her children and by many friends who had collected in her *salon*. As night came on, she grew more uneasy and uncertain what to do; she therefore wrote to Marmont and asked him whether she ought to remain or to try to leave Paris. Marmont replied that he was now arranging the terms of capitulation, and that he strongly recommended her to stay in Paris, which would certainly be the quietest place next morning for twenty leagues around.

The letter arrived at two in the morning (31st), and was read aloud by Laura.

"But," objected one of those present, "if Paris is so very safe, why has the Duchess of Ragusa gone to Fontainebleau? If the duke tells other people to stay here, why does not he give his wife the same advice?"

"And who says he did not?" exclaimed another. "Her departure makes me believe he did, for she always does what he tells her not."

Everyone, however, decided to take the advice of the Duke of Ragusa (Marmont); and in a few hours the Allies entered Paris.

It was a strange Paris to Laura on that and the following days. White cockades and scarfs were seen everywhere; cries of "*Vive le Roi!*" "*Vive les Bourbons!*" were heard in the streets. With the Russians especially came many old friends of hers, amongst others Czernicheff. He came at once to see her, and inquired whether she was well treated by those quartered in her house, to which she replied that it might be better or worse, that she had Platow.

"Platow?" he said. "Why, Platow lodges with Madame de Rémusat."

"The father does, this is his son; and he eats twelve dishes for his *déjeuner*, as my *chef* will tell you, without counting his dessert, which is copious, as my butler will tell you; and his suite let my servants have no peace."

In fact, young Platow gave so much trouble that the housekeeper of the Duchesse d'Abrantès came to complain that he slept in his boots and spurs; which soiled and tore the fine linen, in which she took all the pride of an old servant; and her language was full of curses of the Russian savage. A few days later on, her mistress inquiring if he had improved, as she seemed calmer, the woman replied—

"Not at all, but I now give him the sheets belonging to the stablemen, which are quite good enough."

By way of an experiment, the servants bought some emetic powder and put it into all his food, wine, and brandy; but it had only the effect of making him feel better and hungrier. Laura forbade them to play any more tricks upon him, and M. Czernicheff had him removed and replaced by one of the officers on the emperor's staff, who was rather a protection than an inconvenience.

The Comte d'Artois was expected to arrive immediately at the Tuileries; the Emperor Alexander was at the Elysée-Napoleon, both he and the King of Prussia being carefully guarded.

From the *hôtel* of Madame de Rémusat Laura saw the office of expiation on the place where Louis XVI. and Marie-Antoinette had suffered.

An altar was erected upon the spot, Mass was celebrated, and, as the Emperor of Russia arrived, the *Te Deum* was sung. The Emperor Alexander, the Grand-duke Constantine, the King of Prussia, Prince Schwartzenberg, the English Ambassador, and the 25,000 troops on the place knelt to receive the benediction; and as they rose the Grand-duke Constantine lifted his hat as a signal for the salvos of artillery. It was a touching ceremony, and Laura was deeply impressed.

Within the next fortnight events of the greatest importance succeeded each other with astonishing rapidity.

The Emperor Napoleon signed his abdication at Fontainebleau; the Buonaparte family were scattered.

Caroline was in Italy, Pauline in the south of France, Lucien in England, Joseph and Jérôme starting for America, Madame Mère and Cardinal Fesch on their way to Rome.

The Emperor of Austria arrived on the 15th April. Marie-Louise, no longer empress, but Grand Duchess of Parma and Piacenza, came to meet her father at Trianon, and soon after left for Vienna with her son.

The Princess Catherine of Wurtemberg, on the contrary, refused to desert Jérôme, according to the desire of her father, to whom she wrote an answer saying that, as he well knew, Jérôme was not the husband of her own choice, that she had married him to please her father, but that, having done so, she would stay with him, for she had now become attached to him, and considered that her proper place was with her husband and children.

With the Emperor of Austria came of course Prince Metternich, who was a great friend of Laura's, and called upon her the day after his arrival. He told her that all the *majorats* were lost except those in Italy and Illyria, and on hearing that hers were in Prussia, Westphalia, and Hanover, he shook his head and said he feared she would lose everything. There was, however, one portion of which she showed him the title-deeds, the estate and castle of Acken in Prussia, worth about 50,000 *francs* a year, of which there might be some hope, as it was the property of the King of Prussia, of which he had a right to dispose and which he had ceded by three different agreements.

"You must appeal for that," he said, "and I will support you. But if you take my advice you will address yourself first to the Emperor of Russia, and get his protection; he has great influence over the King of Prussia."

Accordingly, Laura spoke to M. Czernicheff, who promised to ask the Emperor Alexander to give her an audience, but added that he did not; believe he would, and on asking why, only laughed.

"I told you so!" he exclaimed next day. "The emperor will not receive you at the Elysée."

"Eh! *mon Dieu!* why not?"

"He will not receive you at the Elysée because he wishes to have the honour of coming to see you himself. Those were his own words; are they not charming?"

"So much so, that I am deeply touched by them."

"Yes; he wants to see the widow of a man whose name he knows so well. General Junot was one of the brightest jewels in the Emperor Napoleon's crown of glory. The Emperor of Russia will be here to-morrow between twelve and one, if that hour suits you."

"We have not been accustomed to such politeness in imperial manners," observed Laura.

The following day, at about one o'clock, the Emperor Alexander arrived in a *coupé* with only one servant, and leading her eldest boy by the hand, Laura hurried to the great staircase to meet him. (The Emperor Alexander was then about thirty-seven.)

He took her hand and spoke to her with such kindness and courtesy that he won her confidence and attachment at once. She presented her other children, and when they had retired, the emperor led her to an armchair, made her sit down, and placed himself upon an ordinary chair near her.

"But, Sire, it is impossible that I can allow Your Majesty to sit there!" cried Laura, starting up.

"Sit still! sit still!" he said, smiling. "I must sit here to be able to hear you. You know I am deaf of one ear; and now, tell me what you want of me."

Laura explained the desperate condition of her affairs to the emperor, who directed her to make a note of what she wished done, and promised his support and help. He stayed a long time talking to her of many things—of his own romantic affection for Napoleon, of his grief at being betrayed by him, of his hatred and contempt for Savary, in which also Laura sympathised. He declared he would not see Savary, who had been guilty of the murder of the Duc d'Enghien and had the insolence to set spies upon himself in his palace at Petersbourg.

"They say his wife is very beautiful," he continued. "She has asked me for an audience tomorrow. I could not refuse her. But what do either of them want with me?—that I should persuade the Comte d'Artois that he was innocent in the affair of the Duc d'Enghien? It's impossible. As to Savary, I won't see him; that I am resolved. I will attend to your affair, Madame la Duchesse, and I am sure Louis XVIII. will do a great deal for the *noblesse* of the empire. He ought to; and besides, you belong to his kingdom too. Not only that, but you are of his rank. Are you not a Comnenus?"

"My mother was a Comnenus, Sire, but I am not."

"Well! you have royal blood, and for *nous autres souverains* that binds us to help our *relations* who are in trouble. Louis XVIII. was exiled and unfortunate himself a little while ago, and he is still at Hartwell."

The Emperor Alexander talked to Laura as if he had known her for twenty years, and she already felt on terms of friendship with him. He spoke much of Junot, and asked if Napoleon had not treated him with great injustice. Then he told her that he had read a letter of hers to Napoleon from Geneva which had been captured by his Cossacks, and had filled him with admiration and sympathy for her and indignation against Savary, who was evidently the enemy of Junot and herself.

Looking round the room, he inquired if she had no portrait of Junot among so many pictures.

"If Your Majesty would like to see it, I could show you one that is very like him," replied Laura, "but it would be necessary to take the trouble to go all through the apartment."

"Will you show me the way?" asked Alexander, rising and offering her his arm.

They crossed the billiard-room, the library, which was one of the most magnificent collections in Europe, then a large room furnished in antique style, then Laura's bedroom, then another room, and finally arrived in her study or *cabinet de travail*, where hung the portrait of Junot at twenty-seven in the uniform of a general. It was painted by Gros, and given to him by the government as a reward for his gallant conduct when with three hundred men he fought and put to flight four thousand Turks at Nazareth.

When the emperor at last rose to take leave of her, Laura went with him towards the staircase.

"Why, what are you doing?" he exclaimed.

"Sire, your Majesty will allow me—"

"I shall not allow anything at all. What! did you want to come down to the carriage with me?"

"Certainly, Sire," she replied, laughing at his astonished look.

"To my carriage!" he cried, laughing too. "*Eh! mon Dieu!* what would they say of me at *Petersbourg* if they saw me allowing a woman to come down the staircase to accompany me!"

"But we are not at St. Petersburg, Sire," entreated Laura, clasping her hands.

"Well, then, submit to the conqueror," said he, taking her hand and leading her back to the door of the drawing-room, adding, "I warn you that if you persist, I shall come and reconduct you—"

"I like exercise. Sire."

"And if I *command* you not to come any farther?"

"But I am not Your Majesty's subject."

"Well, then I shall not come and see you again. You will not punish me so much as that?"

"The fear of that will make me obey more than all the rest, Sire."

He ran down the staircase, and as he drove away put his head out of the carriage to salute Laura, who stood at the window.

Very soon he came again, walking in one morning unattended, and stayed a long time, conversing upon many subjects. Again, he promised to do all he could for her with the King of Prussia, and tried to persuade her to come to St. Petersburg, where he assured her that she should be well received and entertained.

He asked whether she would have any objection to another lodger; as it would be most convenient if her ground floor, which she was not now using, could be placed at the disposal of Lord Cathcart, the English Ambassador, assuring her that she would like him very much, he would be delighted to be of any use to her, and adding, "And when I come to see him it will be a pretext for me to come upstairs to see his hostess and hear if she has any complaints to make of him."

This apartment, which had only been used for reception, and was now disused, consisted of four large drawing-rooms, two small card-rooms, a large room which could be made a bedroom, a bathroom, and an immense gallery; the rooms opened into the garden.

Lord Cathcart came the next morning, and Laura agreed to let him the apartment and part of the stables, as since Junot's death she had sold all the horses except five.

The rooms on the first floor looking on the garden, which were Laura's when Junot was alive, she let to Sir —— and Lady Cole.

With all of these Laura got on extremely well. She found Lord Cathcart charming, and was on very friendly terms with the Coles. They were all to be found frequently in her *salon* in the evening, as in fact were most of the celebrities then at Paris. Prince Metternich came almost every day; the Duke of Wellington, of whose courtesy and kindness to Junot and herself in Spain she retained a grateful recollection, came to make her acquaintance almost directly he arrived. The only annoyance she experienced was from an insolent fellow who appeared one day when she was out and insisted on being shown over the house, even to the cellars, which were amongst the most celebrated in France, and, regardless of the representations of the *maître-d'hôtel* that the house was already full, proceeded to mark the doors of different rooms as lodgings for various officers of the Prince Royal of Sweden, to whose staff he declared himself to belong.

On hearing of what had happened, Laura wrote at once to the Prince of Sweden (Bernadotte) to complain, and within an hour his *aide-de-camp*, the Count de Brahé, was announced, a remarkably pleasant man about thirty years old in the uniform of the White Hussars, with, many excuses from the prince, who assured her that the culprit should be found and that he himself would call in a day or two to apologise. When he did so he explained that he had known nothing of the affair, and had found that the fellow, who occupied a subordinate post in his household, was a Frenchman.

CHAPTER 24
Laura Visits Joséphine at La Malmaison
1814-1816

Among the English who, although the political enemies, were the personal friends of the Duchesse d'Abrantès, were a very handsome *aide-de-camp* of the Duke of Wellington and his sister, the beautiful Miss Bathurst, who stayed in her house with Lady Cole, and whose melancholy fate soon afterwards has always been remembered in Rome. She was riding with a party of friends along the banks of the Tiber when her horse took fright, reared suddenly, and plunged with her into the river, where she was drowned. The *salon* of the Duchesse d'Abrantès was very much the fashion amongst the foreign diplomatic society.

"Will you promise not to laugh too much if I bring you one of my friends?" asked Metternich one day.

"That depends. You know I am naturally merry. Of what is it a question?"

"Of a friend of mine, who, I warn you, is not handsome. In fact, he is called the monster-prince."

"You are joking."

"Not at all. Of course, he has another name, and that is Wenzel von Lichtenstein. His brother, Prince Maurice von Lichtenstein, has asked me to present him to you; he is very different."

Thus prepared, Laura duly received the prince, whose unfortunately notorious appearance had not been exaggerated, but who was so fascinating as to have caused more than one *grande passion*.

Lord Castlereagh also wished to make her acquaintance, and Lord Cathcart invited her to a great dinner to meet him and Blücher; but she declined, for she had the greatest hatred for Blücher, and did not wish to meet him.

Therefore, having promised to dine quietly another time with Lord Castlereagh, she remained in her own rooms while the banquet went on below. Besides her aversion to Blücher, she felt that she could not bear to be present at the dinner given in her own gallery, where so often she and Junot had entertained the generals and officers of the Empire; and now that it was all swept away, as the martial music of their conquerors rose to her ears melancholy recollections filled her mind and depressed the usually elastic spirits which with her light-hearted, sunny temperament supported her through so many of the trials and difficulties of her chequered life.

A few days later she fulfilled her promise of dining with Lord Cathcart to meet Lord Castlereagh. The Duke of Wellington was also present, and asked if he could see the child born in the Spanish campaign, whom, with his mother, he had certainly on one occasion saved from the brigands. Laura went up and, taking him out of bed, wrapped him up and brought him downstairs. The little one laughed and played with the stars and orders of Wellington and the rest, when suddenly he hid his face in terror on his mother's shoulder as a remarkably ugly man entered.

It was Blücher. Laura ran upstairs with the child, and Lord Cathcart made profuse apologies, saying he had come in by chance.

"Where is he?" said Laura, looking round the room.

"Why, he is gone. I told him that you could not bear to see him, so he went."

"How *could* you?"

"Bah! he is gone to the Cercle. If he wins, the impression will be effaced by his good-humour, and if he loses, by his ill-humour."

In the meantime, preparations were being pushed on for the departure of the Emperor Napoleon for Elba; and having received a letter from Fontainebleau containing many details on the subject, Laura went to La Malmaison to see the Empress Joséphine, whom she knew to be very anxious for news of him.

It was early when she arrived, and Joséphine was still in bed; but on hearing that the Duchesse d'Abrantès was there she ordered her to be instantly admitted. Stretching out her arms to her, she cried, in a voice choked with tears, "Ah! Madame Junot! Madame Junot!"

Laura burst into tears also, for the sight of those rooms and corridors, once so familiar, and where she had spent so many happy days, was too much for her.

When the empress heard that Laura had a letter from Fontainebleau, she asked eagerly that every word should be read to her, as she wished to know *all*.

It was a difficult letter to read her, as it was full of allusions to the Empress Marie-Louise and the King of Rome.

"What do you think of that woman?" she asked, when Laura had finished it.

"What I have always thought, *Madame*: that she is a woman who never ought to have crossed the frontier between France and Germany."

Joséphine seemed pleased with Laura's opinions and sympathy, and presently said—

"Madame Junot, I have a great mind to write to Napoleon. Do you know why? I want him to let me go to Elba with him if Marie-Louise does not. Do you think she will go?"

"I don't think so—she is not capable of it."

Joséphine then asked Laura to get Prince Metternich to use his influence in her favour as he was her great friend, and it was hard to convince her of the impossibility of her plan. Laura represented that it was very doubtful whether Napoleon himself would consent; and on her asking why not, replied, "Because his sisters will certainly go, *Madame*, and Madame Mère too. Let Your Majesty recollect all she suffered even on the throne of France and in the palace of the Tuileries, protected by being a sovereign and wife of the emperor. If even then the sisters of Napoleon did not respect your tranquillity, what would they do now?"

"I believe you are right," said Joséphine sadly, leaning her face upon her hand. "Yes, I believe you are right. Have you seen the Comte d'Artois?"

"No, *Madame*."

Joséphine then expressed her anxiety lest a report should be well-founded which said that she was to lose the title of empress and be called the Duchess of Navarre, but on this point, Laura could give her no information.

The *déjeuner* was in the little dining-room, also full of associations and memories. Afterwards they walked in the conservatory, gardens, and park, where the empress showed Laura many of the plants and shrubs, she had sent her from Spain and Portugal.

Joséphine was extremely fond of flowers, and when Laura asked permission to present Lord Cathcart, who had requested her to do so, she replied—

"Yes! bring him to see me, but let it be at the end of the month. I should like the tulip-trees to be in flower and the park in all its beauty."

Laura remained until late in the afternoon, the empress showing her much affection and sympathy, and saying, "You know, if you don't care to go to the Tuileries, you can always come to La Malmaison, and stay altogether if you like. The emperor has been unjust to you and Junot, it is for me to make reparation. Your daughter is my god-daughter and I ought to do for you and her what I am sure Buonaparte would have done if he had remained upon the throne."

As the time drew near for the departure of Napoleon, Laura's bitter resentment against the man to whom she attributed the death of her husband was swallowed up in pity and regret for the hero of her youth, the greatest commander and statesman of modern times, the extraordinary genius who had saved France from the horrors of the Revolution, given her a magnificent code of laws and placed her, for a few short years, at the head of all the nations in Europe.

Louis XVIII. was approaching the capital, and Buonaparte, after a sorrowful parting with the Imperial Guard and the few friends and followers still faithful to him, was travelling from Fontainebleau southwards, often assailed by the curses and threats of the furious mobs which had once received him with acclamations. More than once he had been in danger of his life, and on one occasion saved himself by putting on an Austrian uniform.

"I lost two of my sons at la Mojaïsk!" cried one woman.

"I lost my father and husband at Wagram!" shouted another.

"I was made a cripple when I was twenty!" called out a man with a wooden leg.

"And the horrible taxes!" yelled another. "Six *sous* for a pot of wine; and all for the sake of the butchery he called 'his wars.' Death to the tyrant! Death!"

Pauline had taken a little house and was waiting to meet him, but when she beheld the Austrian uniform she started back in the midst of the tears and words of affection with which she met him, exclaiming, "What is that uniform?"

"Paulette, would you wish me to be murdered?"

She looked at him for a moment. "I cannot embrace you in that dress," she said. "Oh, Napoleon! what have you done?"

He left the room, and when he came back in the uniform of the Old Guard, she threw herself into his arms.

Outside a crowd had collected, and to the alarm of his escort, he insisted on walking about amongst them.

Suddenly he stopped before a man with a deep scar. "Are you not Jacques Dumont?"

"*Oui, monseigneur! Oui, mon général! Oui,* Sire!"

"You served with me in Egypt?"

"Yes, oh yes. Sire!"

"You were wounded—but it was long ago, I think?"

"At the Battle of Trélia, Sire, with the brave General Suchet, in my leg, and I could serve no longer. But now when I hear the drums beat, I feel like a deserter not to go. I would follow your Majesty again wherever you chose." And he shed tears, repeating, "My name! my name—after fifteen years!"

Napoleon spoke to some others, and suddenly exclaiming, "Marshal Masséna commands at Toulon. I should like to shake hands with him before I go away, perhaps for ever!"

"Will you send a letter, Sire?"

"I will take it!"

"And I!" cried about two hundred voices with eager enthusiasm.

As Laura was sitting alone at work one morning, one of her *valets-de-chambre* came in and said someone wanted to see her. He did not know who it was, as he had only just come from Burgundy, bringing some of Laura's possessions which had been saved from the enemy. He had assured the gentleman that *Madame* did not receive at that hour, but it was no use.

"Is it M. Czernicheff?"

"No, *Madame*, I know M. Czernicheff, it is not him."

"Show the gentleman in," said she and looking up, she started to her feet, upsetting all her things, as the Emperor Alexander walked in laughing heartily.

"Why you are extraordinary in Paris," he said. "Did the Emperor Napoleon never come and see you in this way without ceremony?"

Laura was just going to say "no," when she remembered his visit to Junot in that very room, on one occasion when he had been suffering from an illness brought on by some disagreement between them. She told the Emperor Alexander about it, and he led her to speak of Junot and of the treatment he had received from Napoleon, asking her many questions respecting different persons she had known, especially Bernadotte, now Prince Royal of Sweden, where his wife was not very happy, finding the climate and court alike cold and dull after France. He stayed an hour and a half, and before going assured her that he had spoken to the King of Prussia, who had promised that the estate of Achen and all the arrears should be given her.

The next day M. von Hardenberg, was announced: a stiff, dried-up personage who brought her the deeds of investiture of that property, but to her utter consternation she found that it was only to be granted on condition that her two sons should be naturalised Prussians, which she refused with a transport of indignation.

She wrote to the Emperor Alexander, who came to see her next day, extremely vexed and disappointed; but there was nothing more to be done—the fortune was lost.

There was now no hope, but in the king, and Albert and their uncles all urged Laura to apply to him for assistance.

She was to be presented with the rest of the court, and simplicity in dress was strictly enjoined; Laura found that none of the magnificent toilettes she had worn at the court of Napoleon would be admissible. She looked at her tiara and *rivières* of diamonds, and pronounced them impossible; she tried on *parure* of emeralds and smaller diamonds, which was in the days of the Empire called a *parure du matin*—even that was too brilliant. Her dresses and mantles, heavy with gold and silver embroidery, were not to be thought of She ordered a dress of white satin and white *crêpe* and wore in her hair a *parure* of carbuncles with which she thought no fault could be found.

In the place where she had always been accustomed to see Joséphine and then Marie-Louise, stood the Duchesse d'Angoulême, Dauphine of France. She bowed to each as they curtseyed to her, but when Laura came up, she stopped her, saying, with a gentle manner and voice—

"You are Madame Junot?"

"Yes, *Madame*."

"You suffered very much in your last Spanish journey. Did you save your son?"

Laura was on the point of saying that the boy should be brought up to serve and defend her, but hesitated to do so, and the princess continued, in a tone of kindly interest—

"You do not feel any ill-effects from these hardships still?"

"It is three years ago now, *Madame*."

"Ah, yes, that is true," said the *dauphine* reflecting. She bowed and Laura passed on with a thrill of mingled affection and reverence for the woman who seemed to her at once a princess, a saint, and a martyr—a feeling far different from her liking and friendship for the kind-hearted, frivolous Joséphine, or her indifference to the cold, unsympathetic Marie Louise.

The court was presented *en masse* to the king, whom many of them, including Laura, scarcely saw; but, following the urgent advice of her brother and uncles, she asked for an audience, which was granted for the next day between two and three o'clock.

With mingled feelings of melancholy and embarrassment Laura drove to the Tuileries, so familiar and yet so strange to her. She dreaded the interview in which she must ask for the remnant of their fortune and throw herself and her children upon the generosity of Louis XVIII.; she considered with perplexity how she should call the late emperor when she spoke of him, hesitating between "the emperor," which would perhaps be ill-bred, and "General Buonaparte," which would, she thought, be cowardly.

She had also heard a rumour that the king had promised the *faubourg St. Germain* not to allow the *"noblesse vilaine" i.e.*, of the Empire, to sit down in his presence.

When she entered the room in which she had so often found Napoleon, Louis XVIII. was seated in an armchair, from which he raised himself slowly, excusing himself on account of the gout from which he was suffering, and making her sit in another armchair by his side.

Remarking that he was perhaps overtired, Laura suggested that joy and happiness seldom did anyone real harm.

"Joy and happiness? Those are two things to which I shall have to get accustomed; they have been very strange to me since I left France. They say you are a good Frenchwoman, *Madame la Duchess*e, so you will understand me. You are rather like your mother—she was very beautiful when I last saw her."

"Your Majesty knew my mother?" And she drew nearer to him.

"How should I not have known anyone so lovely? especially when she was a Comnenus and her brothers were at court. Is she still at Paris? Oh! I beg your pardon, I beg your pardon a thousand times!" he added, as Laura's look and silence told him the truth. Then, changing the conversation, he said—

"You are not used to find such an invalid as I am here?" He questioned her about Junot with much kindness and sympathy, took notes, and promised to grant her petition, observing, with a graceful courtesy which touched her—

"The Duc d'Abrantès did not die in my service, but such a man is an honour to his country, and it is for her to pay the debt. I will attend to it."

A sum which had escaped the Prussians and was still in the imperial treasury, bringing her an income of 10,000 *francs*, was restored to her, and a pension promised.

The king also granted the petition she made for her brother, and promised to buy her great *hôtel* in the autumn.

Before the allies left Paris, Laura gave a large dinner-party in honour of the Duke of Wellington.

"Whom would you like to meet?" she asked him.

"Whoever you like—Metternich—he is pleasant and amusing."

But Laura could by no means invite both Wellington and Metternich. Which, in that case, would take precedence of the other? She thought of the Cardinal Maury, who, in spite of his deplorable principles and character, was rather a friend of hers, but a cardinal took precedence over everyone else. In her perplexity she explained the state of things to Prince Metternich, who promised to come after dinner, and with the exception of the two Princes von Lichtenstein, those invited

NEY.

to dine were chiefly French and English.

No one who was present on that evening, seeing the splendour of the house, the masses of flowers everywhere, the perfection of the dinner and of the music which followed it, the magnificent *toilettes*, and the lavish profusion which seemed to pervade every arrangement, would have supposed the hostess to be a ruined person with young children and old uncles depending upon her, and nothing to rely on but the generosity of the king.

The entertainment was brilliant and successful enough, the only *contre-temps* being caused by a French general, who was so anxious to insult the Duke of Wellington that, instead of simply declining to meet him, he tried to assert his dignity by arriving very late, in a morning coat and trousers and dirty shoes—a proceeding which made Wellington laugh, and only annoyed his hostess, against whom he had no spite whatever.

The allies departed—to the festivities in London, and then the Congress in Vienna, whence Laura heard often from Prince Metternich.

She sold her splendid *hôtel* and moved into a smaller one with her family, still sharing in all the stir and excitement, social and political, that went on around her.

The summer and winter passed away and March began: it was almost a year since the fall of the Empire, when suddenly came the news that Buonaparte was again in France.

It was like a thunderbolt in the midst of a clear, calm day. Received with transports of joy in the provinces, his journey from Golfe-Juan to Paris was a continued triumph, and he entered the Tuileries a few hours after the flight of the king and royal family on March 20, 1815.

But at Paris he did not find the enthusiasm he had met with in the country. An immense crowd had gathered before the Tuileries, but he missed many of the faces he looked for, and he was received almost in silence.

The theatres were all closed, and an atmosphere of gloom and depression seemed to pervade the city. Some members of his family met him, amongst others Lucien, who, forgetting his brother's past oppression and injuries, hastened to his side in the hour of need.

During the "Hundred days" of the second reign of Napoleon Laura remained in strict retirement, although it was intimated to her that the emperor wished to see her at his court again. But the same reasons which had before separated her entirely from the man to whom she attributed her husband's death still existed; and besides she now considered herself bound by gratitude to Louis XVIII., who, as she said, had given her the help and sympathy denied by Napoleon.

Few persons of any weight felt much confidence in the duration of the power of Buonaparte; all that seemed to be certain was that the fighting, of which the greater part of the nation were heartily weary, would begin again. Not since the horrible times of the Terror, with which her early years had been so deeply impressed, had Paris presented so melancholy a spectacle as during these three months.

Again, bands of ruffians paraded the streets shouting, "*Vive la République!*" "Death to the Royalists!" Again, revolutionary airs of sinister associations were played in the theatres and fierce, bloodthirsty songs sung on the boulevards.

In anxious fear people waited for the issue of events. It was evident that the crisis must soon come. Napoleon had not a single ally, and all Europe was in league against him.

The energy of former days seemed to have deserted him, and he lingered on in Paris when his most faithful friends were urging him to set off to meet the enemy. It was not till the beginning of June that he left Paris, and shortly after came the news of Waterloo. Napoleon returned to Paris, shut himself up in the Elysée-Bourbon and there signed his final abdication. Again, Paris was filled with the allied troops, and Louis XVIII. returned to the Tuileries.

The *hôtel* in which Laura now lived with her family was in the *rue Saint-Lazare*. She was still surrounded by a large circle of friends, and went occasionally to court, though not as intimately as in the days of the Empire. But wherever she lived all the celebrities of the day were to be found in her *salon*, which was one of the pleasantest in Paris.

There was a famous Bible of the thirteenth century in twelve magnificently illuminated volumes, which Junot, when Napoleon ordered him to seize all the Portuguese art treasures, brought with the rest of the booty to Paris. Being very fond of books and artistic works, Junot asked the emperor to give him this Bible, which he did.

When Laura, after her husband's death, found herself in want of money, she wrote to Napoleon at Dresden asking him to buy the Bible for the *Bibliothèque Royale*. He agreed to do so, but before the matter was arranged came the fall of the Empire and the restoration, which put a stop to the transaction.

But with the victory of the allies of course came the restoration of their property carried off by the French. Statues, pictures, bronzes, gems, art treasures of every description, were sent back to their lawful owners, and amongst other things the King of Portugal wrote for his Bible.

One day whilst the allies were in Paris the Duchesse d'Abrantès received an order to give it up, which she indignantly complained might have been sent to a maid who had stolen her mistress's shawl.

She contended that the Bible was hers, and *must* be hers, as the emperor had given it to her husband and was going to buy it back from herself, apparently not considering whether Napoleon had any right to give her the King of Portugal's Bible. She appealed to the king, who arranged the affair by ordering her to be paid a considerable sum for the Bible, though not the 140,000 *francs* at which it had been valued, and sending it back to Lisbon.

Amongst the relations for whom Laura had great affection was her nephew, Adolphe de Geouffre, son of her sister Cécile, and with his father also she had always remained upon very friendly and intimate terms.

One day in the spring of 1816 her brother-in-law came in with a disturbed air, saying that he wanted to speak to her upon a matter of importance.

He told her that he had just come to Paris, and that in the hotel where he was staying he had made the acquaintance of a young Corsican, who was also staying there with his sister and who had called upon him, saying that his name was Stephanopoli, that he was related to the Duchesse d'Abrantès, to whom he brought letters of introduction from other relations in Corsica, and that he had come to see him, Geouffre, knowing that he was connected with the family.

This seemed natural enough, but M. de Geouffre proceeded to inform her that, although neither Freemason nor Carbonaro himself, he had been at one of their meetings, at which he had met this young Stephanopoli, from whom he had discovered that there were persons in Corsica who believed that Laura had deserted the cause of Napoleon and knew that she had refused to go to the Tuileries during the Hundred days; that for this they owed her a grudge; therefore, knowing the fierceness of the Corsican vendetta, and observing that Stephanopoli talked wildly and wore a dagger, he hastened to warn her of what he felt certain to be a serious danger.

After a little consideration Laura desired him to bring Stephanopoli to see her, to which he strongly objected at first, but afterwards consented.

Soon after he had left her Albert returned from Strasbourg, and, much relieved at his appearance, she told him what had happened, and found that he agreed with their brother-in-law that the situation was alarming.

The next day Stephanopoli was presented to her, and proved to be a dark, handsome, rather wild-looking man of about twenty-seven. He looked at her in silence and evident astonishment, and then stammered a few words of very bad French, to which she replied in such perfect Italian that he changed colour and exclaimed—

"What! you speak Italian like that!"

"Of course, I do; for a very simple reason—I am Italian."

"Your heart is not," he replied, shaking his head. "Our brothers are persecuted, Napoleon is at St. Helena, and you go to see the Bourbons."

"I go because they are necessary for the welfare of the country," she replied. "As to the emperor, I had reason enough to complain of him."

"Ah!" cried this strange guest, grinding his teeth, "how can anyone have cause to complain of Napoleon?"

Presently his eyes fell upon the portrait of Junot, and he inquired if that were the Duc d'Abrantès.

"Ah, he was a brave man," he added, looking earnestly at it; and Laura then related to him the whole history of the treatment her husband had received from Buonaparte, to which Stephanopoli listened with the deepest attention, shedding tears of sympathy and ending by saying—

"Well, I am very glad I have seen you and heard all this, for otherwise—" and he stopped.

Laura invited him to dine and bring his sister, who proved to be a shy, gentle girl, very beautiful and entirely devoted to her brother.

Seeing that her *toilette* left much to be desired, Laura had her hair arranged and a more becoming dress given her, by which her appearance was so much improved that her brother's delight and gratitude were unbounded.

From that time his affection for Laura became as vehement as his hatred had been; he came often to see her with his sister Stephanie, of whom she grew very fond. She told Laura of her monotonous life at the convent in Padua, where she was educated, and of her passionate love for her brother, who was all she had in the world and loved her devotedly. He was like a half-savage, this young Stephanopoli, fierce and hasty but affectionate and impressionable; the sound of music would bring tears to his eyes.

One evening, after Stephanopoli and his sister had been dining with Laura, they were all sitting in a room which opened into the garden. Albert and Stephanopoli went through the glass doors on to the terrace outside and stood leaning upon the balustrade listening to Laura, who was playing dreamily upon the piano.

The air was heavy with the scent of lilacs, and for some time neither of them spoke, but Stephanie whispered to Laura, "Look at my brother; he is crying."

Albert just then spoke to him in a low voice, and they both turned away and disappeared amongst the shady walks of the garden. It was some time before they returned, and after Stephanopoli and his sister had gone Albert told Laura with intense relief that he had at last succeeded in getting Stephanopoli to promise him to leave Paris immediately. His departure would avert a great danger, for it was now certain that he had come to Paris with the intention of murdering not only Laura, but the king.

Albert had gained sufficient influence over him to persuade him to give up his purpose, and was anxious to induce him to go to America. He had offered him letters to Joseph Buonaparte, but it was of no use, he would only go to Germany.

Albert gave him letters to someone there, and Laura took charge of his sister for a time. At first, he sent them news of his movements, but on a sudden all communication ceased.

After five weeks had passed in silence Albert caused inquiries to be made, which resulted in the discovery that he had been murdered in a lonely inn near Ratisbon.

Nothing had been stolen from him and his assassination had evidently been the work of a secret society. He had been warned by Monsieur de Geouffre through a friend, who said that he was also a friend of Metternich, that his life was in danger, and he had apparently been tracked from Paris by the assassins. Two men who seemed to be strangers to him were found to have stopped with him at the inn the night of the murder, and his body was found with two dagger thrusts in the morning.

His sister returned to Padua, and afterwards took the veil in the convent of the Capucines, near the Porta Pia, where Laura saw her on her next visit to Rome.

CHAPTER 25
Her Journey in Italy
1817-1821-1838

In 1817 Laura had a serious illness, after which she passed some weeks in Burgundy, where she recovered her strength and then returned to Paris. The winter and spring were very gay, on account of the marriage of the Duc de Berry with the Princess Caroline of Naples.

The three friends who had been the chosen companions of her girlhood and whose affection had continued unchanged through all these eventful years—Laura de Caseaux, now Madame de Castarède, Melanie de Périgord, and Madame Juste de Noailles, Duchesse de Poix—were living in Paris and were constantly in her society, which consisted of many of her early friends of royalist opinions, besides a number of those of later years and of different nationalities.

With her children, her brother, and her uncles her family was sufficiently numerous and her fortune insufficient, especially for one of her tastes and habits. In 1818 she resolved to spend some time in Italy, where her journey was not entirely one of pleasure; for she hoped by means of influential friends in Rome to be able to recover some more of the property she had lost through the death of her husband, and the political changes by which it had been followed.

She had just refused to marry a Sicilian prince of large fortune but absurd appearance and manners who was very much recommended by some of her friends, but she preferred her poverty and freedom to such a marriage as this, and set off in excellent spirits early in June, accompanied only by her secretary, who had been Junot's, her maid and a valet.

As she drove along the shores of the Lake of Geneva, even the recollection of what she had suffered there five years ago was not enough to prevent her enjoyment of those enchanting scenes. She crossed the Simplon in perfect weather, and travelled from Milan to Florence, where she put up at the well-known Hotel Schneider, and an hour afterwards Prince Metternich arrived to see her.

The Grand-Duke Ferdinand was now re-established, and society was very pleasant in that charming city of flowers and sunshine, which was far more beautiful in those days than now. The vandalism of the modern Italians, their rage for cutting down trees and converting the whole country into a desert or a kitchen-garden, their destruction of ancient walls, towers, and streets, had not then been wreaked upon so many of what were amongst the loveliest scenes in the world, and as Laura sat with Prince Metternich on a balcony looking upon the Arno they contrasted the peace and beauty of the scene before them with the storms and changes they had seen together, and wondered how long this tranquillity would last.

Presently came an enormous bouquet from Prince Camillo Borghese, with a note to inquire when the duchess could receive him, and he shortly appeared and invited her to drive in the Cascine.

That lovely park was thronged with carriages, and as they drove up and down, they met the grand-duke with his two nieces, Leopoldine, soon after Empress of Brazil, and Marie-Louise, whom Laura had not seen since she reigned at the Tuileries.

As she bowed to Laura a flood of recollections rushed into her mind and made her start. For Marie-Louise personally she had never felt either liking or respect, but she thought she ought perhaps to go and see her before leaving Florence, and remarked that evening before various people who had come to tea in her *salon*, that she must do so. Prince Metternich, who was present, made no observation at the time, but sent her a note early next morning advising her not. She followed his counsel, and having been present at the departure of the Archduchess Leopoldine for Brazil, she took leave of her friends in Florence and pursued her journey to Rome.

The country was then exceedingly unsafe on account of the brigands by which it was infested; but having, of course, an escort, and never travelling after dark, Laura arrived safely at the last post from Rome, a lonely inn called La Storta. As it was seven o'clock, it was impossible to go on that night, so she resigned herself to sleep there, though the solitude of the place frightened her, and she asked the landlord, who served her at supper, whether there was not a risk of the inn being attacked in the night.

He assured her that she was quite safe in his house, pointing out that there was a post of *carabinieri* close by and a great bell to ring in case of alarm, and adding what reassured her most—that of course any such event would ruin his inn, for nobody would ever sleep there again, and implying that he averted such a misfortune by paying blackmail to the brigands.

As he waited upon her the host entertained her with stories of their crimes and depredations which were by no means reassuring, and must have reminded Laura of her Spanish journeys in a wilder and more dangerous country, but generally under the powerful protection of her husband.

One of the most terrible of these histories was that of an English family who were wintering in Rome, and whose eldest daughter had just married a Mr. Bischopp.

The young people had set their hearts upon going to Terni, the neighbourhood of which was particularly dangerous. They were warned by their friends against going there without an escort, but persisted in their rash folly, and set off unaccompanied. Mrs. Bischopp tried to persuade her mother and sisters to go too, but they refused (her father was dead).

They slept at the inn, got up early and went to see the waterfall, near which Mr. Bischopp sat down to sketch, whilst Mrs. Bischopp allowed herself to be persuaded by the guide to go up to a higher point at some little distance to see the view.

Her husband sat for some time absorbed in his work, until he was startled by the sound of shrieks and cries mingling with the noise of the water, and, looking up, saw his wife being carried up the rocks by two men. He rushed after them, but slipped upon the stones and fell. When he got up the men with his wife had disappeared, and the guide was coming towards him battered and hurt.

He applied to the *podestà* of the place, who told him that such occurrences were frequent, and the only thing to do was to wait patiently until some communication was made; but scouted his proposal to arrest the messenger, declaring that to do so would be fatal.

During the day a letter was brought saying that the captive would not be harmed, and would be restored if before eight days 30,000 *francs* were put upon a certain stone indicated. If not, her husband would never see her again.

The unfortunate man hurried to Rome to obtain the ransom. There was consternation all over the city. The Duchess of Devonshire went at once to Mrs. Bischopp's mother and offered her purse, but the husband got the money from his banker (Torlonia), and hastened back to place it upon the stone described. But although he kept it there for four days and went back fifteen times, there was no answer, and his wife was never heard of again.

Laura was soon comfortably established in Rome and surrounded with friends and acquaintances. Several of the Buonaparte family had settled there, and received her in their different ways with much affection.

Madame Mère lived in mournful resignation in the great Roman palace, where her chief solace was in the society of such of her children and grandchildren as she could gather round her. Her eldest daughter, Elisa, was in Germany, and she never forgave Caroline for her desertion of Napoleon. Some of her sons were far away, but Jérôme and the Princess Catherine came to Rome; Pauline, the only one of her family who had preserved the rank she was the first to attain, inhabited the huge *palazzo* Borghese; Lucien and his family had returned in peace to the scenes and pursuits in which they delighted; his eldest daughter, Charlotte, was the wife of Prince Gabrielli; and Cardinal Fesch, the brother of Madame Mère, was constantly with his sister, who found the greatest consolation in his presence.

Never had there been a more interesting and intellectual society; and Laura entered into it with enthusiasm. Her *salon* was at once the resort of all the political, artistic, and literary celebrities. She became very fond of the Duchess of Devonshire, and found intimate friends in the Austrian and Swedish ambassadors. Canova, then in the height of his fame, was often at her house. He had not long since finished his famous statue of the Princess Borghese, who eagerly asked Laura if she had seen it and thought it like her, adding that it ought to be, as she stood for it.

"You stood for it!" cried Laura, remembering the scanty drapery of the figure.

"Yes, I did. It was not so disagreeable as you think, for there was a stove in the room."

Pauline was just the same mixture of selfishness, good-nature and folly as ever, and would earnestly inquire of her numerous visitors, "How do you think I look? Am I looking as well as I did last time you saw me?"

At a ball given by Prince Torlonia, Laura sprained her ankle, which caused her to be laid up for six weeks, but her friends came constantly to see her, and her *salon* was just as pleasant as ever; therefore, she was never dull.

The Pope also was very kind to her; he had liked her and Junot in former days. When she was well enough he sent for her to walk with him in the lovely Pamfili gardens. She paid him several visits.

To Lucien Buonaparte, Pio VII. was like a second father, as he remarked when it was suggested that he should settle in Austria to be near his nephew, the late King of Rome, now Duke of Reichstadt.

He said also that his fortune was in Italy, which was the country he preferred, and that his own family must be his first consideration. Certainly, the life they led was an ideally delightful one—a Roman palace in winter and a villa at Tusculum in summer, in both of which Lucien, Prince of Canino, and his wife entertained brilliantly and hospitably the most distinguished and interesting persons of all nations.

In this enchanting climate, in the society of such men as Metternich and Brougham and Byron, with a magnificent library, and surrounded by the majestic ruins of ancient Rome, their lives were like those described by Horace. Lucien would walk in the great gallery of his Roman palace conversing with some kindred spirit, or spend hours in superintending the excavations at Tusculum, or join in an out-of-doors *fête*, or sit immersed in his books, happy and contented in the congenial life from which no dreams of ambition had ever tempted him, while the crowns and sceptres of his brothers and sisters had fallen away, leaving nothing but mediocre men and women mostly discontented and unhappy, distinguished only for having been thrust into and then out of positions they were unfit to fill.

The discovery of some buried treasure was one of the greatest pleasures of the life at La Rufinella, Lucien's estate at Tusculum.

One of the farmers on his property at Canino found one day a small cave containing two thousand exquisite Etruscan vases, and in the course of his excavations at Tusculum Lucien discovered the school of Cicero, to his intense delight. The difficulties and restrictions very rightly imposed in our own days upon the collectors of antiquities in Italy did not exist then, which was all the worse for the country and all the better for the foreign antiquarians, collectors, and travellers.

Laura was exceedingly interested in the excavations, and saw that of the column of Phocas in the Forum. Numbers of exquisite little bronzes and artistic objects were dug up there, of which she brought back a basketful, but she gave most of them away. One, a chariot and horses in a perfect state, she had mounted on *giallo antico* as a paperweight.

The great drawback to this enchanting life was the continual danger from brigands. There was no safety outside the walls of the city. One of the most terrible of their chiefs had been the son of an old shepherd and his wife, named Gasparone. They were simple, pious, respectable people, who lived not far from the villa of Lucien Buonaparte, and their only son, remarkable for his extraordinary strength, height and beauty, was supposed to be equally pious, and was better educated. He carved in wood, recited Tasso, and was a favourite with the priest of the village, who had taught him many things.

Young Gasparone was deeply in love with a beautiful *contadina* who lived close by. This girl was a great favourite with the daughters of Lucien, who foolishly dressed her up in costly clothes and jewels to try the effect upon her beauty, and showed her to young Gasparone, in whose mind this immediately aroused evil and covetous desires to such an extent that he resolved to turn brigand in order to get gold and jewels for Teresa.

He rose early in the morning, left the cottage where his parents were still sleeping, and went to a wood near Canino, which he knew to be the resort of a band who were the terror of the neighbourhood, and where he met their captain, a ferocious miscreant called Luigi, and one of his men. He joined the gang, by whom he was eagerly welcomed, and received with so much favour as to excite the jealousy of Luigi.

Resolved to gain an influence with the men, and aspiring to become their leader, he told them that before the next morning he would give them proofs that he had broken for ever with an honest life.

He went to Viterbo, sought an audience of the *vice-legate*, Cardinal Lanti, and offered to betray Luigi into his hands. The *carabinieri* had for some time been on the track of this band, of whom they had killed several, and the offer was at once accepted.

Gasparone proposed to take a carriage with four horses and six *carabinieri*, three of whom should be disguised as English ladies supposed to be travelling, and promised so to arrange that Luigi should fall into their hands.

They left the palace of the cardinal at ten o'clock on a dark night and drove in silence for some distance. At last the chief of the *carabinieri* remarked that the way seemed long, and asked where they were going.

"Where I promised to take you," replied Gasparone; "we are getting near."

He lighted the carriage lamps, the sign agreed upon with Luigi, and the band of thirty brigands rushed upon them. The *carabinieri* cried, "Treason!" and were at once seized and bound. Gasparone himself stabbed every one of them, and their bodies being thrown into the carriage, the terrified postilion, who had hidden himself in a ditch, was ordered to drive back to the cardinal.

With shouts of "*Viva Gasparone!*" he was made chief of the band, and told Luigi to serve him faithfully or forfeit his life.

A great supper in the robbers' cave followed these murders. The next day a peasant of his own village came with provisions to the cave, and seeing Gasparone giving orders there, uttered a cry of horror, and with some hesitation said—

"Then it is true you are a brigand! Your old father refuses to believe it, and so does Teresa. But do you know what effect the news had on your mother? She fell dead without a word."

Gasparone turned pale and gave a piercing cry.

"Yes," continued the other, "without even a prayer for you. So, you have killed your mother."

This terrible news for some time seemed to increase the ferocity of Gasparone, who became enormously rich and the terror of the countryside. But after a time remorse began to take hold upon him; he grew less cruel and appeared to have a kind of horror of himself

Hearing of this, the priest of his village who had educated him resolved to see him, with Teresa, who still loved him in spite of all that had happened.

When word was brought to Gasparone of their intention, he agreed to meet them in the glade of a wood, and was so far moved by their entreaties, the exhortations of the priest, and the promise of pardon from the Pope, that he assured them he would take the earliest opportunity of leaving the brigands when he could do so with safety. Shortly afterwards he returned to his native village, married Teresa, and was a good husband and father ever afterwards, leading an honest, peaceable life, and, what is the strangest part of this extraordinary story, being allowed to keep his ill-gotten property.

But the most ferocious and terrible brigand in the country just at the time Laura was in Rome was Decesaris, who carried his crimes and depredations not only over all the environs but up to the very gates of the city.

Lucien had married his eldest daughter to Prince Gabrielli, another to an English peer, and a third to the Count de Posset, a Swede, and was now celebrating the betrothal of another to Prince Ecolani, a Bolognese. The prince and several of his family were staying at the Villa Rufinella, near Frascati.

Laura was spending the early autumn in the Palazzo Cerani at Albano, where Madame Mère had also a villa. All that enchanting country, Frascati, Albano, Genzano, Ariccia, Castel Gandolfo, were, and are still, the resort of the great Roman families, whose huge, ancient villas, buried in groves of chestnut and ilex, are scattered about the hills.

The villa Rufinella, which now belongs to Prince Lancellotti, is supposed to occupy the site of the villa of Cicero, and is not far from that of Lucullus.

It stands upon the side of a steep hill, up which the path leads from Frascati to the convent of the Cappuccini and the remains of Tusculum. All around that delightful abode are woods and shady walks, and a little higher up the ruins of the ancient Roman town, now silent, deserted, and grass-grown, were at that time alive with the gang of busy, chattering workmen, engaged in carrying out the excavations which were then the absorbing interest of Lucien Buonaparte.

One evening, a short time before sunset, a *Monsignore*, a friend of the family, arrived at the villa just as Lucien and two or three others came down from the excavations. On his expressing regret at being too late, Lucien said, "Well, go up by this path, and see them; the men are still there, and we will wait dinner."

The old priest walked on, found the men still at work, and remained some time talking to them, and looking at the excavations, in which he was so much interested that he did not notice that whilst he was wandering about, absorbed in the contemplation of the discoveries, the sun had set, the workmen had all gone, and he was alone. The sudden chill which comes after sunset in Italy recalled him from the past to the present; he wrapped his cloak round him and turned to go back, but at that moment a hand was laid upon his shoulder, and a tall, handsome man, of suspicious appearance, desired him to stop.

He was dressed in the manner of the brigands—a coat with an immense number of buttons, leather gaiters, short breeches, a hat adorned with ribbons and a number of watches worn as ornaments. Twelve men at the same time emerged from a thicket close by, and without listening to his representations that he was only a poor priest with no money ordered him to go with them.

They went down to the villa, where, tired of waiting, everyone had gone to dinner, and rang the bell.

The Comte de Châtillon, one of the guests, left the dining-room, and ran down the staircase, at the foot of which he found himself, unarmed and in evening dress, standing face to face with a powerful man, armed with a carbine, who, exclaiming, "*Ah! ecco il principe!*" (Ah! here is the prince), seized hold of him. Châtillon defended himself, knocked the brigand down, and called for help; but the rest of the gang came forward, seized the two or three servants who stood there, and gave Châtillon a violent blow on the forehead, which made him insensible. No one heard what was going on, as the dining-room was at some distance. The priest managed to escape, and by the time the bell rang to summon the peasants to help, Decesaris, and his band had made good their retreat with their captive.

When Châtillon recovered consciousness and asked where he was, Decesaris replied—

"With brigands, who are just as honest as anyone else, *Monseigneur*, and if your highness will give a good ransom you can sup with your family tomorrow night. It is not our fault that you are hurt. Why did you resist so violently?"

"You take me for somebody else," said Châtillon. "I am not 'highness' or 'prince.'"

"You are the Prince of Canino," answered the bandit; and at first, he refused to believe the assertions of Châtillon, who declared he was a poor man with nothing to pay. At daybreak they halted in a wood, and there, by showing some letters in his pocket, Chatillon convinced the brigand chief of his mistake. Decesaris, who had intended to capture the Prince of Canino, swore fearful oaths when he discovered the truth; then, declaring Châtillon to be a brave fellow, he fixed the ransom at 5,000 *piastres* and ordered him to write a letter, dictated by himself, replying to his protestations that he had no money, "Say no more. You must find it."

Cardinal Fesch and Pauline Borghese both offered at once to pay the ransom, but Lucien insisted on doing so himself. The money was placed at the time required under a tree in the forest, and the prisoner released. Whilst he was waiting for its arrival Decesaris told Châtillon the history of his life. He was considered to be the most cruel and remorseless brigand in Italy. He had at one time a love affair with a young girl who used to meet him in the evenings and pass hours with him in a wood. Finding that this *liaison* caused him to be distrusted by the band, he murdered her in order to regain their confidence. He was the terror of the Roman States, a price of 1,000 *piastres* was put on his head, and he never passed two nights in the same place. As time went on he became more and more ferocious, until the country was delivered from him in the following manner:—

Passing on one occasion by a farm where as a lad he used to get fruit and milk, he went in and was received with kindness by the old farmer and his wife, who knew nothing of his present career. They asked him to sit down to the table, where they were at dinner with their daughter, a young girl whom he remembered as a child and who was now engaged to be married. She received her old playfellow in a friendly way, but unfortunately for her Decesaris admired her beauty.

He ordered his band to respect that neighbourhood and representing himself to be only a smuggler, paid several visits to the unsuspecting people. One day when the farmer had gone to Viterbo, he walked into the house, laid his belt and cloak upon a table, and announced that he loved the girl and should stay till morning. The terrified mother, who now knew who he was, he thrust out of the door and locked it as she fell to the ground half stunned.

In a few minutes, however, she recovered herself and got up, hearing the cries of her daughter. "Now God be with me!" she muttered; and looking fearfully around her, she hurried to a wood not far off in which she knew there was a post of *carabinieri*.

"Shall I give you Decesaris?" she asked them.

"*Santissima madre di Dio! lo credo!*" was the answer. (Holy mother of God! I should think so!)

She led them to the farm, where all was silent, hid them in a clump of olives, and having agreed upon a signal, lay down again outside the door.

Presently it opened, and Decesaris came out.

"Come, let us make friends again," he said, "pushing her with his foot. "Perhaps I shall not make such a bad son-in-law. Come, don't sulk, but drink some Montefiascone."

He held out his hand, and as she rose and went into the house with him, she met her daughter coming down the wooden stairs, pale, dishevelled, and tearful. She embraced her, and turning to Decesaris, said—

"Well, yes, I am delighted to have a son-in-law like you. To the success of our wishes!" and she raised her glass—the signal agreed upon.

As the brigand raised his he fell to the ground, shot by the *carabinieri* outside the window. They took his head to Rome, where it was placed over the Porto Pia, and the band was easily destroyed.

When Laura returned to Rome for the winter the Comte de Châtillon came to see her and related his adventures with the brigands. She trembled to hear that while she was at Albano another notorious brigand named Barlone had been close at hand with his troop; but as he happened to be ill just then and was being nursed in a monastery, he had given orders that the neighbourhood was to be left unmolested. Laura, always inclined to be imprudent, had thought of nothing but the enjoyment of that delicious climate and scenery, and had spent her time in rowing upon the lake, taking long walks in the woods and wandering about wherever she chose.

It is difficult to imagine a more enchanting place in which to spend the summer and autumn than the whole tract of country between Frascati and Genzano, of which Castel Gandolfo and Albano are perhaps the most beautiful. Huge, ancient villas, with great, cool halls and colonnades lie buried in half-wild, neglected gardens, where statues stand partly buried in grass and flowers, fountains drip softly on terraces with marble balustrades, and flights of steps lead down into shady walks amongst the tall cypress and spreading ilex groves, whose deep shadows the burning heat of the Italian summer days cannot penetrate; roads shadowed by trees wind up the steep hillsides past woods of pine and chestnut and olive, little lakes sunk deep amongst rocks and precipices, vineyards and strange, lonely villages; ridges of hills look down over a sea of olives upon the Campagna stretching away to the gleaming silver or gold of the Mediterranean.

In the early morning, after sunset, in the brilliant moonlight or, starlight of an Italian night, such scenes are enchanting, and Laura enjoyed them with her whole heart, and lingered until the autumn chills of November and the departure of the other inhabitants of the villas around drove her back to Rome.

Before the end of her stay there she made an excursion to Terni, but with several friends and a proper escort. One of those whom she had most rejoiced to meet again, and from whom she most grieved to part when the time came for her to leave Italy, was Madame Mère, whom she had always loved as her mother's dear friend, for her uniform kindness to herself and her husband, and for the thousand memories and ties they had in common.

Even Pauline Borghese took a mournful leave of her saying, "Ah! Laura, how happy you are! You are going back to France—France!" and she bowed her head upon her hands and cried bitterly.

Laura's position, however, was by no means an especially happy one. She had failed to recover any more of the property, and the future of her children was a subject of much anxiety to her.

In 1819 she was back in Paris, and having decided to take a house for a time in the country where she could economise and get her affairs put in order and arranged to the best advantage, she persuaded an old friend, the Comtesse de la Marlière to join her. They found a place called Orgeval, quiet and peaceful enough though not more than twelve miles from Paris, where they established themselves.

Laura was quite happy and contented there with her four children and Madame de la Marlière, whom she had known from her childhood and looked upon as a second mother. They read, wrote, took long country walks, and received many visits from friends in Paris, many of whom reproached Laura for burying herself in such seclusion and her children too just as her daughters were grown up and ought to go into society.

However, they remained there for nearly two years, and then Laura, who found the place rather too retired for Joséphine and Constance, but could not afford a house in Paris, removed with her family to Versailles, where life was much less expensive and by no means dull.

There was plenty of society, and Joséphine and Constance had friends and amusements to their hearts' content.

They lived there for some years very contentedly. Napoleon, Laura's eldest son, was placed at the College Henri IV. and the younger one, Alfred, at Saint-Cyr.

The elastic spirits which had supported Laura through all vicissitudes and trials never forsook her, although debts and difficulties pressed upon her during the remainder of her life, and often she would bitterly regret that during the time of riches and prosperity she had wasted her money instead of saving, like so many of her friends, a sufficient provision for herself and her children.

No part of Laura's life could have been called dull or uninteresting. Her childhood was filled with storms, dangers, and terrors; her short married life from sixteen to twenty-nine was one of splendour and excitement, and in her later years, in spite of the troubles and anxieties caused by want of money, her buoyant spirits, affectionate nature, and social qualities surrounded her always with numbers of friends. She was devoted to her children and her brother, and strongly attached to a great many other people with whom she continually associated; in addition to which a new interest had arisen in her life, in the literary work to which she now turned her attention.

But the romance and adventures of her career were over, and from the time when at thirty-seven she went to live at Versailles till, her death, which took place when she was fifty-four, there is nothing to relate which would equal the interest attached to the former part of her life, although even these latter years, passed chiefly at Versailles and Paris in times still eventful and amongst persons politically, socially, and intellectually of the most distinguished in Europe, would probably contain many more incidents worth recording than a number of the biographies that are now published.

Most of Laura's children shared her literary tastes. Her daughters took the deepest interest in her writings, in some of which they assisted her, and both of them and their eldest brother wrote novels, essays, and various other books.

Constance married a former *garde-du-corps*, named Louis Aubert, and Joséphine, who, in spite of her turbulent proceedings at her christening, had grown up a gentle, unworldly girl, being anxious to embrace a religious life, was made *chanoinesse*, by Monseigneur Quélen, Archbishop of Paris, a great friend of her mother's. She worked for a time as a Sister of Mercy, but her health was not strong enough for the hardships of such a profession, and she returned to the Duchesse d'Abrantès, with whom she remained until the death of the latter. After they left Versailles, they had an apartment in the Abbaye-aux-Bois, where Laura spent the last years of her life, devoting herself to her children, her friends, and her literary pursuits, in which she was extremely successful.

Her novels were very much the fashion for a time, and the celebrated memoirs of the Revolution, Consulate, and Empire, which came out in 1831-1834 had great success, and are amongst the most delightful existing. The first edition was in eighteen volumes. They were followed by the *Memoirs of the Restoration*. Among her other books were *Les Salons de Paris, Femmes célébres dans tous les pays, Scènes de la vie espagnole, L'Opale, La Duchesse de Valombray, Les deux Soeurs,* &c.

The greatest grief that befell her in the latter part of her life was the death of her brother Albert in 1828. He had been always more like a father than a brother to her, and his loss was irreparable.

She died at the Abbaye-aux-Bois on June 7, 1838. Her daughter Joséphine afterwards married a Monsieur Amet.

Her second son, Alfred, of whom she always spoke with the greatest pride and affection, went into the army and was *aide-de-camp* to Marshal MacMahon and Prince Jérôme Napoleon.

As to her elder son. Napoleon, his military career ended with the Polish lancers of his infancy. He entered the diplomatic service, which he eventually was obliged to leave owing to the scrapes and scandals in which he was continually involved, and spent the rest of his life in Paris, where he wrote novels, essays, articles, &c.

On one occasion during some disturbance in Paris, he was standing on a balcony with his mother when a procession of the rioters passed carrying a *tricolor* flag. As Laura's eyes rested once more upon that ensign, to some so accursed, to others so glorious, all the brilliant days of her youth seemed to rise again before her. Again, she fancied she heard the shouts of victory and saw the glory of France and the forms and faces of those who were gone. "See!" she cried, "there is the banner under which your father fought and conquered! Salute it." And she bowed her head with tears as it passed.

THE DUCHESSE D'ABRANTÈS IN 1836

ALSO FROM LEONAUR
AVAILABLE IN SOFTCOVER OR HARDCOVER WITH DUST JACKET

THE WOMAN IN BATTLE by Loreta Janeta Velazquez—Soldier, Spy and Secret Service Agent for the Confederacy During the American Civil War.

BOOTS AND SADDLES by Elizabeth B. Custer—The experiences of General Custer's Wife on the Western Plains.

FANNIE BEERS' CIVIL WAR by Fannie A. Beers—A Confederate Lady's Experiences of Nursing During the Campaigns & Battles of the American Civil War.

LADY SALE'S AFGHANISTAN by Florentia Sale—An Indomitable Victorian Lady's Account of the Retreat from Kabul During the First Afghan War.

THE TWO WARS OF MRS DUBERLY by Frances Isabella Duberly—An Intrepid Victorian Lady's Experience of the Crimea and Indian Mutiny.

THE REBELLIOUS DUCHESS by Paul F. S. Dermoncourt—The Adventures of the Duchess of Berri and Her Attempt to Overthrow French Monarchy.

LADIES OF WATERLOO by Charlotte A. Eaton, Magdalene de Lancey & Juana Smith—The Experiences of Three Women During the Campaign of 1815: Waterloo Days by Charlotte A. Eaton, A Week at Waterloo by Magdalene de Lancey & Juana's Story by Juana Smith.

NURSE AND SPY IN THE UNION ARMY by Sarah Emma Evelyn Edmonds—During the American Civil War

WIFE NO. 19 by Ann Eliza Young—The Life & Ordeals of a Mormon Woman During the 19th Century

DIARY OF A NURSE IN SOUTH AFRICA by Alice Bron—With the Dutch-Belgian Red Cross During the Boer War

MARIE ANTOINETTE AND THE DOWNFALL OF ROYALTY by Imbert de Saint-Amand—The Queen of France and the French Revolution

THE MEMSAHIB & THE MUTINY by R. M. Coopland—An English lady's ordeals in Gwalior and Agra during the Indian Mutiny 1857

MY CAPTIVITY AMONG THE SIOUX INDIANS by Fanny Kelly—The ordeal of a pioneer woman crossing the Western Plains in 1864

WITH MAXIMILIAN IN MEXICO by Sara Yorke Stevenson—A Lady's experience of the French Adventure

AVAILABLE ONLINE AT **www.leonaur.com**
AND FROM ALL GOOD BOOK STORES

www.ingramcontent.com/pod-product-compliance
Lightning Source LLC
Chambersburg PA
CBHW031620160426
43196CB00006B/212